Possum in the Pawpaw Tree

POSSUM

in the Pawpaw Tree

A SEASONAL GUIDE TO MIDWESTERN GARDENING

B. Rosie Lerner
& Beverly S. Netzhammer

Purdue University Press / *West Lafayette, Indiana*

98 97 96 95   5 4 3 2

The paper used in this book meets the minimum requirements of American National
Standard for Information Sciences—Permanence of Paper for Printed Library
Materials, ANSI Z39.48-1984.

Printed in the United States of America
Design by Chiquita Babb
Illustrations by Mary Lou Hayden and Chiquita Babb

LIBRARY OF CONGRESS CATALOGING-IN-PUBLICATION DATA

Lerner, B. Rosie, 1956–
    Possum in the pawpaw tree : a seasonal guide to midwestern
gardening / B. Rosie Lerner and Beverly S. Netzhammer.
        p.   cm.
    Includes index.
    ISBN 1-55753-053-X (cloth : alk. paper) —ISBN 1-55753-054-8 (paper : alk. paper)
    1. Gardening—Middle West. 2. Gardening—Middle West—Calendars.
    I. Netzhammer, Beverly S., 1963– . II. Title.
SB453.2.M54L47   1994
635'.0977—dc20   94-12066
                                                  CIP

Contents

Preface   xiii

Introduction   1

JANUARY

Garden Calendar   5

    Forcing Branches to Bloom Brings Spring Indoors   6

    Garden with Garbage!   7

    Amaryllis Require Special Care   9

    Winter Can Be Hazardous to Houseplants   11

    A Tropical Touch: Ferns for Indoors   12

    Properly Potting Your Plants   13

    Didn't Get Your Bulbs Planted?   14

    Be a Skeptical Shopper   15

    How Plants Are Named   16

    De-icing Salts Harmful to Plants   18

    Wood Ash in the Garden   19

    Saffron Comes from Crocus Flowers   20

    Gardening Questions   21

CONTENTS

FEBRUARY

Garden Calendar   31
Precocious Bulbs   32
Winter Injury of Landscape Plants   33
Gifts for Your Valentine   35
Cut-Flower Care: Myths and Facts   37
The Vanilla Orchid   38
Loamy Soil Ideal for Gardening   39
Grow Your Own Transplants   40
Designing a Flower Bed with a View in Mind   41
Finocchio   43
Spots on African Violet Leaves   43
Gardening Questions   44

MARCH

Garden Calendar   53
Harbingers of Spring   55
Gardening Tips for Beginners   56
Cool-Season Gardening   58
Coriander, the Versatile Herb   59
Late Winter Recommended for Pruning Chores   60
Pruning Evergreens   61
Topping is Hazardous to Your Tree   63
Spring Pruning of Roses   64
Fertilizing Woody Plants   65
Chlorophyll: Why Plants Wear Green   67
Irish Shamrock   68
Gardening Questions   69

APRIL

Garden Calendar 77
Cauliflower Demands a Cool Season 78
Lettuce: A Cool Crop for Midwestern Gardens 79
Intensive Gardening Techniques Stretch Garden Space 80
Celebrate Arbor Day 82
Start an Asparagus Bed 83
Grow Your Own Strawberries 85
Planting a Rose Garden 86
Flowering Annuals versus Perennials 88
Herb Gardening 89
Don't Bag Those Grass Clippings 91
Gardening Equipment Includes the Microwave 92
Easter Lily Symbolizes the Season 93
Gardening Questions 94

MAY

Garden Calendar 105
Wildflowers Can Be Alternative to Lawn 106
Landscapes Aren't Just for Looking Anymore 108
Be Choosy When Selecting Ground Covers 109
Fruit Trees Need Company 111
Warm Soil Key to Early Planting 112
The Tomato: Queen of the Home Garden 113
Leggy Tomatoes 115
Sweet Corn Isn't Just for Large Gardens 116
Container and Raised Bed Gardening Can Ease the Pain 117
Mulching Controls Weeds, Conserves Soil Moisture 119

CONTENTS

Houseplants Migrate Outdoors   121
Gardening Questions   122

JUNE

Garden Calendar   135
Off with Their Heads!   137
How to Water the Garden   138
Trickle Irrigation Eases Watering Chores   138
Premature Fruit Drop   139
Bacterial Wilt Deals Fatal Blow to Cukes and Melons   140
Iron-Starved Leaves Turn Yellow   141
Poison Ivy: A Variable Pest   143
Geraniums Repel Mosquitoes??   144
Storing Leftover Garden Seed   145
Plan Now for Your Halloween Pumpkin   146
Propagating Trees and Shrubs from Cuttings   147
Give Asparagus and Rhubarb a Break   148
Gardening Questions   149

JULY

Garden Calendar   157
In Times of Drought   159
Tomato Troubles   161
The Bitter Truth about Cucumbers   162
Why Fruit Trees May Fail to Bear   164
Improper Use of Pesticides Can Be Harmful to Plants   165
Renovating the Strawberry Patch   166
Potatoes Grow Tomatoes?   168
Squashkins and Cucumelons   169

Gladiolus for Summer Flowers 170
Edible Flowers for the Gourmet Gardener 171
Gardening Questions 172

AUGUST

Garden Calendar 181
Harvest Winter Squash in Summer 182
Saving Seeds from the Garden 183
Plant Now for Fall Harvest 184
Brussels Sprouts Best as Fall Crop 185
Cover Crops or Green Manure—What's in a Name? 186
Dividing Perennials 188
Pruning and Propagating Raspberries 189
Time to Start Your New Lawn 190
Herb Propagation 191
Potpourri: A Fragrant Memory 193
Brighten Your Garden with Sunflowers 194
Plants Have Allergies, Too! 196
Gardening Questions 197

SEPTEMBER

Garden Calendar 207
Harvest Your Roses? 209
Harvesting Grapes 210
Pears Best Ripened off the Tree 211
Dig Those Potatoes 212
Early Pumpkins 213
Vegetable Spaghetti 213
Peanuts for Midwestern Gardens 214

CONTENTS

Gardeners Prepare to Avoid Frost   215
Fall Ideal for Planting Trees   217
Plant Garlic This Fall   218
Fire Up for Hot Peppers   219
Bringing Houseplants Back Indoors   220
Some Landscape Trees Should Be Weeded Out   221
Evergreen Needles Don't Last Forever   222
Gardening Questions   223

OCTOBER

Garden Calendar   231
Storing Apples for the Winter   232
Harvesting and Preserving Gourds   234
Luffa: The Natural Sponge   234
Cool Potatoes to Prevent Sprouting   236
Horseradish Will Awaken Your Tastebuds   237
Pawpaw: The Midwestern Banana?   238
Tender Perennials Need Indoor Protection   239
Fertilize Woody Plants This Fall   241
Poinsettias Can Rebloom for the Holidays   241
Fall Color Signals End of Season   242
Backyard Composting   243
Plant Spring-Flowering Bulbs This Fall   244
Forcing Bulbs for Indoor Color   245
Gardening Questions   246

NOVEMBER

Garden Calendar   251
Anti-freeze for Roses   252

Preparing Landscape Plants for Winter 253
Strawberries Need Winter Protection 255
Mulch for Winter Protection 256
Please Don't Burn Autumn Leaves 256
Wood Preservatives for Gardening Structures 258
Prepare Your Spring Garden This Fall 259
Popcorn without the Pop 260
Growing Trees from Seed 261
Gardening Questions 262

DECEMBER

Garden Calendar 269
Holiday Greenery 270
Be Choosy When Selecting Christmas Trees 271
Cut Your Own Christmas Tree 273
Living Christmas Trees 273
Poinsettia Care 274
Holiday Gift Plants 276
Pomanders Make Fragrant Gifts 278
Gardening Questions 279

Appendix A: Midwest Plant Hardiness Zone Map 285
Appendix B: Public Gardens and Arboreta of the Midwest 287
Appendix C: State Cooperative Extension Service Offices 295
Glossary 297
Index 303

Preface

Over the years, we have encountered a wide array of gardening questions through our work with the Cooperative Extension Service. We would like to thank those gardeners who prompted us to gather our advice into a book.

Indeed, the title of this book was inspired by one of our readers. In our "Growing Concerns" gardening column, we once responded to an inquiry about poor fruit set in pawpaw. We suggested several possible causes, but a reader wrote to add another solution to our list. He claimed that the insects responsible for pollination in pawpaws are attracted to rotting flesh, and so one should hang a dead animal in the tree. (There was no mention of what the neighbors or their dogs might have thought of this practice.) It is true that pawpaws may be pollinated by carrion flies, but not all gardeners are willing to take such drastic steps to raise these uncommon fruits.

The pawpaw discussion reminds us that there isn't necessarily one right way to garden; there may be several approaches that all lead to successful results. What is a reasonable effort to one gardener might be out of the question to another. One thing is certain: gardening is never boring. Each year brings new experiences, and gardeners will continue to come up with challenging questions and solutions.

We must confess that we thought about changing the book's title more than once. Since most of our inquiries seem to revolve around problems, including lack of flowers, crop failure, winter injury, drought, pests, and diseases, we considered titles such as

"The Miseries, Disappointments, Trials, and Tribulations of Gardening," "Nothin' Bloomin'," and "Gardening Is Hell."

Despite numerous obstacles, most gardeners seem to be determined to keep trying. We think this book is a testament to the indomitable spirit of the midwestern gardener.

Possum in the Pawpaw Tree was brought to harvest under the care of many "gardeners." We wish to acknowledge: Carolyn McGrew for planting the seed to publish this collection; ScapeArt, Inc., and the Purdue University Department of Horticulture for giving us the time and space to allow the book to grow; Margaret Hunt for pruning the book into a productive form; and Mary Lou Hayden for making the book blossom with her artistry. Throughout this process, our families, friends, and critters have been our trellis; our heartfelt thanks for their perennial support.

Possum in the Pawpaw Tree

Introduction

Each season brings welcome delights to gardeners in the Midwest. In the country's heartland, the changes in temperature and the length of day bring constant newness to the garden's appearance and to our activities. We may envy those who garden in a warmer climate, but most of us admit we like the variety of our midwestern home. We eagerly anticipate the sight of the first buds as they burst into soft green leaves, the bright daffodils, the taste of midwestern corn, the brilliant fall color, and the blanket of snow decorating the evergreens. We also cherish the opportunities to sow seed in the spring, harvest crops in the fall, and finally put away the weed whip in the winter. Friends in the Sunbelt may wonder what midwestern gardeners do when the snow flies, but we enjoy this chance to sharpen the mower blades, pamper our houseplants, and plan for the season ahead.

Possum in the Pawpaw Tree is written as a seasonal guide for the Midwest, which encompasses Ohio, Michigan, Indiana, Illinois, Wisconsin, Missouri, Iowa, Minnesota, North Dakota, South Dakota, Nebraska, and Kansas. Many gardening authors live in the western and eastern United States and so often write about plants, soils, weather patterns, and pests that are alien to our midwestern experience. Our weather can be unpredictable, and we can expect extremes in temperature and moisture.

For each month, we have provided a short calendar, which the reader can use as a quick reference to determine the month's activities. A section of short essays introduces the reader to a variety of techniques, problems, and new plants to try. The final section for each month consists of questions and answers that target specific difficulties commonly encountered in the Midwest. Although we share many garden experiences in this part of the country, our climates are different enough to make the timing of garden activities in this book variable. We only suggest appropriate months. You may need to adjust your schedule by a few weeks, depending upon local conditions. The calendar, especially, is a checklist that you should modify to your climate, and we encourage you to add your own ideas and activities to it.

For the sake of readability, we use common names of plants when they are readily recognizable and unambiguous. Latin (botanical) names are used only when necessary for clarification. References to specific pesticides and products are omitted, since the labels and availability change from year to year. Finally, *Possum* is not intended to be all-inclusive; rather, it is a collection of seasonal essays, tips, and ideas. Your county and state extension services, libraries, garden centers, nurseries, magazines, botanical gardens, and arboreta can supply additional information.

So let's set off to celebrate the seasons, starting in blustery January . . .

JANUARY

The short days, chilly winds, and snowfall keep most gardeners indoors for what seems like endless weeks. You can ward off cabin fever with the bright colors and foliage of indoor gardening projects and the enticing photographs in the gardening catalogs that are arriving in your mailbox. Now is the time to plan for the spring and summer and carefully select plant material to ensure healthy plants for years to come. Be a discerning shopper; as Vita Sackville-West reminds us, "I have grown wise, after many years of gardening, and no longer order recklessly from wildly alluring descriptions which make every annual sound easy to grow and brilliant as a film star. I now know that gardening is not like that."

If winter gets you down, remember it brings a necessary chilling period to cheerful yellow daffodils and glowing pink peonies slumbering under their blanket of snow and mulch. We'll be enjoying them soon.

Garden Calendar

HOME

Keep holiday poinsettias and other plants near a bright window and water as top of soil dries.

Check houseplant leaves for brown, dry edges, which indicate too little relative humidity in the house. Increase humidity by running a humidifier, grouping plants, or using pebble trays.

Repot houseplants as they outgrow current pots.

Check stored produce and tender flower bulbs and roots for rot, shriveling, or excess moisture. Discard damaged material.

YARD

Check young trees for rodent injury on lower trunks. Prevent injury with hardware cloth or protective collars.

Keep road and sidewalk salt away from plants. To keep salt spray off of plants, construct a burlap screen if necessary.

Leaf through nursery catalogs and make plans for landscape and home orchard additions. Order plants early for best selection.

Cut branches of forsythia, pussy willow, crab apple, quince, honeysuckle, and other early spring-flowering plants to force into bloom indoors (see pages 6–7).

GARDEN

Send for seed catalogs for your flower and vegetable gardens.

Sketch your garden plans on paper, including what to grow, spacing, arrangement, and number of plants needed.

FORCING BRANCHES TO BLOOM
BRINGS SPRING INDOORS

Winter days may be gloomy and dull, but you can give your home a touch of spring color by forcing landscape branches to bloom indoors.

Spring-flowering trees and shrubs set their flower buds the previous fall. Once the buds have been exposed to cold for several months (usually by mid-January), a branch can be cut and forced to bloom indoors. The easiest branches to force include forsythia, pussy willow, honeysuckle, crab apple, redbud, magnolia, and flowering dogwood.

Generally, shrub branches are easier to force than tree branches. Buds take from one to five weeks to open, depending on the plant you choose. The closer to the natural blooming time you cut the branches, the shorter the wait.

When selecting branches, choose healthy ones that are free from disease, insect, and other injury. Treat the plant as you would when you are pruning. Cut the branch just above a side bud, being careful not to leave a stub. Take branches from crowded spots or other areas where they will not be missed.

The length of the cut branch can vary, but between 6 and 18 inches is a good length. Look for branches with many flower buds, which are usually larger and fatter than leaf buds. Cut the stem with a sharp knife or pruners. Recut the stems just before placing in water. If you cut the branches when temperatures are below freezing, immerse the stems in cool water for several hours to prevent the buds from opening too soon.

Next, place the branches in an upright container and add hot water to cover no more than 3 inches of the stem. Allow to stand about ½ hour, then fill the container with cool water. Flowers will last longer if kept in a cool (60–65° F) location away from direct sunlight. Be sure to keep the container filled with water. Floral preservatives may help extend the vase life of the blooms.

GARDEN WITH GARBAGE!

Instead of throwing out that inedible pineapple top, turn it into a houseplant! Carrot tops and avocado pits can also be salvaged from the garbage pail and elevated to the ranks of houseplants.

To grow a pineapple plant, cut off the leafy top, leaving about a ¼ inch of the fruit attached. Scoop out the pulp and let the top air dry for a few days. Then press the top into a pot or pan of moistened rooting medium, such as vermiculite or perlite. Keep the medium moist at all times, and in about a month or two, roots should begin to form. Then repot the top into potting soil and place in a sunny windowsill.

Carrot plants can also be started from what we usually throw away. Cut off ¾ to 1 inch of the top of the root with the green stalks attached. Set it in a shallow dish of water and wait for the new fibrous roots to develop. When roots are about 1 inch long, plant it in potting soil so that the top of the old root is just barely visible and place it in a bright location.

Avocado pits produce attractive houseplants. Wash the pit to remove the fruit pulp and insert 4 toothpicks at quarterly intervals about halfway up the pit. The toothpicks should only be inserted as deeply as necessary to provide support. Place the pit in a glass of water with the broad end down, resting the toothpicks on the rim of the glass. Replace lost water daily and provide a complete change of water weekly. Roots, and eventually a shoot, can take up to three months to appear. Plant the pit in potting soil

The top of a fresh pineapple can be rooted to grow a pineapple plant.

with the top of the pit exposed and pinch off the tip of the shoot when it is about 6 inches tall. Several side branches will form along the remaining stem.

Fruit trees, such as apple, orange, and cherry, can be grown from the seeds of ordinary fruit. Since these trees are not normally propagated by seed, the resulting plants will likely be of inferior quality compared to the plant that produced that tasty fruit (see page 261). However, seedling fruit plants can make fun houseplants or novelty yard plants. Many tree seeds must be stored in cool, moist conditions for up to 3 months before they will sprout; pack the seeds in moist vermiculite, peat moss, or sand for the duration of the cold treatment. Then plant the seeds in good-quality potting soil. Once the temperature is above 50° F, you may want to place the emerged plant outside to get maximum growth.

AMARYLLIS REQUIRE SPECIAL CARE

The amaryllis is a tender bulb that won't survive outdoors even in the mildest of midwestern winters. But they can be grown indoors to provide a dramatic burst of color during those dreary winter months.

The showy flowers range from crimson, scarlet, rose, lavender, white, or bicolor combinations. Although each bulb may only produce one cluster of 2–4 blooms, each flower can reach up to 8 inches in diameter during their peak of bloom. The flowers are borne on a tall, stout stem about 2 feet tall.

The plants are easy to care for but may require a little special handling to rebloom next year. Cool temperatures—about 55–65° F—and a sunny window are most conducive to a sturdy bloom. Weak stems may need to be staked. Water the plant thoroughly when the top inch of soil begins to dry and then allow the soil to dry again before rewatering. Watering too frequently can cause the bulb to rot. Flowering should begin about 6–8 weeks after you first pot the bulb.

After the flower fades, you can cut the flower stalk off, but the plant's health is still important if reblooming is desired. Water and fertilize it as you would other houseplants and place it near a sunny window.

After all danger of frost is past in the spring, you can plunge the pot into the soil outdoors with an eastern or western exposure. Late in summer, as the leaves begin to yellow, cut back on watering gradually until the leaves fade completely and the soil is dry.

The bulb is now dormant and should be left in the pot and stored in a cool, dark location at about 40–55° F. Amaryllis do not require a chilling period like many other flowering bulbs, but they do require a period of cool, dry dormancy. After about 2 months of rest, water the soil, set the pot in a sunny window, and resume normal care.

Amaryllis in bloom.

Dormant amaryllis bulb.

Though you may feel quite cozy in your heated home, the typical house in winter is a hostile environment for most houseplants. Many of our houseplants are outdoor plants in their native tropical climates—which means they prefer warm, humid air.

Although the room that the plants are growing in may be warm, leaves in contact with cold windowpanes can be injured and may even be frozen in the condensation that often collects on the glass. Cold blasts of air from doors being opened to the outdoors can eventually take their toll on houseplants.

Overly warm rooms can also present a problem. The air becomes extremely dry as the furnace forces warm air throughout the house. The warm temperatures coupled with low humidity have a devastating effect on your houseplants.

All plants lose water through their leaves continuously through a process called transpiration. Normally, this water is replaced through water taken up by the roots. When the surrounding air is excessively dry, the rate of transpiration can become so high that the roots can't supply sufficient water. Thus, even if soil is wet, plants may begin to wilt or show brown edges and tips.

There are a number of ways to relieve houseplant suffering. The first choice would be to run a humidifier, which would increase *your* comfort as well. Many different models are available, ranging from small tabletop to large floor models that service several rooms. There are also humidifier attachments for your furnace unit.

If buying a humidifier sounds too extreme, or if you just have a few plants, there are some less complex methods. Simply grouping plants together helps increase relative humidity by taking advantage of the water vapor emitted during transpiration. Putting the plants on top of a tray of wet pebbles will increase the humidity further. When using the pebble tray, be sure the level of the water on the pebbles is below the holes in the plant's pot, so that the water will not be sucked up into the soil. Soil that is constantly wet becomes starved for oxygen, which is just as important to root life as adequate moisture.

Misting your plants isn't likely to help the plants much. Misting with a spray bottle adds such temporary moisture that it does not effectively change the relative humidity.

Some plants, such as ferns, mosses, and other tropical plants, require even higher humidity than other plants. Such moisture-loving plants often grow better in an enclosed container, such as a terrarium or miniature greenhouse. Enclosing the plant helps keep humidity up by preventing moisture loss through evaporation. And the more humid the air, the less water will be lost through transpiration.

Almost any type of container can be used as a terrarium. Old glass jars, goblets, fish bowls, and aquariums can all be used. A cover will help control the humidity, although tightly sealed containers may need to be ventilated at times to prevent too much moisture from accumulating. The size of the container is flexible, but the opening should be wide enough to allow small plants and tools inside.

Although many types of plants will adapt to terrarium life, some plants, such as cacti and succulents, will rot because of the high humidity. Plants of similar cultural requirements should be placed in one container, since only one climate can be achieved.

A TROPICAL TOUCH: FERNS FOR INDOORS

Many indoor gardeners love the lush, exotic appearance of ferns but are disappointed to find that the plant that looked so fabulous in the nursery's greenhouse just doesn't do well at home.

Most ferns are native to tropical climates, where they develop as understory plants in the rain forests. That means that ferns will thrive where temperatures are relatively cool, humidity and soil moisture are high, and light is filtered.

Now consider what the average home environment is like, particularly in winter. Many homeowners keep their thermostats set at 72° F during the day and perhaps 65° F at night. Ferns are best adapted to daytime temperatures of 65–70° F and night temperatures of 55–60° F. Relative humidity in the home often drops to 10–15% during the winter heating months, while most ferns can just barely tolerate 30% (40–50% is the ideal range).

It's easy to see why ferns often suffer in the home. Their fronds turn brown and dry at the tips, and the inner leaves turn yellow and drop.

Ferns aren't a hopeless case, but you'll need to modify their environment for a successful plant. Place ferns in the cooler rooms of the house and especially avoid hot drafts from heating vents. Don't allow the soil to become overly dry; once a fern wilts, it does not recover as well as many other types of plants. The best way to determine when to water is to poke your finger into the soil; water when the top surface just begins to feel dry. Increasing the room's humidity will help slow down the loss of water.

The so-called asparagus ferns are not ferns at all but members of the lily family. They generally require brighter light year-round than do true ferns. But asparagus ferns are also very sensitive to soil moisture and will drop many leaves if allowed to dry. Follow the same procedures for increasing humidity as you would for true ferns.

PROPERLY POTTING YOUR PLANTS

Interesting containers for your houseplants can enhance the decor of a room, but whether you choose brass, ceramic, or plain old terra-cotta, be sure to pot your plants properly to keep them healthy. Almost any container can be used for potting plants, as long as drainage holes are provided because plant roots must have some oxygen in order to take up water and nutrients. If the soil surrounding the roots is thoroughly filled with water for extended periods, the roots will suffocate. Once the roots start to rot, the top of the plant may wilt, a symptom that well-meaning gardeners interpret as a signal to get out the watering can. But this overwatering just aggravates the problem.

A plant in an unglazed clay pot is less likely to suffer from too much water than a plant in a glass or plastic container because water can move out from, and air can move into, the soil through the clay. But even clay pots should have drainage holes in the bottom.

Unglazed clay containers do, however, tend to accumulate unsightly salt residue as water evaporates from the surface. This residue is generally not harmful to the plants

unless it builds up in the soil. Plastic containers weigh considerably less than clay ones, which makes it easier to move the plant from one location to another, and they don't tend to accumulate as much salt residue. However, plastic containers can be too light, so that large plants easily tip over. Decorative containers often do not allow excess water to drain away from plants. With such a container, use the double-potting method. Pot your plant in a properly sized unglazed clay pot with drainage holes and then slip the pot into the decorative container. Discard the drainage after watering.

Take special care to select a pot of the correct size. A plant in a pot that is too small does not have room to grow and dries out quickly. One that is in an oversized pot may suffer from too much water and too little air.

To determine if a plant needs to be repotted, examine the root system by removing the plant from the container. If only a few roots are visible from the outside of the soil ball, the plant does not need repotting. If many roots are visible, it is time to repot. Use a pot just the next size larger, so that the soil will not stay too wet too long.

DIDN'T GET YOUR BULBS PLANTED?

If you didn't get your spring-flowering bulbs planted, you're not alone. Many gardeners found that other chores, as well as autumn rains, delayed their planting. Your best bet to salvaging your investment is planting them as soon as possible.

Waiting until spring to plant the bulbs will not satisfy the chilling and rooting requirements of the bulbs, so no flowers will bloom on spring-planted bulbs. Most bulbs require 10–13 weeks of cold temperatures, about 40° F, in order to initiate flower buds. Cool autumn weather is ideal for root formation before the top growth begins.

Flowering bulbs do not store well, so saving them for planting next fall is not a good option, either. Proper storage conditions to keep the bulbs cool and dry are often hard to find in the home environment. The bulbs usually begin to soften and rot or may actually sprout before they get planted. Even under ideal storage conditions, the bulbs will lose some of their food reserves through the natural process of respiration, the breaking down of stored carbohydrates as fuel for growth and maturation.

If you haven't planted your bulbs yet, there are two ways to salvage your investment. You could get them planted as soon as possible, as long as the soil is still unfrozen. Mulch the bulbs over after the ground freezes to prevent them from being heaved or pushed out of the soil from alternate freezing and thawing. The bulbs may not bloom this spring, but with any luck, many will survive to bloom the following year.

The other alternative is to force the bulbs into bloom indoors. Remember that the bulbs will need to be chilled for as long as 13 weeks to initiate flowers. Bulbs that have been forced are not very productive when replanted outdoors, but at least you will have had some enjoyment from the bulbs.

BE A SKEPTICAL SHOPPER

There seems to be no end to advertisements for plants that are not only horticultural breakthroughs but are bargain priced as well. Are they for real? It's best to trust the old saying "If it sounds too good to be true, it probably is."

Mail-order houses can be a good source of high-quality, unusual, and/or inexpensive plants. Most local garden centers cannot afford to stock the large range of cultivars or exotic plants that a mail-order firm can. The majority of these companies are legitimate and reputable. However, a few unscrupulous dealers are out there, so it pays to take the time to find a reliable source.

Many a gardener has been misled by fabulous photos of fantastic "new" plants. Somehow, many of the facts were missing or in very fine print. New horticultural breakthroughs are few and far between, and you can bet they won't be available at bargain prices. However, high prices don't necessarily mean a great plant, either.

Examples of recent disappointing "breakthroughs" include gopher purge plants, mosquito-repellent plants, Populus Giganteus shade trees, and tree tomatoes. The so-called gopher-repelling plant not only does not repel gophers, it can become a nasty weed in the garden. The mosquito-repellent plant is nothing more than a citrus-scented geranium, certainly not new to the gardening world. One plant cannot provide

protection from mosquitoes. Fast-growing shade trees sound great, but unfortunately, these poplars are weak-wooded and susceptible to disease, making them very short-lived. The tree tomato is a tropical plant that will not overwinter outdoors in the Midwest. If given sufficient light—in a greenhouse, for example—it will produce fruit through the winter. However, the fruit is more tart and jellylike than our garden tomato and likely to disappoint the taste buds.

The best way to avoid disappointment is to determine exactly what plant you are ordering. Most advertisements list both the plant's common name and scientific (botanical) name. Common names alone can be deceiving because many different plants can have the same common name, and one plant may have several common names.

Beware of any plant advertised as a wonder plant or a breakthrough. Plants that boast of miraculous growth, yield, or bloom may not be hardy in the Midwest or at least may not perform as advertised when grown in midwestern conditions. Other disappointments may include plants that require special treatments or long dormancy periods that weren't mentioned in the advertisement. Exotic, unusual plants often have different cultural requirements than commonly grown plants. Also, gardeners can be frustrated when they receive a tiny seedling or possibly a packet of seeds rather than the lush, mature plants shown in the colorful pictures of the ad. Compare several different companies' catalogs and note differences in size, age, warranties, packaging, and shipping details. These factors can account for differences in prices.

HOW PLANTS ARE NAMED

Plant names can be quite confusing and downright misleading in some cases. The common names that everyday folks use for plants do not necessarily follow any rules. Some plants may have more than one common name, and the same common name may apply to more than one plant.

A good example of just how confusing plant names can be is the spider plant, which conjures up the image of a commonly grown houseplant for some, but a very different garden flower for others. To make matters worse, the houseplant that some call spider plant is called airplane plant by others.

In the scientific community, all plants are given a unique two-part name that is based on Latin so that the name will be recognized throughout the world no matter what the native language. This scientific name is also known as the botanical or Latin name. Although Latin can be difficult to pronounce for the layperson, knowing the scientific name can be very helpful, particularly when one is trying to locate cultural information and sources of plants.

Plants are classified according to similar botanical characteristics, such as flower, fruit, and leaf structure. Different plants that have similar structures are grouped into classes known as families. For instance, the rose family, known botanically as Rosaceae, is comprised of more than 2,000 different plants, yet all have similar flower structures.

Within a family, individual plants have a two-part scientific name, much like our own names. A plant's first name identifies the genus and functions like our surname. For example, the group of plants within the rose family that is characterized by fruit with a hard pit in the middle carries the genus name *Prunus*. Plants in this group include peach, cherry, almond, plum, nectarine, and apricot.

A plant's second name indicates its species, which identifies a specific group of plants within a genus. For example, the scientific name for peach is *Prunus persica*. The sweet cherry is known as *Prunus avium*, the apricot is *Prunus armeniaca*, and so on. Generally, the scientific name should be italicized or underlined, the genus name is capitalized, and the species name is lowercase, except when the species is named for a person or place.

Either in nature or as a result of human intervention, a species of plant may exhibit forms that are different in some characteristic, such as plant size, flower color, fruit size, or flavor. When these differences continue to occur in nature, the subgroup of plants is known as a variety. The variety name is often, but not always, a Latin name.

POSSUM IN THE PAWPAW TREE

The nectarine is actually a variety of peach known botanically as *Prunus persica* var. *nucipersica*.

When differences within a species are the result of artificially made hybrids or other specialized propagation techniques, the unique plant is known as a cultivar (a shortening of the term "cultivated variety"). The cultivar name is usually in the native language of the horticulturist responsible for naming the plant. The cultivar name can be set off in single quotes or preceded by the word "cultivar" and is always capitalized. For example, the redhaven peach can be written *Prunus persica* cultivar Redhaven or *Prunus persica* 'Redhaven.' Naturally occurring varieties may be further developed by horticulturists, resulting in new cultivars. Thus, although the original nectarine was a variety, there are cultivars of nectarines, such as 'Red Gold,' 'Sunglo,' and 'Independence.'

In everyday usage, the terms "variety" and "cultivar" are often incorrectly used interchangeably. The difference is subtle but important to horticulturists, particularly those responsible for introducing new plants.

DE-ICING SALTS HARMFUL TO PLANTS

De-icing salts can save your neck this winter, but they can spell disaster for landscape plants. Salt spray from passing traffic can splash onto the plants' limbs. Salt may be inadvertently shoveled onto plants when sidewalks are cleaned. It can then accumulate in the soil surrounding the plants, resulting in possible root damage.

Salts can adversely affect a plant in several ways. They can be taken up by the plant and accumulate to toxic levels. Salts can cause excessive drying of foliage and roots. They can also cause a nutritional imbalance by changing the chemistry of the soil and can directly harm soil structure. The most apparent damage from salts is death of buds and twig tips as a result of salt spray. As the tips of the plant die, it responds by growing an excessive number of side branches.

Accumulation damage is more slowly manifested and may not be noticeable for many months. Sodium salts are the most common type used for de-icing, while cal-

18

cium salts are used to a lesser extent. Both these types of salt can cause direct plant damage, but calcium is less harmful to soil chemistry than sodium. Effects usually appear as stunting, lack of vigor, dieback of growing tips, leaf burn, or leaf drop. Winter and spring rains can help prevent accumulation by washing the salt out of the root zone. Supplemental irrigation is advisable when natural rainfall is scarce.

Protect your plants by constructing burlap or durable plastic screens to shield them from roadway splash. If screening from traffic is not practical, or if you find it too unsightly, try to use salt-tolerant plants, such as maple, buckeye, hawthorn, juniper, Siberian pea shrub, Russian olive, poplar, and honey locust.

Avoid throwing sidewalk residue onto nearby plants, including shrubs and ground covers. Use alternatives such as clean clay cat litter, sand, or sawdust to help improve traction on ice.

WOOD ASH IN THE GARDEN

Winter's chill winds keep many a wood-burning stove working overtime, leaving owners with the ashes to dispose of. Many gardening books advise throwing them in the garden. But how do these ashes affect soil and plants?

Wood ash does have fertilizer value, the amount varying somewhat with the species of wood being used. Generally, wood ash contains less than 10% potash, 1% phosphate, and trace amounts of micronutrients such as iron, manganese, boron, copper, and zinc. Trace amounts of heavy metals such as lead, cadmium, nickel, and chromium also may be present. Wood ash does not contain nitrogen.

The largest component of wood ash (about 25%) is calcium carbonate, a common liming material, which increases soil alkalinity. Wood ash has very fine particles and thus reacts rapidly and completely in the soil. So although small amounts of nutrients are applied with wood ash, the main effect is that of a liming agent.

Increasing the alkalinity of the soil does affect plant nutrition. Nutrients are most readily available to plants when the soil is slightly acidic. As soil alkalinity increases and the pH rises above 7.0, nutrients such as phosphorus, iron, boron, manganese,

copper, zinc, and potassium become chemically tied to the soil and less available for plant use.

Applying small amounts of wood ash to most soils will not adversely affect your garden crops, and the ash does help replenish some nutrients. But because wood ash increases soil pH, adding large amounts can do more harm than good. Moreover, wood ash that has been exposed to the weather, particularly rainfall, has lost a lot of its potency, including nutrients.

Specific recommendations for the use of wood ash in the garden are difficult to make because soil composition and reaction vary from garden to garden. Distinctly acidic soils (pH less that 5.5) will probably be improved by adding wood ash. Soils that are slightly acidic (pH 6.0 to 6.5) should not be harmed by the application of 20 pounds per 1,000 square feet annually. However, if your soil is neutral or alkaline (pH greater than 7.0), find another way to dispose of the wood ash. If you don't know the acidity or alkalinity of your soil, have it tested for pH.

Crop tolerance to alkaline soil also should be considered. Some plants, such as asparagus and junipers, are more tolerant of slightly alkaline conditions than acid-loving plants such as potatoes, rhododendrons, and blueberries. Wood ash should *never* be used on acid-loving plants.

SAFFRON COMES FROM CROCUS FLOWERS

Saffron, one of the world's most expensive spices, is reported to wholesale for about $100 per pound and retail for $365 per pound! If you've ever wondered why this yellow powder is so expensive, consider the source.

Saffron comes from a portion of the flower of *Crocus sativus*, an autumn-flowering crocus. Actually, only the dried stigmas constitute the saffron we use. The stigma is the female part of the flower, which receives the pollen produced by the male part. Each blossom has only 3 stigmas, which must be picked by hand. About 210,000 stigmas from 70,000 plants are needed to gather one pound of dried saffron; the stigmas loose about 80% of their weight upon drying. Saffron has a pleasantly spicy, pungent flavor and a distinctive, long-lasting odor. Just a little pinch goes a long way, which is fortunate, considering its price.

Saffron was used extensively in the past as a yellowish-orange natural dye but has since been replaced by today's synthetic dyes. In some areas of the world, the corms of this and other crocus species are eaten.

The saffron crocus is native to southern Europe and Asia and is grown commercially in Spain, Portugal, France, and India. This petite perennial grows 6–10 inches high and produces blue-violet, lily-shaped flowers. The saffron species should be hardy in southern areas of the Midwest, but survival would be questionable in northern gardens.

Gardening Questions

2. I saw beautiful dish gardens filled with cacti while traveling in the Southwest. I couldn't carry one home on the plane. How do I make one for myself?

Saffron crocus.

A. Cacti and succulents, plants that store water in their leaves and stems, are good candidates for dish gardens, since they grow slowly. Dish gardens with tropical plants usually only last for several months, as the plants will rapidly require more space, but your desert dish garden can remain undisturbed for much longer.

The most important step is choosing plants with similar water and light requirements. Since you'll probably purchase the plants in individual containers, take the opportunity to learn about their cultural requirements by caring for them in separate pots. Gradually group them by their water and light requirements. When you have enough candidates with similar needs, you can assemble your dish garden.

Choose a container with drainage holes in the bottom. Make a potting mix of one part sand, one part potting soil, and one part leaf mold or compost and fill the container. Gently plant the cacti, adding soil as needed. You can put a layer of gravel on top for decoration, but it will make it more difficult to see if the soil has dried out. A clever ornament such as petrified wood can add the finishing touch.

Since you educated yourself about the individual plants ahead of time, you know how much to water your dish garden. As always, make sure you don't over-water.

Q. My plumosa asparagus fern is turning brown. What causes this, and what can I do for it?

A. There are several kinds of asparagus houseplants, and they are all particular about soil moisture. They will inevitably lose foliage if the potting mixture ever dries out completely. During the active growth period, water plentifully as often as necessary to keep the potting mixture moist, but never allow the pot to stand in water. Trim out any dead material and pay careful attention to soil moisture.

Place asparagus plants in bright, indirect light and transplant them every spring into a larger pot until they are the largest size you want. Since these are not true ferns, they do not demand the high humidity that ferns require.

$\mathcal{Q}$. I have a 4-year-old lipstick plant, still in its original pot. I fertilize and water once a week and keep it by a south window in a room kept at 65° F. I get lots of leaves on it but no blooms. What does it take to get this to bloom?

Also, I have a 3-year-old Kaffir lily. It hasn't put on any new leaves in that time, but it looks healthy. It's in a pot quite a bit larger than the bulb, and I have it in an east window with filtered light. The temperature ranges from 70° F to much higher when the curtain is open and it gets direct sunlight.

I'm quite successful with most plants, but these two have me baffled. Can you help me?

A. Convincing houseplants to bloom can be a challenge. You must carefully meet their individual growing requirements before they will flower.

The possibilities for a lack of blossoms are the same for houseplants as they are for flowering plants in your yard. These include improper pruning or temperature, insufficient light, and excessive nitrogen fertilizer.

Lipstick plants require higher temperatures than you are providing. Daytime temperatures of 72–75° F with night temperatures of 65–70° F are optimum. Make sure the bright light is indirect or filtered by a sheer curtain to prevent scorching. Keep the plant evenly moist and fertilize it with a blooming plant fertilizer during the spring and summer. If you choose to repot it, use an acidic growing medium of equal parts of peat moss, perlite or vermiculite, and soil.

The Kaffir lily needs to be in a smaller pot because it prefers to be potbound. Provide a cooler temperature of 60–65° F during the day, dropping 10° at night. Allow the plant to rest in early winter by providing temperatures just below 50° F and reducing water for 6–8 weeks, then resume normal care.

$\mathcal{Q}$. For several weeks our two jade plants have been dropping leaves (or shedding?) until one of them is almost bare. Both have been putting out new leaf nubs. The severe leaf-dropping worries us. It is the worst case in the several years they have been growing. Both of them are about 30 inches high and 30 inches across.

Multiple, sturdy trunks are up to 2 inches in diameter. They are in clay pots 9 inches high and 9 inches across, with drain holes and commercial potting soil. Until now, the leaves were beautifully green and glossy. There is no evidence of pests. We always keep them indoors, in an uncurtained window with a full day of indirect light and some direct sun. Because they seemed so healthy, we never fertilized them. The affected leaves look shriveled and lose normal color before dropping.

What are we doing wrong? What were we doing right? Should we fertilize them? If so, with what? (For instance, are they an acid-loving plant?) Although they have shallow roots, do they become potbound?

A. There are several possibilities, including insufficient water and nutrition. Insufficient potassium, nitrogen, or magnesium will cause defoliation. Apply fertilizer every month or so during the active growth season. Follow label instructions, as overfertilization can be as damaging as inadequate fertilization.

When you water, does the water rush right through the soil and roots and out of the pot? Sometimes soil dries out too much, and it requires a good soaking to wet it again. This can also indicate the need for a larger pot. Transplant it into a pot the next size larger and pay careful attention to watering. Jades prefer a good drenching, but allow them to dry out between watering.

A sudden change in the environment, such as rapid temperature changes, drafts of dry, hot, or cold air, or a change in light will cause leaves to drop suddenly. The new growth is a good sign your plants will survive.

2. Underneath the leaves of many of my houseplants, there are white fuzzy things with legs. I suspect they are an insect that could harm the plants. What should I do?

A. Mealybugs can pose a serious threat to your plants. They are white, cottony insects found underneath the leaves or where the leaves connect to the stems. They harm the plants by sucking out the sap.

If only a few mealybugs are present, wipe them off with a damp towel, or remove them with cotton swabs dipped in rubbing alcohol. Sometimes you can prune them back and discard the heavily infested portions of the plant. With luck, the plant will survive the pruning and put out new growth. Keep a close eye on it, since mealybugs and their eggs are probably present to reinfest the plant. It may be best to discard severely infested plants.

Repeated applications of an insecticide or insecticidal soap may be necessary. Make sure the product is labeled for your plants and follow label instructions carefully. Inspect the plants and their containers regularly for mealybugs or their cottony egg masses.

In the future, inspect any new plants you bring into your home to be sure they are free of insects. Make sure you check the houseplants you bring indoors at the end of the summer, too.

Q. I can't keep my cat from eating my houseplants. I've read that some plants are poisonous. Which ones are dangerous? Is there something I can grow for him to munch on?

A. Many plants are poisonous if specific parts of the plant are eaten in sufficient quantity. Some plants are particularly dangerous, including dumbcane, oleander, philodendron, and mistletoe. Outdoors, watch out for morning glory, lily of the valley, rhubarb, tomato vines, and mushrooms.

Cats don't need vegetation in their diet; they're carnivorous, but we all know curiosity killed the cat, and some cats like to nibble on foliage. Try to break the habit by squirting your cat with a toy water gun when he shows interest in the plant, or simply remove the plant from his reach.

Your local pet supply store or veterinarian can recommend safe plants for your cat to nibble. There are safe "kitty grass" products on the market, but if your cat is like mine, he prefers the forbidden houseplant over the most expensive kitty grass available. As a cat owner, I choose not to provide a home for these toxic houseplants.

Q. I recently moved to the Midwest from the West Coast. How can I find out which plants are hardy here?

A. Knowing the U.S. Department of Agriculture plant hardiness zones will help you select plants that will survive winters in your area. The United States is divided into zones based on long-term studies of temperatures. (See Appendix A). Plants are then assigned a hardiness zone, which is mentioned on many plant tags or in garden catalogs and reference books. If a plant is hardy to zone 5, for example, that means it will survive the average minimum temperatures of those places on the map that are rated zone 5 or warmer. A quick glance at the map will tell you your hardiness zone.

Many garden books refer to the USDA map, while others use a slightly different map developed by the Arnold Arboretum. One word of caution: some retailers will omit mentioning or exaggerate a plant's hardiness in the interest of promoting sales. Any time you purchase from a new source, check a few of their hardiness claims against a reference book that has no interest in selling plants until you know if the new source is trustworthy.

Just because a plant is hardy does not mean it will thrive or even survive in your garden. Other factors must also be taken into account. Frosts, rainfall, soil types, soil pH, summer heat, and sunlight will also affect your plants. Combine your knowledge of hardiness maps with your own observations of plants doing well in your area.

Q. We enjoy the squirrels and birds in our garden, especially in the winter. Can we grow certain plants to entice them into our yard?

A. You can create a wildlife habitat in your yard by providing food, water, and cover. Plants that form acorns, nuts, berries, buds, catkins, fruits, nectar, or seeds all provide food for animals. Animal favorites include viburnum, crab apple, firethorn, and hawthorn. The thorns of firethorn and hawthorn also provide protective cover for animals. Porcelain vine, Boston ivy, and Virginia creeper also provide food and cover.

Flower seeds are a valuable source of nutrients for birds and small animals. Globe thistle (*Echinops*), purple coneflower (*Echinacea*), sunflower, and goldenrod offer plenty of seeds.

Add a pond or set the basin of a birdbath into the ground to give wildlife a water source. A brush pile and a stand of tall grass or flowers will protect smaller animals from wind and predators.

Q. We have large hickory and oak trees on our property. The trees are old but healthy. A recent ice storm broke off some limbs, leaving ragged stumps on the tree. How should we treat these to prevent insects and rain from entering the trees?

A. Prune off the dead branch stubs so the bark can grow over the wound to protect the underlying tissue. The final cut should not go into the ringed ridges at the base of the branch, called a branch collar.

Many arborists now reject the old practice of painting wounds. Sunlight and warmth cause the paint to expand and contract, forming cracks in the paint. These openings allow moisture, insects, and diseases into the plant, where the remaining shield of paint provides a protected, damp environment that is perfect for insect and disease growth. Tree specialists recommend that no dressing be applied to pruning cuts. Left untreated, the tree forms new tissue over the pruning cut which eventually encloses the entire wound.

Q. A honey locust in my front yard has roots that come up out of the lawn, which makes walking and mowing difficult. Is this typical of honey locusts? Can I fix it by adding soil, or should I remove the tree? It is probably 30 years old.

A. Silver maples, poplars, elms, and sweet gums are more likely to produce surface roots. Honey locusts are less likely to have protruding roots but may on occasion. Surface roots in the lawn are encouraged to form by light sprinklings of water, compacted soil, confined root space, or waterlogged soil. Trees will grow best when given plenty of space in well-drained soils and watered deeply.

Slowly raising the level of the soil 1 inch (no more!) per year is one possible

solution, but it has its drawbacks. You may need to do this for some years, since the roots will continue to grow in diameter and then break the surface of the soil again. If too much soil is added each year, the roots will become starved for oxygen, and the tree may die. Raise the soil level only as the last resort.

If you can't live with the surface roots, you might want to have the tree removed. Make sure soil drainage and root space are adequate before planting a new tree. Oak and ash rarely have surface roots. An easier—and more attractive—solution is to plant a permanent ground cover under the tree, so you don't have to walk or mow there.

FEBRUARY

There seems to be so much more winter than we need this year.
—Kathleen Norris

As the wind howls, gardeners sometimes lose patience. We have waited so long for the season to begin, but it still seems far away. We anxiously approach the second of February asking if the groundhog will see his shadow. Whether he does or not, a midwestern February is predictable in its very unpredictability. The erratic weather this month—welcome thaws followed by subzero temperatures—can be hard on your outdoor plants as well as on your frame of mind.

Valentine's Day offers the opportunity to bring flowers and plants into the house, reminding us of the wonders of nature and brightening our spirits. There is still time to plan your spring and summer plantings. With the prospect of new life outdoors, make sure you remember to care for your houseplants, too.

If there is a warm day near the end of the month, venture into the garden. Look carefully for emerging snowdrops, winter aconites, or blooming hellebores and help prepare your woody plants for the growing season as you enjoy the crisp, fresh air.

Garden Calendar

HOME

Refill water levels daily in vases of flowers.

Early blooms of spring-flowering bulbs make good gifts for a sweetheart. Keep the plant in a bright, cool location for longer-lasting blooms.

Because growth slows or stops in winter months, most plants will require less water and little if any fertilizer. Check soil for dryness before watering. Increase humidity in the home to make up for dry, heated air.

Houseplants may not receive adequate light because days are short. Move plants closer to windows but avoid placing foliage against cold glass panes. Artificial lighting may be helpful.

YARD

Check mulches, rodent shields, salt/wind screens, and other winter plant protections to make sure they are still in place.

Prune landscape plants, except early-spring bloomers, which should be pruned after their flowers fade. Birches, maples, dogwoods, and other heavy sap bleeders can be pruned in early summer to avoid the sap flow.

Choose appropriate species and cultivars of plants, and begin drawing landscaping plans.

GARDEN

Test leftover garden seed for germination. Place 10 seeds between moist paper toweling or cover with a thin layer of soil. Keep seeds warm and moist. If fewer than 6 seeds germinate, then fresh seed should be purchased.

Order seeds before it's too late for this year's planting.

Start seeds indoors for cool-season vegetables so they will be ready for transplanting to the garden early in the season. Broccoli, cauliflower, and cabbage seeds should be started 5–7 weeks prior to transplanting.

Prepare or repair lawn and garden tools for the upcoming season.

PRECOCIOUS BULBS

Hardly a year goes by that spring-flowering bulbs don't send up some leaves in winter. However heartening this sign of approaching spring is, gardeners always fret over whether the plants will be injured and whether they should try to cover them.

Bulbs that were planted too early in autumn often produce leaves before winter sets in. But even those planted at the proper time may send up leaves when a spell of balmy weather warms the soil sufficiently. In the Midwest, the soil freezes and thaws frequently, and it is during the thaws that bulbs start to grow. Gardens in protected locations or close to a warm building are likely to thaw more often.

Once the foliage has broken through the ground, the leaf tips may be damaged by hard freezes. But the plant will be able to grow more leaves and the flowers should come up at their "usual" time. Most bulbs need at least 10 weeks of cold temperatures before the flower buds are formed. Even after flower buds have been initiated, they are still safely tucked away inside the bulb below.

As "normal" flowering time grows closer, there is always a chance that flowers will begin to emerge during warm spells, only to be nipped by a late freeze. In most cases, the flowers do recover. The worst-case scenario is that your spring show will be curtailed for a year. But take heart: even if the flowers are damaged, the plant will survive. Some anxious gardeners temporarily cover emerged flowers to protect them through a hard freeze, but often the weight of the cover does more damage to the flowers than the cold weather.

Applying winter mulch to keep the ground cold *after* the ground freezes may help prevent the frequent thawing caused by fluctuating temperatures. But if the weather remains warm for several days or longer, the bulbs may poke through, anyway. Applying mulch after the bulbs have started to come up will not provide adequate protection for the foliage and may actually encourage disease.

The bottom line is, no action is required when bulbs come up in winter. They've been doing it for years and seem to manage just fine without our intervention!

WINTER INJURY OF LANDSCAPE PLANTS

Cold snaps can injure even the hardiest of landscape plants. Most of them will survive, but damage can show up later in spring and summer.

Prolonged periods of zero or subzero temperatures can kill buds (both flower and leaf), twigs, or entire branches. Tender or marginally hardy plants will suffer the most. Plants that have been hardy in previous years can be damaged if they've been subjected to a period of warm weather before the temperature drops or to inadequate soil moisture in the fall.

Some plants tend to start breaking bud during early warm spells. These buds are then damaged or even killed when temperatures drop back below freezing. Cherry, peach, apricot, and forsythia are among the most likely candidates for this type of injury.

High winds can cause damage that is not visible until later in the growing season. Plants continue to lose water through their twigs and buds throughout the winter. The greater the wind, the faster the plants lose water. When the ground is frozen, the plant's roots cannot replace the lost water, resulting in desiccation of the twigs, buds, and leaves.

Evergreens, particularly broad-leaved evergreens—such as rhododendrons—have a greater surface area through which to lose water compared to deciduous plants and so

are particularly susceptible to injury. Young or newly transplanted plants that did not establish an adequate root system are also at a disadvantage.

Severe drying will show up as dead twigs and buds when spring growth begins. Some twigs will leaf out in spring, only to die back later in the summer as heat stress sets in. Symptoms include yellow, brown, or purple discoloration of leaves and branches. Broad-leaved evergreens typically have beige to brown leaf edges that are curled.

Yet another winter injury is known as frost cracking or southwest injury. The bark of young, thin-barked trees can split open as a result of a quick temperature drop. This type of injury most commonly occurs on the south or southwest side of the trunk on cold, sunny days in January or February. The trunk and bark heat as the sun shines, causing expansion. Then as the sun sets, the temperature of the trunk drops, and the bark contracts more rapidly than the wood below. A vertical split in the bark is the result. A young, fast-growing tree can often cover such an injury by producing callous tissue. However, the wound can be a site of infection by disease or insects.

Prevention is the best cure for winter injury. Use plants that are known to be hardy in your area. Avoid planting in low spots, where cold air settles, or areas subject to high winds. If autumn rains are sparse, water plants thoroughly before the soil freezes. If plants are particularly susceptible to desiccation, make a burlap or canvas screen to break the wind. Wrap trunks of young trees in late November and remove the wrap in March to prevent splitting of the bark (see page 247).

If you discover injury in the spring, prune out dead twigs and branches. Water plants thoroughly during dry spells and apply a 2–3-inch layer of mulch to help conserve soil moisture. A light application of fertilizer in early spring will help encourage recovery.

There is no effective treatment for split bark. Wound dressings have been shown to be of no benefit. Healthy trees can tolerate all but the most extreme bark injuries.

Valentine's Day is just around the corner, and you may be searching for a meaningful gift for that special someone. Why not say it with flowers?

Nothing expresses your affection like cut flowers, particularly roses, but their elegant beauty fades fast. If you're looking for something that will last a little longer, there are several blooming plants that will fit the bill.

Cyclamen, with its heart-shaped leaves, is made for the occasion. But the real attraction of this plant is its flowers, which can be white or many shades of pink, red, or lavender. The flowers have a striking form that has been likened to butterflies, birds in

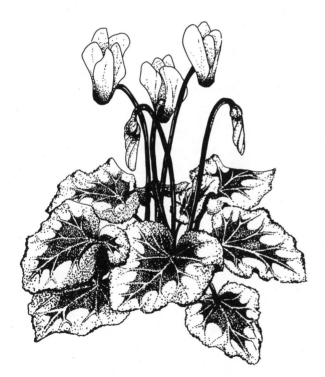

Cyclamen's heart-shaped leaves and dainty flowers make it an ideal gift.

flight, and even falling stars. And if the plants weren't already attractive enough, the leaves are finely detailed with silvery or light green markings. The cyclamen most often stocked at your florist's is large and showy, but mini-cyclamen are also available. Look under the leaves to find plants with the largest number of flower buds. To enjoy this beauty well into spring, provide cyclamen bright light and very cool temperatures—about 65° F during the day and 45° F at night. Water thoroughly when the top layer of soil begins to feel dry to the touch.

An azalea in bloom is sure to drive away the winter blahs of just about anyone. Plants are available in a wide range of colors, including white, pink, salmon, crimson, magenta, orange, and even bicolor forms. The azaleas most often grown for holiday gifts bear large blossoms, up to 3 inches across. They are not hardy outdoors in the Midwest, although they can be placed outdoors in summer. Water thoroughly when the top layer of soil is just beginning to dry. A sunny east or west window is ideal indoors, and, as for cyclamen, cool temperatures are a must.

Calceolaria, also known as pocket-book plant, bears unusual, pouchlike flowers, hence its common name. Flower color ranges from red and maroon to bronze and yellow, and the texture is soft and rich, like velvet.

Cineraria produces a striking mass of daisy-like flowers in rich shades of pink, red, blue, and violet, all with bold white centers. Both calceolaria and cineraria are cared for in much the same way. Again, keep them cool to encourage continued flowering and place them in bright indirect light, such as a clear northern exposure. Water when the top layer of soil begins to dry and avoid splashing water on the leaves and especially flowers of calceolaria, as they will spot easily.

Plants don't have to flower to be a good Valentine's Day messenger. String of hearts, or *Ceropegia*, is a trailing vine that—as you might guess from its name—has heart-shaped leaves borne on long, threadlike stems. The thick, succulent leaves are dark green with whitish veins for contrast. Although the plants do bear interesting pink or purplish tube-shaped flowers, they are quite small and don't provide much of a show. Little tubers form from the trailing stems and can be used to start new plants.

A sunny window is best for *Ceropegia*, but it will tolerate lower light intensity. Allow the top layer of soil to dry slightly between waterings.

Whatever your choice of gift, be sure to have the sales clerk wrap your plant to protect it from cold winter weather. Plants can be injured by even a brief period of freezing temperatures, so keep the car warm and make the florist your last stop before going home.

CUT-FLOWER CARE: MYTHS AND FACTS

Many gardeners have their own recipes for extending cut-flower life, including dropping a penny in a vase of roses. However, many commonly held beliefs probably do more good for the gardener than for the flowers.

Adding a penny to vase water isn't likely to prolong flower life. The belief probably comes from the fact that pennies contain copper, which was commonly used in pesticides at one time, but it isn't likely to dissolve in water. Another common belief is that adding aspirin to vase water will keep flowers fresh. There is no evidence to support this assumption, either.

Commercially packaged preservatives generally include sugar, bactericide, and an acidifier. The sugar provides carbohydrate for the flowers, the bactericide prevents decay, and the acidifier prevents growth of organisms that can clog the vessels that carry water through the stems.

Lemon-lime soda pop can make a reasonable alternative to commercially formulated preservatives. The lemon-lime pop contains sugar and acidifiers. Mix 2 cups soda pop with 2 cups water and add ½–1 teaspoon of chlorine bleach. However, commercially packaged preservatives are likely to be less expensive and more effective.

Recutting stems and changing vase water daily will help prolong flower life. Cutting the stem at an angle has often been recommended to promote uptake of water, but a straight cut actually takes up water at the same rate. Angle-cut stems, however, are easier to insert into floral foams and other items used for flower arrangements.

Although many old books recommend splitting or smashing the ends of cut twigs to allow better absorption, stems are best left intact. Woody stems are typically slow to take up water, and mashing them will only destroy their structural integrity. Recut the stems daily and cut back to greener growth when possible.

Since rotting leaves encourage bacterial and fungal growth, which can clog the stem's plumbing system, always remove the stems' lower leaves so they will not sit in the water and rot. Use clean containers for arrangements and change water daily.

Flowers kept in a cool location out of direct sunlight will have a longer vase life. Don't store flowers near fruits or vegetables, since ripening produce gives off ethylene gas, which causes both produce and flowers to mature faster.

Cut flowers from your garden in the early morning or late evening, when they are the most turgid, or filled with water. Before arranging garden flowers, condition them by placing the cut stems in warm water for two hours and store them in a cool area overnight.

THE VANILLA ORCHID

Although much of the vanilla used for flavoring today is produced synthetically, natural vanilla comes from the seedpod of an orchid plant. The vanilla orchid is a vigorous vining plant that can reach up to 300 feet in its native tropical environment.

The vine produces 2-inch green flowers that must be individually hand-pollinated to ensure a good set of pods. The pods grow to about 6–9 inches long and are harvested when fully grown but not yet ripe. The vanilla flavor is then further developed by curing and fermenting the pods.

Today, most cooks purchase vanilla in extract form, but occasionally one can find the whole seedpod, often called a vanilla bean. Most commercial production of vanilla takes place in the tropical regions of Mexico and Madagascar, where the climate is warm and humid, the soil is rich with organic matter, and the plant is provided with constant shade from other tropical plants. In fact, the vanilla orchid is often grown on the trunks of shade trees to support the vines.

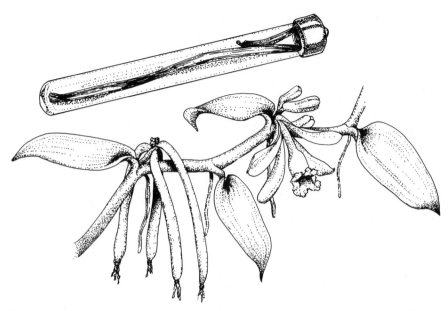

Top: A vanilla bean packaged for sale. Bottom: The vanilla orchid with immature pods.

Although green-thumbed gardeners may be successful at raising orchids, the vanilla plant is not as showy as other types. Midwestern gardeners can best appreciate vanilla as an import.

LOAMY SOIL IDEAL FOR GARDENING

Gardeners are always advised that a loamy garden soil is best for just about all plants. But just what is a loamy soil? And what can you do to get that perfect soil if you weren't blessed with it?

In general, soil is composed of many particles of varying sizes. Soil scientists have classified soil particles into 3 major groups: sand, silt, and clay. Sand particles are the largest and tend to hold little water but allow good aeration. Clay particles are very small and tend to pack down, so that water does not drain well, and little or no air can

penetrate. Silt particles are medium sized and have properties in between those of sand and clay.

A loamy soil combines all three of these types of particles in relatively equal amounts. Loamy soil is ideal for most garden plants because it holds plenty of moisture but also drains well, so that plenty of air can reach the roots.

Heavy clay or compacted soils can be rescued by the persevering gardener. Add a good amount of organic matter, such as compost, animal manure, cover crops, or organic mulch, each year as the soil is worked. It may take several years, but eventually the soil will be improved. Although adding some sand along with the organic matter is acceptable, adding sand alone is not advised. The organic matter offers several advantages that sand does not, including increased water- and nutrient-holding capabilities.

Highly sandy soils can be a problem, since they hold little water and few nutrients. Adding organic materials to a sandy soil will improve its ability to hold water and nutrients. You'll need to add at least a 2-inch layer of material to make a marked improvement. This translates to about 18 cubic feet of organic matter for a 100-square-foot area.

Soil improvement is a program, not just a one-shot deal. You'll need to continue applications at least once a year for several years to really change the nature of the existing soil. But there's no better long-term investment you can make in your garden.

GROW YOUR OWN TRANSPLANTS

Growing your own garden transplants may take some extra work, but it does have its advantages. You'll have a much wider choice of cultivars to choose from, since most garden centers can stock only a limited number.

Start out with high-quality, fresh seed; look for the freshness date on the packet. Most any clean container can be used, as long as excess water can drain out the bottom. Use a fine-textured, well-drained medium such as a peat moss–vermiculite mixture. Seeds need high relative humidity for good germination, so place a plastic bag around the container until plants are growing. Too much humidity can also be a problem, so be sure to poke a few holes in the plastic to allow ventilation. Although plants vary as to optimum temperature, most garden seeds will germinate faster in warm temperatures—65–70° F. Seeds of cool-season plants, including peas, cabbage, broccoli, and cauliflower, should be kept at about 55° F.

Be sure to check your seedlings frequently for moisture needs. The planting medium should be kept reasonably moist throughout the germination period. Water gently to avoid damaging the tender seedlings. Once plants are up and growing, allow the medium to dry slightly between waterings.

Most home growers get into trouble after the seeds come up by not supplying the plants with enough light. Low light causes plants to become spindly and weak. Place them in as sunny a location as possible or use artificial lights if necessary.

Proper timing is crucial if you want to have transplants at the right size at planting time. Seeds of tomatoes, peppers, and eggplant should be started about 7 weeks before your outdoor planting date. Pumpkins, melons, and squash should be started about 4 weeks before planting outdoors. Flower seeds will need anywhere from 4 to 14 weeks, depending on the species. Most seed packets have growing information on the back.

In addition to providing you with exactly what you want when you want it, growing your own seedlings is a marvelous way to cure winter doldrums.

DESIGNING A FLOWER BED WITH A VIEW IN MIND

While it is true that beauty is in the eye of the beholder, there are some basic design principles to keep in mind when designing a flower bed.

The most important consideration that drives the rest of the design is function. How will the garden be seen? Will it be enjoyed primarily by those looking out of a window from inside the house? Is it to be viewed by passing cars and pedestrians? Is the bed a part of an outdoor room? Do you want to view the bed while sitting out on the patio, or is it meant to entice one to walk through it?

The size of the flower bed will be determined by factors such as function and, of

course, budget. If you're new to gardening, it is probably best to start small at first—you can always expand later.

Most garden books advise three basic design rules. Tall plants to the back, complementary color schemes, and massing of flowers for effect. In general, you won't want taller plants to block the view of shorter flowers. However, if the bed can be viewed from all directions rather than just one side, perhaps the tallest plants should be placed in the middle, with smaller plants toward the perimeter. For those with a taste for the extraordinary, dare to defy the rules and create a surprise garden by tucking some smaller flowers behind the taller-stemmed plants. This technique can be effective for gardens that invite intimate visits.

Once you've determined a function, decide on a focal point, a center of attention. The focal point can be a plant or group of plants, a pond, a statue, or any other object you want to catch the eye. The other elements of your design should serve to enhance that focal point, not compete with it. Because of the seasonal nature of gardens, the focal point can change through the year.

Certain color combinations tend to be more pleasing than others, but what is harmonious to one observer may be less so to another. A useful tool for color design is known as the color wheel. Colors that are directly across from each other on the wheel are known as complementary. Purple and yellow, blue and orange, and red and green are considered to be complementary color combinations. Analogous harmony uses colors directly next to each other on the wheel. For example, blue and green or blue and violet are also considered to be pleasing combinations. A color scheme using various shades of a single color is known as monochromatic. A multicolored design will tend to have a more informal look.

Grouping many plants of the same texture and color is known as massing. This technique will give greater emphasis to that color and texture and will tend to be more dramatic.

Don't think of your flower garden as a permanent exhibit. Annual flowers will need to be planted new each year. Perennial flowers will come back on their own, but they can be moved when necessary. Think of your garden plants much like the furniture in a room. If you're unhappy with the arrangement, change it!

FINOCCHIO

If you're looking for a new crop to liven up your garden, why not try finocchio? Also called Florence fennel, finocchio has long been a popular vegetable in Europe but has somehow fallen out of circulation from most American gardens. You may have tasted this unusual vegetable on an antipasto tray in some Italian restaurants. It's the one with the mild licorice flavor.

Finocchio, which is a relative of celery, parsley, and carrots, is grown for the thick swelling at the base of the leaf stalks. It is a cool-season plant that thrives in moist, highly organic soil. You'll probably have to order seeds from mail-order houses, particularly those that offer culinary specialties. The plant requires about 100 days from seeding to maturity, so starting the seed indoors will help give you a head start and get the crop in before the season warms too much.

The part you harvest is the bottom of the main stalk, sometimes referred to as the "bulb." This swollen base should be covered with mulch to block out the sun when about 1 inch thick to keep the flavor mild. Finocchio is ready to harvest when it's about the size of a baseball. The bulb can be stuffed or sliced up for salads, stir-frying, grilling, or steaming. The leaves can be harvested any time and used to liven up dressings, dips, and sauces and for an exotic garnish. Even the seeds of this plant are tasty for flavoring baked goods and tomato dishes. But don't allow too many sprigs to go to seed; this will take much of the plant's energy away from stem formation.

SPOTS ON AFRICAN VIOLET LEAVES

Those who grow African violets often become alarmed when their prized violets develop spots on their leaves. Although there may be other causes, these spots are usually just the result of splashing water.

African violet leaves are sensitive to cold water and will form spots where the water contacts the leaf tissue. Watering from below has often been recommended as a remedy.

Placing water in the bottom dish and allowing it to be drawn up into the soil should avoid the splashing of water onto the leaves. However, watering from the bottom can lead to a buildup of salt residue in the soil. Most tap water contains some mineral salt, and some water sources may have a considerable amount. Fertilizing the plants will also add salts to the soil. As water evaporates from the top of the soil, the mineral salts are left behind. This is the white, crusty material that is often seen on houseplants.

An occasional heavy watering from above will help flush those salts out of the pot. About every fourth watering, apply enough water from above so that some runs out of the drainage holes at the bottom of the pot. Be sure to discard that excess so that the salty drainage water is not reabsorbed into the soil.

Spotting of African violet leaves can also be avoided by using lukewarm water rather than cold tap water. Then you can always water from above, preventing the salt buildup. You will still have to ensure that the drainage water does not become reabsorbed. A simple way to prevent reabsorption is to set the pots up on rocks, bricks, or some other support, so that the bottom of the pot is out of the reach of the drained water.

Gardening Questions

Q. We have a family of groundhogs that have taken up residence in our vegetable garden and orchard. They make enormous tunnels and consume an incredible amount of vegetables. We can't bring ourselves to shoot them. Any thoughts?

A. We all hope the groundhog won't see his shadow on groundhog day, but most of us hope he looks for it in someone else's garden! One or two woodchucks, as they are also known, can ruin a small garden in 24 hours. On the other hand, they are one of the only large wild mammals active during the day, and their burrows aer-ate the soil and provide refuge for other animals. If their damage is tolerable, enjoy them. If it is intolerable, as it often is, some form of control is necessary.

Try to control woodchucks in early spring when the young are still at home. Live trapping is the most effective means of nonlethal control. Convince your neighbors to participate, too, or your yard will be reinfested by neighboring wood-chucks. Woodchucks are fairly easy to entice into a trap. Set a live trap in the trail immediately in front of the burrow entrance and bait it with apple slices, carrots, or sweet corn. Check the trap in midmorning and at dusk to avoid stress or injury to the trapped animal. Relocate them, if it is legal in your area, at least five miles from the trap site in an area where they will not cause a problem for someone else. Good luck locating such a site! Your local branch of the Department of Natural Resources can help you determine if/where you can relocate the animal.

Fencing could keep the groundhogs out of the garden, but since the fence would have to extend into the ground several feet, it is only a viable solution for small gardens and strong gardeners.

$2.$ I would like to know how to get rid of flies and worms on my apple trees. What and how many sprays should I apply each season? I ordered a spray from a cata-log. It did nothing.

$A.$ Multipurpose Fruit Sprays (MPFS) will give adequate control of insects and dis-eases under average conditions. They are available in most retail garden depart-ments or through the mail and usually contain a fungicide and one or two insecticides. Healthy fruit production typically requires one application of a dor-mant oil spray and regular MPFS applications throughout the season. Spraying once or twice a season without regard to timing is ineffective.

A typical schedule begins with an application of dormant oil before the leaves start to protrude from the buds. Make MPFS applications when the leaves show ½ inch of green tissue and again when the first hint of pink shows in opening

blossoms. Be sure to omit the insecticide from your applications while the trees are in bloom. Otherwise, you may injure bees, which you need to pollinate your fruit crop. Apply a fungicide (no insecticide!) when 50% of the blossoms are open, then an MPFS when 75% of the petals have fallen and again 7–10 days after petal fall. Repeat the MPFS applications at 2-week intervals until the harvest restriction date. Maybe all that work explains the price of a good apple!

You can use an MPFS on pears, stone fruits, grapes, and berries, but each requires a different spray schedule. Follow all label instructions carefully.

Q. When is a good time to prune fruit trees?
A. Tackle most pruning chores during the dormant season. The best time to prune is early spring, just before the beginning of active growth. During this period, healing is rapid, shoot growth is promoted, and it is easy to detect flower buds, enabling you to quickly decide the location and number of cuts (see page 60).

Q. When is the best time to prune old, overgrown grapes, and what is the best way to do it? I would like to repair the arbor. Should I cut the plants way back for easier access to the arbor?
A. Prune grapes in the winter or very early spring, while they are dormant. To rejuvenate an older plant or gain access to the arbor, select a sturdy cane originating near the base of the plant. Allow a 3–4-foot length to remain. After this cane completes its second growing season, cut off the old trunk just above the attachment of the renewal cane. This renewal cane is now the new trunk.

Q. We have a passive solar home with a sunroom/greenhouse on the front. We filled the planters with topsoil and added sawdust for a nice loose soil. We added fertilizer and lime to control the acid from the sawdust. We have tried to grow lots of vegetables from seed, including lettuce, broccoli, snow peas, beans, and tomatoes. The plants get about 3 inches out of the ground and stop growing. We are not heating the sunroom with anything but sun. Some days it gets as high as 120° F and as low as 38° F. Could this be our problem?

A. It would be convenient to have a solar greenhouse *and* sunroom, but the room cannot serve both purposes unless you are willing to make some modifications. Plants will not grow with such wide temperature fluctuations! Most seedlings, including tomatoes and beans, prefer a temperature of 65–75° F. Some cool-season plants, such as broccoli, lettuce, and peas, germinate best at 55° F. Consider installing blinds, shade cloth, or fans to regulate the temperatures.

The soil mix may be another problem. Fresh sawdust ties up the available nitrogen in the soil, and it is difficult to counteract this process with the addition of fertilizer. Try replacing the soil with a sterile medium recommended for seedlings, available at most garden centers.

2. My garden space is limited, and I grow only 6 tomato plants each year. The seed packets usually contain several dozen more seeds than I need. Should I plant the 6 largest seeds to get the best transplants?

A. Even the 6 largest seeds won't guarantee 6 strong transplants. Instead, start more seeds than you will need. For example, you could sow 18 seeds. After they germinate, discard the smallest plants to reduce the competition for nutrients and water. The number to discard will depend upon how many germinated. Try to leave 12 plants to grow on until it's time to transplant them outdoors. This gives you extras in case some fall victim to damping off or another misfortune. Choose the largest transplants to set out in your garden, and dispose of the others. You might give them to a gardening friend if it breaks your heart to throw them on the compost pile.

2. When is the best time to plant onion seed so I can later plant my own onion sets? I've heard that years ago people planted this seed in August. I would like to try this, but don't know how to follow through. Can you help?

A. Onions may be planted from sets, seeds, or transplants. Sets are small, dry onions usually used to produce green onions. Onion plants grown from sets are more prone to bolting, and their mature bulbs do not store as well as those grown from seed or transplants.

To grow sets from seed, scatter seeds in a row 2 inches wide in early spring. Do not thin the onions, as crowding keeps them small. Pull the plants in late July before they are ¾ inch in diameter. Smaller sets will give you larger bulbs and are less likely to bolt next year. Place the sets in the sun until the tops are completely dry and then remove the tops. Store the sets in a dry, cool place.

Plant sets in the garden the following spring. Push them into the soil just enough to hold them in place. Pull green onions and use them for fresh eating any time while they are young. Onions for drying mature in 3–5 months.

2. Several years ago, I planted a perennial garden and am disappointed when each plant blooms for a week or so and then quits. Which ones bloom for a long time?

A. Most perennials bloom for several weeks during the growing season. You can design colorful gardens by carefully selecting plants that bloom at different times of the year or by choosing plants with an extended period of bloom.

Coreopsis 'Moonbeam' blooms from June to frost with tiny pale yellow flowers. Veronica 'Sunny Border Blue' sends up purple spikes from July to frost. 'Stella de Oro' is a golden miniature daylily that blooms for 4 months. Since these plants begin blooming in the summer, bring early color to your garden by including spring bloomers such as peony and iris.

There is no law against including a few annuals in your perennial garden. Add some annuals for constant spots of color during the growing season and to cover the bare spots before your perennials fill in.

2. I bought a weeping fig tree, and all its leaves are dropping. The greenhouse employee told me how to care for it, and I am following her instructions. I put it in a southern window as she suggested. What is wrong?

A. Probably nothing! Weeping figs are not good travelers. They will drop almost all of their leaves every time you move them. With proper care, they will produce new leaves that are better suited to the light in their new home. Weeping figs prefer even moisture, regular fertilization, and high light levels. Protect your plant from drafts and don't move it to new locations very often!

2. The other day I saw a jade plant blooming at a friend's house. I've had one for years, and it has never bloomed. Does she have a different kind? The leaves looked the same.

A. If it resembles yours, it is probably the same, although several species exist. Encourage your plant to flower by imitating the desert conditions that cause jades to flower in nature. You'll need to provide cool night temperatures of 50–55° F and very bright days. Jades will flower after they are 4 years old and prefer to be slightly potbound.

MARCH

Now the greening begins. Slowly, patiently, we find signs of life in the garden and in nature. Buds are swelling, and the bulbs begin to show their spring color. The first warm day in March lures gardeners outdoors, eager to be in the sunshine and to dally in the dirt. Our muscles may have rested during the winter months, but planting some cool-season crops will get us back into shape. We also need to provide some mainte-nance for our established plants. They need to shape up, too, and some fertilization and pruning will aid their long-term survival.

Garden Calendar

HOME

Keep spent leaves and flowers of houseplants removed to improve appearance and encourage more blooms.

Prune, repot, and clean houseplants as needed.

Begin fertilizing houseplants as new growth appears.

YARD

Rake the lawn to remove leaves, twigs, and trash.

Prune trees and shrubs while plants are still dormant, except those that bloom early in spring.

Remove winter coverings from roses as soon as new growth begins. Prune and fertilize as needed.

Fertilize woody plants before new growth begins but after soil temperatures have reached 40° F.

Remove trunk wraps that were applied earlier to prevent bark from splitting.

Apply superior oil spray to landscape plants and fruit trees for control of scale insects and mites when tips of leaves start to protrude from buds.

Plant new trees and shrubs as soon as soil dries enough to be worked. Plant bare-root plants before they leaf out.

Seed bare spots in lawn.

Apply crabgrass preventer when grass starts active growth in southern areas of the Midwest; wait until April in northern areas, as active growth is later.

GARDEN

Watch for blooms of early spring bulbs, such as daffodils, squill, crocus, dwarf iris, and snowdrops.

Remove old asparagus and rhubarb tops and side-dress the plants with nitrogen or dried manure.

Remove weak, diseased, or damaged canes from raspberry plants before new growth begins. Remove old fruiting canes if they were allowed to overwinter, and shorten remaining canes if necessary.

Prune grape vines.

Remove winter mulch from strawberry beds as soon as new growth begins, but keep the mulch nearby to protect against frost and freezes.

Follow last fall's soil test recommendations for fertilizer and pH adjustment. It's not too late to test soil if you missed last year.

Gradually harden off transplants by setting them outdoors temporarily during the daytime for about a week before planting.

Plant cool-season vegetables and flowers as soon as the ground has dried enough to work. Do not work the soil while it is wet.

Plant or transplant asparagus, rhubarb, and small fruit plants.

Start seeds of warm-season vegetables and flowers indoors.

Spring officially begins in March, but it seems it's the flowers that let us know when spring really begins.

Flowering is quite dependent on the weather, so the timing of the blooms varies from year to year. But regardless of the weather, the sequence in which plants bloom should remain the same.

Some bulbs may show their stuff long before spring is officially proclaimed. Winter aconites and snowdrops often pop up during the brief warm-ups that February brings. Some species of crocus tend to be right on the money, blooming about the third week of March. Bulbous iris and some species of squill follow along toward the end of the month. Next come daffodils and spring beauties (*Claytonia*). As spring progresses, more daffodils, grape hyacinths, and early tulips grace our gardens.

Local weather conditions and microclimates can affect the season of bloom. Southern areas of the Midwest can be up to 4 weeks ahead of northern areas. Urban areas tend to be warmer than rural areas, and even certain areas of one garden can be warmer than others. Flowers that are planted close to buildings and in sunny spots tend to bloom before those that are out in the yard or in shady areas.

Bulbous plants have a distinct advantage over some other types of plants due to the large amount of food reserves stored in the bulbs. These plants usually have enough reserves to see them through the spring blooming season. But if you want to keep these bulbs healthy and productive in the years to come, you may have to give them some help.

In many cases, the bulb's foliage is not much to look at once the flowers have faded. However, it is essential that the foliage be allowed to grow so it can manufacture the food reserves that are then transferred to the bulb for storage. The leaves should never be cut off before they've begun to yellow and wither on their own. Bulbs can be planted among ground covers or intermingled with annual or perennial flowers to focus attention away from the bulb's foliage. Spent flowers should be removed to prevent the production of seed, which uses up considerable food reserves from the bulb.

A light side-dressing of fertilizer helps keep the foliage thriving. Apply a nitrogen-containing product such as ammonium nitrate, bonemeal, or manure according to label directions. The fertilizer should be placed alongside the plants, not directly on the foliage.

If you want to move your bulbs to another spot in the garden, wait until after the foliage fades to dig them up. Replant them as soon as possible to protect them from exposure to light and excessive heat and drying.

GARDENING TIPS FOR BEGINNERS

If you're just starting out in the world of gardening, don't be overwhelmed by your neighbor's 1000-square-foot "patch." It isn't difficult to be a successful gardener, but it will take some time and elbow grease.

Good planning is essential to successful gardening. Start your garden off right by selecting a location that receives at least six hours of direct sunlight daily. Check the site for good drainage by making sure water doesn't tend to stand after a rain or irrigation. Try to steer clear of trees and shrubs that would compete with your garden plants for water, light, and nutrients. Walnut trees in particular produce a substance called juglone that is toxic to some garden plants (see pages 196–97).

Once you've selected your site, sketch your plans on paper. Decide how big the garden will be, what crops you want to grow, and where to place them. Beginners have a tendency to go overboard at first, not realizing how much work lies ahead. It's best to start out small and gradually add to your patch each year as needed. A 100-square-foot plot should be plenty for your first venture.

Many different vegetables will produce well in the Midwest. Most new gardeners start out by picking up a few seed packets at their local grocery store, which is an acceptable way to get started, although there is no guarantee that the cultivars of vegetables being sold are best suited for your area. More experienced gardeners usually shop at garden centers or order from seed catalogs, taking time to pick out cultivars that are recommended for the Midwest and that have the particular characteristics they're interested in.

Before heading out to the garden to plant, you'll need to gather some tools and properly prepare the soil. A hoe, rake, spade, sprinkler, string, and stakes are about the minimum tool supply you'll need. It's a good idea to have your soil tested as early as possible to learn how much fertilizer to apply.

Next, you should prepare a good planting bed, but make sure the soil has dried sufficiently before you work it. Working wet soil will damage the soil's structure by forming hard, durable clumps that will be difficult to break apart. Squeeze a handful of soil, and if it crumbles away easily, it's ready. If it sticks together in a muddy ball, you'd better hold off. When it's ready, work the soil at least 6 inches deep. A tiller makes this job easy, but for small plots, a spade and strong arms will do. Then rake the surface level.

Most seed packages will list planting directions, such as depth and spacing. When setting out transplants, you'll need to dig a hole larger than the soil ball of the plant to aid root establishment. Most transplants are sold in containers that must be removed before planting. The exception is those sold in peat pots (brown fibrous pots), which can be planted but do need a little modification. Tear off the rim of peat pots to insure that no part of the pot will stick out of the soil, which would promote excess evaporation. Because peat moss tends to repel water when dry, be sure the pots are moist when planted. And if roots are not growing out of the bottom of the pot already, it's helpful to tear or poke holes through the bottom of the pot to allow for easier root penetration. Transplants dry out and wilt rapidly, so be sure to get them watered in thoroughly as soon as possible.

The job doesn't end with planting. There are always weeds, insects, and diseases to battle. There are numerous cultural types of controls and preventive measures, such as mulch, floating row covers, and disease-resistant cultivars, that complement, or even replace, chemical controls. No one chemical will control all problems on all crops, so you'll need to identify your problem correctly and then choose the proper control.

If all this sounds overwhelming, don't despair. Your local libraries and bookstores abound with gardening books that can help you plan, plant, harvest, and troubleshoot your garden. Every neighborhood has at least one green-thumbed gardener; all gardeners love to share their expertise and brag about their know-how. Check with local Extension Service offices for gardening publications. And, of course, if all fails, there's always next year!

COOL-SEASON GARDENING

Gardeners, start your engines! Cool-season crops such as lettuce, potatoes, peas, cauliflower, and onions actually prefer the cool, moist conditions of spring.

Many cool-season crops, including peas, carrots, beets, lettuce, spinach, radishes, and turnips, can be started by sowing seeds directly in the garden. Each crop has its own optimum planting instructions. Most gardeners make the mistake of planting the seed too deep; a general rule of thumb is that the planting depth should be about 1½ times the size of the seed. When in doubt, most seed packets list the proper planting depth and spacing for that particular vegetable. If your soil tends to be heavy or form a hard crust, try placing a light mulch over the seeds as you plant them. Vermiculite, finished compost, or potting soil allows the young seedlings to come up easily after germination.

Other cool-season vegetables are best transplanted to the garden to give them a head start on the growing season. This group includes cabbage, cauliflower, broccoli, and brussels sprouts. Transplants should be set at the same depth they were grown in. If they are planted too deep, their roots may be too cold and starved for oxygen. Don't forget to give the transplants a drink of water as soon as possible after planting. Young transplants can dry out very quickly, especially if weather is sunny, warm, and windy.

Potatoes are an unusual crop in that they are started from buds of last year's crop. The tubers used to start a new crop are often called seed potatoes, although they are not seed at all. The tuber that grows underground is a modified stem. Each "eye" on the potato is actually a vegetative bud that will produce a new stem and leaves. In turn, the new stems will produce a root system. Cut the seed potatoes into pieces, making sure that each piece has at least one healthy bud. Plant the pieces about 4 inches deep and cover with soil.

Some fast-growing cool-season crops will be harvested by the time it is warm enough to plant tender crops. Replace spring plantings of radish, lettuce, and spinach with snap beans, sweet corn, or other summer crops.

CORIANDER, THE VERSATILE HERB

Today's gourmet cook is likely to have a good supply of coriander on hand, but there's nothing new about this herb. Coriander's use has been documented back to biblical times.

Actually, only the seeds are referred to as coriander. The fresh leaves of the plant are sold as cilantro or Chinese parsley. Coriander is related to parsley, and the early leaves are quite similar in appearance. However, as the plant branches out before flowering, the newer leaves become more divided and lacy, resembling dill leaves.

It is the larger, parsley-like leaves that are used as cilantro in a variety of Mexican, Oriental, and Mediterranean dishes. The flavor is distinctively bold, so it's best to use it sparingly at first.

The round seeds should be harvested as they mature to a light brown color. As with dill, the seeds will shatter onto the soil if allowed to become too mature on the plant. A paper or cheesecloth bag can be placed over the developing seed heads to collect the seeds as they fall. After harvest, the seeds can be ground and used in pastries, sausage, pickles, salads, and curry.

Although native to Asia, coriander is easy to grow in midwestern gardens. It does not transplant well, so it is best to sow the seed directly into the ground. For a continuous harvest, make successive plantings about 2 weeks apart. Thin the seedlings to

about 8–10 inches apart. You can begin harvesting the leaves when plants are about 6 inches tall. If mature seed is desired, allow the plants to continue growth. If both leaves and seeds are desired, it's best to have separate plantings for each purpose.

LATE WINTER RECOMMENDED FOR PRUNING CHORES

If you're itching to get outdoors and work on your garden, now's a good time to survey your landscape and decide what needs pruning. But not all plants need to be trimmed, and some shouldn't be pruned at this time.

Landscape plants should be pruned to maintain or reduce their size, to remove undesirable growth, to remove dead or damaged branches, and to rejuvenate older plants to produce more vigorous foliage, flowers, and fruits. In some cases, pruning is necessary to prevent damage to life and property.

Pruning isn't as difficult as most people think, but there are proper techniques to keep in mind. Late winter or early spring, before new growth begins, is generally considered to be the optimum time to prune most plants, since the plant's wounds heal quickly without threat of insect or disease infection. However, plants that bloom in early spring, such as forsythia, magnolia, and crab apples, should be pruned later, after their blooms fade. These early bloomers produce their flower buds on last year's wood, so pruning early would remove many potential blooms. Trees that have large quantities of sap in the spring, such as maple, birch, and dogwood, are not harmed by early-spring pruning but can be pruned in late spring or early summer to avoid the sap bleeding.

It's best to allow a tree or shrub to develop its natural shape as much as possible. However, removing selected branches because they are weak or formed at a poor angle to the trunk will help the rest of plant receive more sunlight. Thin this type of growth by removing unwanted branches at their point of origin. Cut the branch just beyond the swollen area of the junction to the main branch (known as the collar) to avoid injury to the main branch or trunk.

If reduction in size is desired, a technique called heading back is recommended.

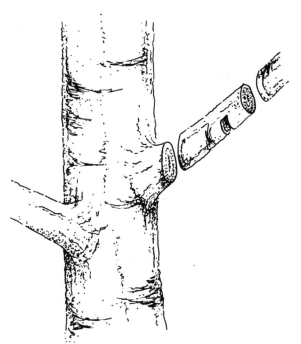

*Prune branches just beyond
the collar.*

Shorten branches by cutting back to a healthy side bud or branch that is pointing in the direction you want future growth to occur. Make your cut about ¼″ above the bud or branch.

Whatever the tree or shrub, topping, or haircut trimming, is not a sound pruning practice (see pages 63–64). Use the heading-back technique to reduce the plant's height. This technique may be more costly in time or money, but the results are worth the extra effort.

PRUNING EVERGREENS

Although a plant is not likely to die from improper pruning, it is important to note that most evergreens are not pruned the way other plants are. Many evergreens cannot

replace lost growth the way deciduous plants can, so an errant pruning cut can have long-lasting results.

Evergreens that have been shaped to formal or artificial shapes require frequent pruning to keep that shape. However, many evergreens may never need pruning. Individual plants should be assessed for pruning needs. Spruce and pine trees have very different pruning requirements than yew and juniper shrubs.

When pruning any plant, the first objective is to remove any dead or damaged wood. Prune back to a branch or bud that is pointed in the direction you want the new growth to go, always making sure to cut back into healthy wood.

You can improve light penetration to overgrown shrubs by using a technique known as thinning. Remove selective branches at their point of attachment rather than giving a "haircut" to several branches at once. Thinning will not harm the plant's natural beauty or stimulate excessive new growth. Some plants must be thinned occasionally to prevent lower branches from dying back due to heavy shade from upper growth.

The best time to thin evergreens is in late winter or early spring before new growth begins. Light pruning may be needed later to shorten branches, especially if shrubs are in formal shapes or hedges. Broad-leaved evergreens that flower in spring should be pruned after they have bloomed. Even if you choose not to prune, spent flowers should be removed to prevent seed formation and encourage new growth. Overgrown broad-leaved evergreens that have become bare at the bottom can be rejuvenated by pruning several of the oldest branches to the ground each year in early spring. This practice encourages new growth at the base of the plant.

Pine, spruce, and fir trees, which produce all of their yearly growth in one spurt, generally require less pruning than other evergreens. Pruning is generally limited to removing dead or damaged branches close to their points of attachment or just above a healthy branch.

To encourage more compact growth of these trees, the tips of new shoots, called candles, can be cut back halfway before the needles unfold. Candling usually occurs between late April and mid-May, depending on the weather. Use a sharp knife or your fingers to pinch instead of shears, which can damage the needles surrounding the candle. Cutting the shoot tips after the needles have developed will result in a misshapen plant, as these trees cannot replace the growing tips. To preserve their natural beauty, pine, spruce, and fir trees should be planted where they will have ample space to grow.

TOPPING IS HAZARDOUS TO YOUR TREE

Tree topping is an all too common practice among homeowners, particularly when their trees become too tall and pose a possible threat to the house or overhead power lines. Some have their trees topped because they've been led to believe that topping is a good pruning practice.

Obviously, some situations require the removal of large limbs for the sake of safety. But topping is a drastic step and ultimately endangers the tree's life. Removing such a great quantity of growth in one shot throws off the balance of roots to shoots that the tree has gradually developed over the years. The much-reduced leaf surface will not be able to manufacture sufficient food reserves to feed the large root system. As the roots starve, the rest of the tree will suffer from insufficient moisture and nutrients.

Another drawback to topping is the stimulation of numerous branches that grow straight up. These shoots are typically very soft, weak growth and break easily and are more susceptible to attack by diseases and insects. They are rapid growers, so the tree will soon be back to its original height. Moreover, the stubs left by topping are usually too large for the tree's natural production of callous to cover over. Thus the stubs also become easy prey for insects, diseases, and decay.

There are alternatives to topping when size reduction is required. Thinning out the canopy by removing selected branches completely back to their point of origin will reduce the tree's size while maintaining more of its natural shape. The cuts will be less conspicuous and should heal more rapidly. Thinning is a much more time-consuming process and requires a more skilled hand, which usually translates to more expense.

If the tree isn't worth the money to do the job right, it's probably better to remove the tree entirely rather than to top it repeatedly. In the case of overhead power lines, it really is best to remove the tree and replant with a more appropriately sized plant. But if the tree is worth saving, make the investment in a healthy future.

SPRING PRUNING OF ROSES

Now's the time to prepare your garden roses for the coming growing season. Winter mulch and Styrofoam covers should be removed as soon as new growth becomes apparent. Since a late freeze is still possible, it's a good idea to keep the winter mulch nearby for quick protection.

If you have older, overgrown plants that produce few if any flowers, it's best to cut them off at ground level (except grafted roses) and allow new, vigorous canes to develop. You may have to sacrifice the flowers, and even the plant, for a year or so, but the results will be worth the effort.

The next step is to remove any dead, diseased, or otherwise damaged canes and to control the quantity and quality of flowers produced. Cut back badly damaged or dead canes down to the base of the plant. Completely remove any suckers (shoots that arise from the rootstock). Slightly damaged canes only need to be cut back to healthy tissue. Be sure to cut back to an outward-facing bud, so that new growth will occur toward the outside of the plant. This will insure good air circulation around the plant, which helps prevent disease.

For bush-type roses, select 4–8 strong canes that spread out away from the center of the plant in the shape of a V and cut them to a uniform height. Remove all other canes completely back to the trunk. This will prevent overcrowding inside the plant framework.

Climbing roses are pruned differently, depending on what type of climber it is. Everblooming climbers, which bloom throughout the growing season, should need little pruning the first few years. As with all roses, remove any dead or weak wood. Thereafter, remove the older, longer canes that have become unproductive. Younger canes (2–3 years old) produce the most flowers and should be cut back to 2–3 healthy buds.

64

)

Climbers that bloom only once a season should be pruned immediately after blooms fade, since next year's buds form only on canes produced this summer. As with raspberries, canes that bear flowers this year should be completely removed to allow space for the new canes to develop and produce buds for next year's season.

The popular large-flowered climber is often less winter hardy than some other types, so care should be taken to lay the plants down and cover them in winter. Because large-flowered climbers bloom on current season's growth, they should be pruned in late winter or early spring, as you would most other woody plants. Remove dead or damaged wood first. Then remove the older, thicker canes, which have become unproductive, by cutting them at the base. Cut lateral branches on the remaining canes back to 2 or 3 strong buds.

The old-fashioned ramblers have thinner canes that bear clusters of smaller flowers in late spring or early summer on one-year-old canes. Ramblers should be pruned after flowers fade. Pruning in fall, winter, or early spring will remove the flower buds before they have a chance to bloom.

Shrub roses rarely need to be shaped, and heavy pruning may just destroy the plant's natural beauty. Pruning of shrub roses should be limited to removal of dead or damaged wood and thinning of excessive growth. (For information on the various types of roses, see pages 86–87.)

FERTILIZING WOODY PLANTS

Trees and shrubs need a properly balanced diet to grow big and strong, just as people need their nutrients. Vigorous plant growth that will be resistant to diseases, insects, and an adverse environment is dependent on good nutrition. Most plant nutrients come from the soil and are probably sufficient for healthy, mature trees. But young plants or those under stress may need a booster of fertilizer to help them grow.

The three nutrients that most often need to be applied as fertilizer are nitrogen, phosphorous, and potassium. Nitrogen is quite water soluble, which causes it to move out of the root area with drainage water rather quickly. Nitrogen generally should be applied every year or perhaps in smaller applications 2 or 3 times a year. Phosphorous and potassium stay in the soil longer than nitrogen, making their application necessary only every 3–5 years.

Fertilizer should be applied to the area where roots are growing. Research has shown that most of the feeder roots of a tree will be at and beyond the dripline rather than next to the trunk. If nitrogen fertilizer alone is to be applied, it can be spread over the surface of the ground and watered in if roots are not restricted by soil compaction, pavement, buildings, or other obstacles. Alternatively, fertilizer can be placed in holes 1–2 inches in diameter and about 1 foot deep that are drilled into the soil at spaced intervals.

The amount of fertilizer to apply is critical. Too little will not adequately serve the plant, but too much can burn the plant's roots as well as the surrounding turf. In general, a rate of 2–4 pounds of actual nitrogen applied over 1000 square feet per year is ideal. But to prevent injury to the surrounding lawn, the fertilizer should be split into two or more separate applications, such as early spring just as buds are breaking and again in fall after leaves drop. In fact, trees may already be receiving adequate nutrition if the surrounding lawn is fertilized.

Fertilize a woody plant at the feeder roots, which extend beyond the dripline.

CHLOROPHYLL: WHY PLANTS WEAR GREEN

St. Patrick's Day seems to bring out the "wearin' o' the green" among human folk. But many plants wear their green throughout the year, and it is the green that makes plants such unique life forms.

Plants get their green color from a pigment called chlorophyll. Chlorophyll appears green because it absorbs red and blue wavelengths of light and reflects green wavelengths. Green plants produce their own food supply through a process called photosynthesis, which can only take place when chlorophyll is present. Thus the very life of a green plant is dependent on chlorophyll.

Other ingredients are also essential for photosynthesis to take place. The plant uses light and chlorophyll to manufacture carbohydrates from carbon dioxide and water in the plant environment. The leaves produce most of the carbohydrates, but stems and buds are also contributors.

Chlorophyll is only able to use a portion of the light that reaches it. On a sunny day, only about 1% of the light received by a leaf will be used in photosynthesis. The rest will be reflected, transformed into heat, or used for other plant processes. Photosynthetic production will be dramatically cut back during cloudy weather or other low-light situations.

Fortunately, not all plants must have maximum light intensity for good plant growth. The optimum light level depends on the species of plant. Some plants require as little as $^1/_{10}$ of full sunlight. This is why some plants, such as impatiens, are considered shade plants, while others, such as petunias, are considered sun plants.

Houseplants also vary in their light needs. Because light levels inside the home are generally quite low compared to outdoors, we often think of houseplants in terms of how well they adapt to low light. Most houseplants will grow best in as much light as you can supply in the typical home.

But there are a few plants, such as pothos, snake plant, dracaena, and Chinese evergreen, that can adapt quite well to relatively dark conditions. Of course, even these

plants do need some light in order to survive. If light is bright enough to read by, these low-light plants will get by.

IRISH SHAMROCK

The holiday of St. Patrick conjures up images of dancing leprechauns, pots of gold, and, of course, shamrocks. Although sometimes referred to as clover, the shamrock is not, botanically speaking, a clover, but a species of *Oxalis*. In fact, shamrocks and clover are not even in the same plant family.

Shamrocks normally have leaves that are divided into 3 leaflets, so you would indeed be lucky to find one with 4. The *Oxalis* that is most commonly grown as a shamrock has small white flowers with purple veins, but some of the other species vary in flower and leaf color and shape. The shamrock's flowers close at night and during cloudy weather, making it an interesting plant for youngsters of all ages.

The shamrock's low, trailing habit makes it a good specimen for a hanging basket or tabletop planter. The roots like to stay close to the soil surface, so they should not be planted too deeply. Water the plants when the top of the soil feels a little bit dry, but be careful not to let the soil get too dry, since the roots are shallow. Use a fertilizer for blooming houseplants according to label directions.

Shamrocks grow well in average house temperatures and especially prefer cooler temperatures at night. Bright, indirect light is acceptable, but a few hours of direct sunlight will help encourage blooming. A sunny east- or west-facing window is ideal.

After blooming, it's a good idea to allow plants a rest, otherwise known as a dormant period. During this time, let the soil dry a bit more than usual and discontinue fertilizing. Resume normal plant care in about 2 months.

Gardening Questions

Q. I see products in the garden catalogs that protect early transplants from frost and freezing temperatures. I know some people who put their plants out weeks before I do. Is there some advantage to planting tomatoes outdoors so early?

A. Some gardeners plant tomatoes early so they can have the first tomato on their street. Others are just eager for the garden season to begin. With protection from frost and freezing temperatures, the plants will produce fruit a few weeks earlier, but it's not just the top of the plant that gardeners should worry about. Cold root temperatures stunt growth through the entire growing season.

Warm the soil by covering it with black plastic for a few weeks before setting out transplants and then provide protection for the leafy portion of the plants. Plant protection can take many forms. Make your own small greenhouse with hoops of wire bent over the transplants. Cover this with polyethylene and weight the edges down. Open the ends on warm days and close them during the cooler nights. Or purchase hot caps, clear tents that sit over the plants, providing the same kind of cozy environment. Water walls are plastic teepees with walls filled with water. The water serves as an insulation from the cold. Most of these season extenders are available through garden mail-order catalogs or at your local garden center.

Q. Twice I have purchased a pawpaw tree from different nurseries. Neither has lived. Somehow, I don't think it was the fault of the nurseries, although I didn't inform them. Should I purchase a tree in person rather than by mail?

A. A pawpaw tree is difficult to transplant because of its brittle roots. When purchasing a pawpaw, look for small plants grown in a container. Some nurseries sell bare-root divisions from pawpaw thickets, which rarely survive. A local garden center or nursery probably can order a container-grown plant for you this spring.

It is even easier to raise the trees from seed. Pawpaw seeds possess a dormant embryo and possibly an impermeable seed coat. To break dormancy, the seeds must be stratified, or exposed to cold temperatures for a certain period of time, in this case 60–90 days. Nature provides the stratification if you plant the seed outdoors in the fall and let it overwinter. Germination will occur in late summer the next year. Or stratify the seeds yourself by placing them in moist vermiculite or sand and storing them in a refrigerator for 60–90 days. Sow the seeds in their permanent locations and give the seedlings some protection from direct sun. Germination may be inconsistent.

If you try moving plants from the wild (with the owner's permission, of course), transplant dormant trees in the spring when they are 12–18 inches tall. You may try adding some soil from the original hole into the new hole, since some sources believe the pawpaw has a symbiotic relationship with a fungus that should be found in the original soil.

2. A reader recently complained of a green vine overtaking her yard, which you identified as either ground ivy or creeping charlie. I live in the woods, and one side of my yard is constantly in the shade. I have a year-round damp, muddy mess. If this plant is prolific and hardy under these conditions, I would love to have some as a ground cover. Is it strictly a weed, or can I purchase the seeds somewhere?

A. Creeping charlie, or *Glechoma*, is truly a weed in most situations, but you could use it as a ground cover in an extreme case. It thrives in shady areas with damp, rich soil.

Proceed with caution! This plant spreads quickly and is difficult to keep under control. There are more attractive ground covers for your conditions, including lily of the valley, hosta, Chinese astilbe, and spotted dead nettle. These are available at most garden centers or through many mail-order nurseries and should cover the area within a couple of years.

$\mathcal{Q}$. My neighbor said to fertilize my spring bulbs with bonemeal. The clerk at the store tried to sell me a bulb fertilizer that cost more. Who is right?

$\mathcal{A}$. The clerk gave you the best advice. Bonemeal isn't all it's cracked up to be. It is falsely rumored to be the ideal fertilizer for spring bulbs, but it is an incomplete fertilizer. Supplement bonemeal with well-rotted manure for an organic alternative or use an inorganic fertilizer such as 6-12-6 or 5-10-5.

Side-dress existing bulbs after they have flowered. Don't let the fertilizer remain on the foliage, or it will damage the tissue.

$\mathcal{Q}$. My azaleas and rhododendrons survive the winter but will not bloom. I would appreciate any helpful hints.

$\mathcal{A}$. Certain early-blooming rhododendrons and azaleas may be damaged by late frosts. Warm spells in the spring encourage buds to swell and break, only to be killed back by late frosts. Improper pruning is another cause for a lack of blooms. It is safe to cut out dead wood throughout the year, but all other pruning should be done immediately after flowering to avoid pruning off flower buds.

There are many kinds of rhododendrons, and some are much more likely to do well in the Midwest. 'P.J.M.' hybrids are one of the hardiest broad-leaved rhodos. The purple-pink flowers are a bit much for some people, but it is quite striking with bright yellow daffodils and white-flowering shrubs.

Most azaleas and a few rhododendrons are deciduous, which means they are not susceptible to the winter drying of the broad-leaved evergreens. 'Exbury' hybrids are hardy to at least zone 5, and the 'Northern Lights' series is hardy to -45° F.

Rhododendrons require cool, moist, acid soil with a 2–3-inch layer of mulch. Mulch derived from pine needles, peat moss, and oak leaves add to the acidity of the ground as they decompose. Water rhododendrons well during droughts and just before dormancy and protect them from strong winter winds.

Q. I have an old clematis that flourished for years with no special attention. For the past two years, the plant has grown well and produced leaves in the spring, but soon after the leaves appear, they turn yellow. Also, the plant does not grow nearly as large, and last summer it produced few blossoms.

A. Age is a likely culprit. The plant may benefit from rejuvenation pruning before it begins growth in the spring. This involves gradually cutting out old wood and encouraging new shoots. Each year, remove ⅓ of the oldest, largest vines at the base of the plant for three years. This method of pruning also effectively rejuvenates overgrown shrubs.

Q. My hedge is open at the bottom, and the woody stems look scraggly. I wanted a formal box-shaped hedge. What should I do?

A. The most common mistake in maintaining a hedge is improper pruning. Many gardeners allow the top of the hedge to become wider than the bottom, which shades out the lower branches. The lower branches then defoliate, making the entire hedge unattractive. For an established hedge, prune back nearly, but not quite, to old wood each time. Begin to correct pruning mistakes by pruning so the bottom becomes the widest portion.

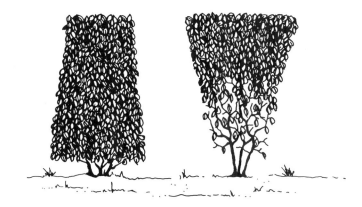

A properly pruned hedge is wider at the bottom (left).

You can cut many deciduous hedges back to the ground and start over if it is necessary. Butterfly bush, forsythia, rose of Sharon, spirea, and lilac may all be cut back.

Q. We have 2 walnut trees approximately 10 years old that badly need trimming. About 1 foot above the ground, 3 limbs about 6 inches in diameter branch out. Should we cut them off? Since they finally produced nuts this year, maybe we should leave the limbs alone.

A. As you have discovered, you should train trees when they are young. It will require serious trimming to correct the problem now. Severe pruning will reduce nut production, and the pruning wounds will provide points of entry for diseases and insects. Unless it is absolutely necessary for mowing purposes, do not prune the lower limbs off. Next time, get them while they are young.

Q. I pruned my trees this spring, and some of them lost plenty of sap. Should I be alarmed?

A. Some trees produce large quantities of sap in the spring and are known as "bleeders." This doesn't hurt the tree in any way but may not be pleasant for people and objects underneath it. Maple, birch, dogwood, elm, walnut, and yellowwood are well-known bleeders. Avoid the problem by pruning these trees in midsummer or late fall.

Q. A maple tree in my yard has liquid oozing from under the bark at waist height. What is the cause, and what can I do about it? Will it kill the tree?

A. It is probably slime flux, a bacterial infection of the tree's vascular system. Sap from a wound or pruning cut runs down the branch or tree, attracting bacteria, fungi, and insects, which turn it into a malodorous mixture. The slime can be quite potent, destroying the tissues it flows over.

Treatment is limited to good cultural practices, such as regular fertilization

and watering during dry periods to help the tree overcome the infection with its own natural defenses. If the goo comes from an improper pruning cut or bark wound, prune it properly to speed healing. If the oozing is persistent or comes from a cavity, you may need to drill a "weep hole." Bore an upward-slanting hole through the heartwood in the tree below where the slime appears. Insert a short length of ½-inch pipe to carry the drip away from the trunk. This will keep the toxic sap off the tree and will relieve its internal pressure.

2. I would like to know how to get rid of moles. My yard is riddled with tunnels. I have tried traps and poisons, but with no success.

A. Attempting to kill moles with poison or bait is usually ineffective. Trapping is the most reliable method of mole control, but it requires patience, practice, and persistence. Traps must be set properly and checked often.

Begin by locating a main runway. Look for runways that: follow a fairly straight course for some distance; appear to connect two mounds or two runway systems; follow fences, walls, or other artificial borders; or follow a woody perimeter of a field or yard. Poke small holes into the runway. Moles will repair these within a day or two if you have actually located a main runway.

Moles use deeper burrows when the ground freezes, so trapping is most effective in the spring and summer. Harpoon traps should be set on the main runways and checked daily. Tamp the soil down with your foot before placing the trap. Be sure the trap is centered over the runway and the supporting spikes do not cut into the tunnel below. Take care not to tread on or disturb any other portion of the runway system.

Home remedies, including plastic spinning daisies, chewing gum, and moth balls, do little to reduce the mole population.

APRIL

A garden can be likened to a stage, with each plant playing a role. Enter the blooming witch hazels stage left as they co-star with star magnolias. The minor characters—creeping phlox and Virginia bluebells—blossom at their feet. As the first characters fade, ornamental pears burst onto the scene, accompanied by tulips and serviceberry.

We certainly enjoy the outdoors this month, but we need to be patient and not rush into upcoming scenes. The vision of juicy, vine-ripened tomatoes is tempting, but it's risky to put out tender vegetables. Instead, coax along some budding new actors, including the many cool-weather crops that can be planted safely. Early spring is a good time for starting a variety of plantings, whether your ultimate goal is food, summer shade, or beautiful flowers. Take pleasure in your own role as the garden drama unfolds.

Garden Calendar

HOME

Apply fertilizer to houseplants according to label directions as days grow brighter and longer and new growth begins. Foliage plants require a relatively high-nitrogen fertilizer, while blooming plants thrive on formulations that are higher in phosphorous.

YARD

Complete pruning chores, removing dead and injured branches first.

Apply preemergent herbicide to control crabgrass in lawns.

Apply a prebloom multipurpose fruit spray to fruit trees.

Plant a tree in celebration of Arbor Day. Bare-root stock should be planted before new top growth begins. Balled-and-burlapped and containerized stock can still be planted later in the spring.

GARDEN

Allow foliage of spring-flowering bulbs to remain in place after blooms fade. Leaves manufacture the food reserves, which are then stored in the bulb for a repeat showing next year.

Prune grape vines and repair support trellises as needed.

Plant or transplant strawberries, raspberries, and other small fruit.

Plant seeds of cool-season crops directly in the garden as soon as soil dries enough to be worked. Cool-season crops that can be direct seeded include peas, lettuce, spinach, carrots, beets, turnips, parsnips, and Swiss chard.

Plant transplants of cool-season crops, such as broccoli, cauliflower, cabbage, brussels sprouts, kohlrabi, and onions.

Plant sections of certified disease-free potato "seed" tubers.

Plant hardy perennials, such as daylilies and delphiniums.

Start tuberous begonias and caladiums indoors for transplanting to garden later.

CAULIFLOWER DEMANDS A COOL SEASON

Cauliflower, like its close relatives, broccoli, cabbage, and brussels sprouts, is a cool-season vegetable. Cold weather is not necessary to produce the cauliflower head, but quality is greatly affected by temperature.

The optimum temperature for curd development is about 63° F, but results will be satisfactory until temperatures reach the upper 60s to mid 70s, depending on the cultivar. High temperatures can cause small leaves to form inside the curd or may cause the texture of the curd to be somewhat velvety (ricey).

It is important to plant cauliflower early in the spring to allow the plants to mature while temperatures are still cool. Using transplants rather than starting from seed will give you a considerable head start on the growing season. When choosing transplants, look for relatively small plants because large plants with very thick stems tend to produce "buttons," or very small curds.

Freezing temperatures can also be damaging to cauliflower by causing "blindness," that is, a plant with no head. If late freezes are predicted, cover plants with newspaper tents, hot caps, blankets, or insulating mulch overnight.

Cauliflower curds develop an off color such as yellow, brown, or even green upon exposure to light, so it is necessary to exclude light from (or blanch) the curds in order to preserve that snow-white appearance. As soon as the head starts to form, gather the leaves of the plant up and around the head and secure in place with a soft cord, rubber band, or strips of nylon stockings.

Heads will be ready to harvest 2–3 weeks after tying. Cauliflower will store up to 4 weeks at 32° F with high relative humidity. Perforated plastic bags will help keep humidity high. If you manage to raise more than you can use in a few weeks, the excess can be frozen for longer storage.

LETTUCE: A COOL CROP FOR MIDWESTERN GARDENS

Lettuce sometimes demands a high price at the grocery store but is actually very easy to grow in the Midwest. The key to growing a successful crop is to plant and mature the lettuce in cool weather.

Lettuce is an annual plant that will bolt, or produce a flower stalk, in hot weather. As lettuce begins to bolt, the leaves develop a bitter flavor. It's best to pull up and discard bolted plants and replace them with a warm-season crop.

The iceburg—more correctly called the crisphead—type is the predominant head lettuce in grocery stores. Unfortunately, crisphead cultivars require a fairly long, cool growing season of 70–85 days. The cool season in the Midwest is usually too short to produce the crisphead types. Fortunately, there are many other kinds of lettuce that do well in the Midwest and whose superior flavor and texture are preferred by gourmets.

Leaf type lettuce requires only half the growing time, generally 40–50 days, so it is an excellent choice for home gardeners. Leaf lettuce produces a loose arrangement of leaves on the stalk. Leaves may be green, as with the cultivars 'Black-Seeded Simpson' and 'Grand Rapids,' or red, as with 'Ruby' and 'Red Sails.' Leaf lettuce can be cut whenever the leaves are large enough to use. You can harvest just a few leaves at a time and allow the plants to keep producing more leaves, or you can harvest the entire plant.

There are non-crisphead types of lettuce that can also be grown successfully in the Midwest. Some cultivars, often called butterhead lettuce, produce a loose-leaf head and

in general take 60–70 days from seed to harvest. Butterhead types tend to have very soft, pliable leaves that have a delicate texture and flavor. 'Bibb,' 'Boston,' and 'Buttercrunch' are just a few examples. Using transplants instead of directly seeding into the garden will get the plants off to a good start before warm weather arrives.

Cos, or romaine, lettuce forms elongated, stiff leaves that form an upright, loose head. 'Paris Island' and 'Paris White' are common cos cultivars that need about 70–75 days to mature. As with butterhead types, transplanting is recommended.

If you've missed out on planting lettuce this spring, don't dismay. Leaf lettuce makes an excellent planting for a fall crop. Planting in late August or September should allow plenty of time to harvest before killing temperatures arrive.

INTENSIVE GARDENING TECHNIQUES STRETCH GARDEN SPACE

More city dwellers than ever are growing their own vegetables, but they often find that space is limited in their urban garden. Some would-be gardeners have no home garden space. As a result, garden plots are springing up in backyards and front yards, on balconies and rooftops, and in container planters. Rental plots are also popular in some areas.

Although space may limit the amount of vegetables you can grow, you can stretch space with intensive gardening techniques. For example, you can make the gardening season last a little longer by using such materials as row covers, cloches, tunnels, hot caps, and mulches. These devices insulate the plant from cold air and can increase the growing season on each end.

Succession planting will double or triple the amount of produce a garden can yield in one year. With this technique, one replants a crop after the earlier crop is finished. For instance, when cool-season crops such as lettuce, spinach, radishes, and peas have finished producing, replant the area with green beans, beets, or turnips. When these crops are harvested, replant again with a cool-season crop for a fall harvest. Radishes, green onions, and leaf lettuce are particularly fast growers.

Interplanting, or alternating rows of fast- and slow-growing crops, early in the season may double the amount of produce you get. When the fast-growing crop is harvested, the row spacing will then be widened to allow more room for the slow-growing crop. For example, you could plant radishes, green onions, spinach, or lettuce between rows of cabbage, brussels sprouts, or broccoli.

Intercropping is just a variation of interplanting. Sow seeds of a fast- and slow-growing crop together in the same row. For example, if you sow radish and carrot seed together, you'll thin the carrots to wider spacing as you harvest radishes. And you'll have harvested two crops instead of one in the same amount of space.

Many planting charts recommend wide pathways between rows of different or even the same vegetables. However, in small plantings where mechanical equipment is not used, wide paths between rows simply wastes valuable space. Small vegetables, such as lettuce, spinach, beets, and radishes, are especially suited to planting in bands or several closely spaced rows. Allow the same amount of space between rows as you do within the row. For example, if lettuce should be thinned to 4 inches between plants, then space the rows 4 inches apart within the band.

Many vegetables, including peas, pole beans, cucumbers, squash, melons, and tomatoes will naturally climb a support or can be trained to grow upwards, leaving ground space for other crops. Support structures include cages, stakes, trellises, strings, teepees, chicken wire, or existing fences—let your imagination take over!

Most fertilizer recommendations are based on more traditional row spacings. To maintain intense production, midseason applications of nitrogen may be needed. Ammonium nitrate is a potent form of nitrogen (33%). Sprinkle about $^1/_5$ cup of ammonium nitrate per 100 square feet alongside the plants and water in. Be sure to wash any fertilizer off the foliage immediately to avoid burning the leaves. Dried animal manure can be applied instead of ammonium nitrate for those who prefer a natural product.

Vegetable breeders have been emphasizing small, yet productive plants for container and small-plot gardening. Although some of the dwarf or mini-plants produce smaller fruits, often the number of fruits per plant yields a good total harvest. Tomatoes,

squash, cucumbers, and melons are among the vegetables that are available in compact or dwarf cultivars. Some crops, including some cultivars of tomatoes and cucumbers, have a compact, trailing habit, which makes them ideal for hanging baskets.

CELEBRATE ARBOR DAY

There's no better way to celebrate Arbor Day and add beauty and value to your home landscape than to plant a new tree. Trees can provide shade and wind protection for many years to come if given the proper start. The last Friday in April is National Arbor Day. Local dates may vary from state to state.

The first step in planting a tree is to select an appropriate species. Keep in mind such characteristics as plant size at maturity, growth rate, cultural requirements, and plant hardiness. Once you have narrowed down your list of desirable trees, check local nurseries and garden centers for availability. Trees can be purchased either as bare-root, balled-and-burlapped, or containerized plants. Bare-root stock should be planted while dormant, before leaves break bud. Containerized and balled-and-burlapped stock can be planted any time the soil can be worked, but waiting until hot summer days arrive will put additional stress on young trees.

Prepare the soil where the tree is to be planted well ahead of time so that the tree's roots will not be in danger of drying out before you get them in the ground. If planting must be delayed, be sure to supply moisture to the roots. Dig an area that is larger than the root system. The hole should be at least a foot wider than the root spread or soil ball, and the sides of the hole should be vertical, not sloping. Plant the tree at the same depth it was grown in the nursery. If the hole is too deep, replace some of the soil at the bottom but be sure to firm the soil to prevent the tree from slipping down later.

Refill the planting hole with the same soil you took out of the hole. Do not amend the backfill with organic material, as it only makes root establishment more difficult once the roots grow beyond the amended soil, particularly in clay soils. To avoid burning the roots, do not mix dry fertilizer or manure in with the soil.

Firm the soil around the roots with your hands and continue to add soil until the hole is three-fourths full. Then fill it with water to settle the soil around the roots. Straighten the tree if necessary and finish filling the hole with soil. For ease in watering the new tree, construct a basin by forming a 2–3-inch-high rim of soil around the edge of the planting hole. Then water the tree with several gallons of water. A soluble fertilizer may be applied with the water to get the roots off to a good start. Use about 1–2 tablespoons of 20-20-20 or similar analysis fertilizer per gallon of water. No additional fertilizer will be needed the first year. Applying a 2–3-inch layer of mulch such as shredded or chipped bark will help conserve soil moisture and keep weeds to a minimum.

If balled-and-burlapped stock is planted, make sure you cut the twine that binds the ball to the trunk. If left in place, the wire or twine will cut through the trunk as it expands in diameter, which strangles the plant. The damage may take several years to show up, but by then it will be too late to rescue the tree.

Staking the tree is generally not recommended unless the site is particular windy. Unstaked trees tend to develop stronger root systems than those that are staked. If support is needed, use 2 stakes—one on either side of the tree. Where the wire will be in contact with the tree trunk, it should be padded with a section of old garden hose or similar material. Remove the stakes as soon as possible after new roots become established.

START AN ASPARAGUS BED

One of the first vegetables you see poking its head through the cool ground in the spring is asparagus, and what a welcome sight! The climate in the Midwest is perfect for asparagus. In fact, asparagus needs to be planted where the soil is cold enough to freeze at least a few inches deep.

Plants can be started from seed or crowns, but crowns are the preferred method. Seedling plants can be quite variable in quality, and they take several years to establish. Crowns are vegetatively propagated by division of the plants into smaller pieces. Each

piece is genetically identical to the original plant, so you know exactly what type of plant you'll have.

Choose a site that is well-drained; asparagus will not tolerate soggy soil. A loose, sandy soil is ideal. Asparagus is one of the few vegetables that actually prefer a neutral to slightly alkaline soil pH.

Asparagus benefits from a good fertilization program. When establishing a new bed, work 2–3 inches of well-rotted manure into the soil before planting or apply a balanced fertilizer such as 12-12-12 at the rate of about 2 pounds per 100 square feet of bed area.

Dig a trench about 6 inches deep and lay the asparagus crowns so that the buds are facing up. Refill the trench with soil, tamp lightly, and water thoroughly.

Newly planted asparagus beds may produce a few harvestable spears the first year, depending on the quality of the planting stock. Check the size of the spears as they emerge. Spears the diameter of a pencil or larger are a good catch. Spindly spears should be allowed to mature.

Even for established plantings, stop harvesting about the middle of June to allow the plants to rebuild food reserves. The spears will become feathery, fern-like shrubs, and this growth is important for the plant to make a good comeback next year. After the

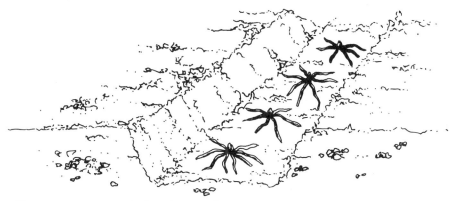

Plant asparagus crowns bud-up in a trench.

foliage fades in the autumn, it can be removed down to soil level. Or the dead foliage can be left over the winter to collect leaves, snow, and other insulation. Your asparagus bed is an investment that will give you many years of enjoyment.

GROW YOUR OWN STRAWBERRIES

If those store-bought strawberries leave you yearning for fresh, home-grown flavor, now's the time to prepare the garden. Strawberries are relatively easy to grow compared to most other fruit crops. Proper site selection and preparation are the keys to a good crop.

Strawberries will adapt to many different types of soil but prefer well-drained, loamy soils. Choose a site that is on high ground because cold air tends to settle in low spots, leading to frost injury. Avoid sites where strawberries, tomatoes, peppers, eggplants, or potatoes have grown within the past 3 years. These plants are all susceptible to a fungal wilt disease.

The ground should be prepared much as for a vegetable garden, preferably the previous fall. All weeds and other plants should be thoroughly removed before planting. In the absence of soil test recommendations, work in 2–3 pounds of 12-12-12 or similar fertilizer per 100 square feet.

Choose cultivars that are hardy and disease resistant. For an early-season harvest, 'Earliglow' and 'Sunrise' are good performers. Midseason cultivars include 'Redchief,' 'Guardian,' and 'Surecrop.' 'Sparkle,' 'Marlate,' and 'Delite' are suggested for late-season harvest. 'Ozark Beauty' is still the cultivar of choice for everbearing strawberries. Disease-free plants are crucial to a successful planting, so buy healthy, virus-free plants from a reliable nursery rather than using plants from old, established beds.

Most strawberries are considered to be June-bearers, which flower during short days in May and ripen in June. There are a few strawberry cultivars that are known as everbearers, which flower during both short and long days, producing their fruit gradually throughout the season.

Planting depth is important to establishing a healthy patch. Plants should be set so that the fleshy base of the plant known as the crown is right at the soil surface. Space the plants 1–2 feet apart, depending on how much space you have available. Allow 3½–4 feet between the rows.

Pinch off any blooms that form the first spring to allow the plants to spend their food reserves on establishing healthy roots and shoots. Horizontal stems (runners) will form new crowns as they fill in the space between the rows. Allow about 5 plants per square foot to remain and remove any excess plants.

Plants can benefit from a side-dressing of about 1 cup of 12-12-12 fertilizer per 25 feet of row. Flower buds for next year's crop are formed beginning in mid-August, making irrigation critical during dry summers. Apply enough water so that the plants receive a total of 1–1½ inches of water per week.

All your hard work will be rewarded next year with a bountiful supply of luscious berries. Pick the fruit when it is fully colored, leaving the cap of leaves and a short piece of stalk attached to avoid injury to the berries. If you can resist eating all of your harvest on the way back to the house, the fruits will keep up to 1 week at 32° F and high relative humidity. Strawberries will also freeze well for a welcome winter treat.

PLANTING A ROSE GARDEN

The rose is one of the oldest flowers in cultivation and is so popular that in 1986 the U.S. Congress named the rose as our national floral emblem. Most modern roses need some special assistance to survive our harsh growing conditions. But for the dedicated gardener, roses can be a very rewarding hobby.

Generally, roses can be grouped into four classes, based on their growth habit: bush, climbing, tree, and shrub. Bush roses are self-supporting and bear most of their flowers at the top of the plant. Height may range from several inches to 6 feet. The many types of bush roses are distinguished by their flowering habits.

Hybrid teas, the most popular bush roses, feature long, pointed buds that open to large double, often fragrant blooms. Hybrid teas usually bloom throughout the growing season and need winter protection in the Midwest. Hybrid perpetuals predate hybrid teas and are generally more winter hardy. These roses flower once in June and may rebloom sporadically throughout the summer. Floribunda roses bear many clusters of single or double flowers that are smaller than hybrid tea blooms. Floribundas provide masses of color throughout the summer. Grandifloras are the result of crosses between floribundas and hybrid teas, producing small clusters of large blossoms on long stems. Miniature roses offer petite versions of the larger hybrid teas and floribundas. Plants generally reach up to 18 inches tall.

Climbing roses have vigorous, long canes that require strong support. Canes range from 5 to 20 feet, depending on the cultivar. Climbers can be further classified as everbloomers (flowers throughout the summer), ramblers (huge canes that usually flower only once), large-flowered climbers (large flowers throughout the summer), and trailers (small flowers on sprawling plants). Some climbers are hardy, while others may need special winter protection. The most popular type is the large-flowered climber, which has strong, heavy canes that grow 8–15 feet tall and bear flowers up to 6 inches across in summer. Large-flowered climbers often occur as a natural mutation of a regular garden rose such as the hybrid teas. These plants produce the greatest number of flowers when trained horizontally rather than vertically.

Tree roses, also known as standards, are formed by grafting a bush rose onto a long, upright trunk. These small trees range from 3 to 6 feet tall and provide a formal accent to the garden. Weeping roses are formed by grafting a climber onto an upright trunk. Tree roses are not hardy in the Midwest and must be laid down on the ground for winter protection each year.

Shrub roses are large, dense plants that require little pruning. Many of the old-fashioned, fragrant roses belong to this group. Most shrub roses are not grafted and are very winter hardy, but they only bloom once each year.

Roses grow best in full sun but will perform adequately with a minimum of 6 hours of direct sunlight daily. Early-morning sun is most important, as it enables the foliage

to dry off quickly. Damp conditions encourage fungal diseases such as black spot. Climbing roses will need to be grown next to a trellis or other means of support.

Roses can be grown in almost any soil that will support other plants, but good drainage is essential. Heavy, clay soils can be modified with organic matter to increase aeration and drainage.

If plants are purchased as bare-root stock, get them planted as soon as possible. Be sure to prevent the roots from drying out if planting must be delayed. Container roses can be held for longer periods, but again, be sure to check for watering needs. Don't forget to remove metal or plastic pots before planting. Pressed-peat and papier-mâché pots can be planted but should be slashed with a sharp knife on the bottom and sides.

Dig a planting hole that is somewhat wider and deeper than the root system. The Midwest's harsh winters can damage or kill many roses, particularly grafted types. Plant grafted roses so that the union (the swollen, knobby area near the base) is one or two inches below ground. Then set the plant in the hole and fill loose soil in around the roots. Water the plants thoroughly following planting. A 2–3-inch layer of organic mulch, such as chipped or shredded bark or compost, will keep down weeds and help retain moisture during dry spells.

FLOWERING ANNUALS VERSUS PERENNIALS

Comparing annuals and perennials is a little like comparing apples and oranges. Each type of plant has its own characteristics and advantages.

Annuals complete their life cycle in just one growing season. In other words, you plant a seed (or a seedling plant), and it flowers and dies all in the same year. Annuals tend to bloom from spring until autumn frost. They must be replanted each year, but they are hard to beat in terms of showy color.

Popular flowering annuals include petunias, marigolds, zinnias, and impatiens. If you're looking for something a little more exotic than these traditional bedding plants, try spider flower (*Cleome*), *Gazania*, and *Lisianthus*. Some annuals are grown for their attractive foliage rather than flowers, including coleus, Joseph's coat (*Amaranthus*), and snow-on-the-mountain (*Euphorbia*). Even some plants normally grown for vegetables can be attractive in the flower garden, including ornamental peppers, flowering cabbage, and okra.

Perennials grow for 3 or more years. Although most perennials tend to have a relatively short season of bloom, proper planning of combinations can yield season-long color. And some perennials rebloom a second time later in the season.

Some of the most popular perennials include daylilies, hostas, peonies, and garden mums. But the selection of flowering perennials is endless at many garden centers. For a spiky show of purple, try blazing star (*Liatris*). Or for a delicate bouquet of yellow, try *Coreopsis* 'Moonbeam.' Nothing matches hot pink creeping phlox for drama in early spring. There is no end to the colors, textures, and sizes available in perennial plants.

To help you decide which of the many beautiful flowers to grow, check your local library and bookstore for a good book with color photos. And don't forget to draw on mail-order catalogs for inspiration and as sources of harder-to-find plants. Regular visits to a botanical garden will give you a good idea of what a particular plant looks like throughout the growing season.

HERB GARDENING

What makes an herb an herb? An herb is defined as any plant that is used whole or in part as an ingredient for health, flavor, or fragrance. With today's interest in creative cookery, most gardeners grow herbs for culinary purposes, but herbs have other uses besides tickling taste buds. They are grown for their fragrance for use in potpourris, sachets, pomanders, and nosegays. Some are used to scent other products, such as soaps, oils, perfumes, and candles. Even breath is sweetened by herbs such as parsley and mint. Many herbs are quite attractive in the landscape and may help attract wildlife to the garden. Other uses include natural dyes and self-medication.

Culinary herbs, like other garden plants, grow best in a sunny, well-drained

location. Although many herbs will produce luxurious growth in partial shade, abundant sunlight is necessary for maximum production of the volatile oils responsible for the rich flavor and aroma of the herbs.

Most herbs thrive in relatively dry, infertile soil, requiring irrigation only during long periods of drought. Herbs such as basil, parsley, and chives, which are cut frequently during the growing season, may benefit from a side-dressing of fertilizer.

Herbs are rarely plagued by serious insect or disease problems in a home garden, but weeds can certainly be troublesome. Some herbs may themselves become a weed problem, such as dill, which self-sows large quantities of seed, or mint, which is notorious for its spreading habit. A summer mulch will help keep weeds and herbs under control.

The time to harvest herbs is when the oils responsible for flavor and aroma are at their peak. Most herbs are cultivated for their foliage, which should be harvested just as flower buds form. Many herbs, including parsley, mint, basil, chives, and oregano, can be harvested throughout the growing season. Harvest herbs grown for their seeds, such as dill, caraway, coriander, and cumin, as the fruits change color from green to brown or gray, but before they scatter to the ground. Collect herb flowers, such as borage and chamomile, just before full flowering. Herb roots, including bloodroot, chicory, ginseng, and goldenseal, should be dug in the fall, after the foliage fades.

Nothing beats fresh-snipped herbs from the garden, but you may want to preserve some of the harvest for later use. Drying is the most common method of preserving. Leafy herbs can be tied in bunches and hung upside down in a warm, dry, well-ventilated location. Electric drying units and ovens can also be used for drying herbs on racks or cookie sheets. Microwave drying is quick, easy, and preserves the natural color of the herbs. Place the herbs between layers of paper toweling and dry on medium to high power, checking for dryness at one-minute intervals. All dried herbs should be sealed in airtight containers, such as jars or sealable bags, and stored away from heat, light, and moisture.

Freezing is a good way to preserve an herb's fresh flavor. Herbs should first be blanched (heat treated) in boiling water for a few seconds to stop enzyme action, which causes decay. Then cool them immediately in ice water and package them into plastic freezer bags or containers. Herbal cubes can be made by placing chopped herbs into an ice tray, filling it with water, and freezing.

DON'T BAG THOSE GRASS CLIPPINGS

As you rev up your lawn mowers this spring, consider the following. Many landfills are rapidly reaching their capacity, causing cities and towns to work toward reducing the amount of trash taken to the landfill. In fact, many states have passed legislation that bans the disposal of yard waste in landfills.

Yard waste, such as tree leaves, grass clippings, and garden trimmings, occupy up to 20% of landfill space. Although these materials are biodegradable, they need moisture and air to break down. Landfills are constructed to be air- and water-tight, so that none of its contents actually break down.

Gardeners can have a great impact on the environment by reducing the amount of yard waste set out for trash collection. One simple technique is to leave grass clippings on the lawn rather than bagging them. A moderate-size lawn can generate more than a ton of grass clippings over the course of a growing season!

Grass clippings left on the lawn are not harmful to the turf if the lawn is mowed frequently and at the proper height. In fact, the clippings actually return some nitrogen and other nutrients back to the soil. Clippings are mostly made up of water, and the rest decomposes very quickly. In fact, it has been estimated that returning clippings to the soil is the equivalent of one fertilizer application per year.

The key is to maintain the lawn at about 2½–3 inches tall, removing no more than ⅓ of the height at any one time. This will require mowing more often, but the total time spent will be considerably less if you don't have to stop to empty the bag.

Mow only when the grass is dry to prevent the clippings from matting down and smothering the grass plant below. If the lawn is excessively tall when you mow, you should remove the clippings and either use them as a mulch around garden plants or

add them to the compost pile. If you do use them as mulch, make sure the lawn hasn't been treated with a weed killer within the past 2 months, which would injure garden plants. Another alternative is to use a mulching lawn mower, which chops up the clippings before it deposits them back on the lawn.

GARDENING EQUIPMENT INCLUDES THE MICROWAVE

It's time to garden—get out your hoe, rake, tiller, and microwave oven. Microwave oven?

Yes, microwaves have joined the ranks of gardening tools. Conventional cooking ovens have long been used to pasteurize garden soil before using it to grow houseplants or start garden seeds. So why not the microwave?

Pasteurizing soil destroys undesirable insects, diseases, and even many weed seeds that are often brought in with the garden soil. Heat the soil to 180° F and hold that temperature for 30 minutes.

To microwave your soil, simply spread some soil in a microwave-safe container. Damp, but not soggy, soil will heat faster than dry soil because the water turns into steam. Soil should be "cooked" on high for about 15 minutes. Stir the soil and rotate the container occasionally, just as you would a food dish. Remember, outside areas will heat faster than the middle.

You can also pasteurize used clay pots (but not plastic ones) in the microwave. First, scrub pots to remove excess grime and then soak them in warm water to thoroughly moisten the clay. Microwave on high for 5 minutes or until the pot is nearly dry.

Your microwave can also be used to dry herbs (see page 90), flowers from your garden, or a special bouquet. In fact, microwave-dried flowers are often less fragile and hold their color better than those dried by traditional methods. You'll still need a drying medium, such as silica gel or plain clay cat litter. Stand the flower (stem up) in about an inch of drying medium spread in a microwavable container tall enough to accommodate your flower (you may need to shorten the stem). Very gently fill in around the flower with additional drying medium until it is completely covered. You'll have to experiment with drying times, but in general, small, thin-petaled blooms take about 1½ minutes on high power. Large, full flowers may need up to 5 minutes or longer, but check on their condition frequently. You may need to leave a small cup of water in the oven while flowers dry to maintain enough moisture for proper operation (see your owner's manual). After microwaving flowers, it's a good idea to leave them undisturbed in the drying medium for another day or so.

And don't forget perhaps the most useful function of the microwave to the gardener—for quick, crisp-cooked vegetables from the garden! Check your microwave cookbook for recipes and cooking times.

EASTER LILY SYMBOLIZES THE SEASON

The Easter lily, *Lilium longiflorum*, is the fragrant floral symbol of the Easter holiday and of the spring season. The large, white, bell-shaped flowers bring a bit of spring into the home but can also be enjoyed outdoors later in the season.

Like other lilies, the Easter lily grows from a bulb that stores food reserves used by the plant to produce foliage and flower growth. If encouraged to build up food reserves, the bulb will be able to make a second show later in summer.

Most gardeners tend to kill their plants with kindness, that is, by overwatering. Water only when the top inch or so of soil becomes dry to the touch. Apply enough water that some drains from the bottom of the pot. The Easter lily often comes with the pot wrapped in decorative foil. Either remove the foil or poke holes through the bottom to allow excess water to escape. Discard this drained water.

Easter lilies last longer in moderately cool temperatures. Keep flowers out of direct sunlight and away from drafts, such as an entry door or heating vent.

The bright yellow pollen borne by structures called anthers inside the flower can stain the petals and reduce flower life. To avoid these problems, remove the anthers with tweezers or your fingertips as soon as the flower opens.

After the blooms have faded, you should fertilize the plant to help rebuild the bulb's food reserves. Use a fertilizer labeled for flowering plants according to package instructions or a general-purpose balanced fertilizer such as 12-12-12 at the rate of ½ teaspoon per gallon of water. Move the plant to a sunny window.

After danger of frost is past for your area, plant the Easter lily outdoors in a sunny, well-drained location so that the top of the bulb is 6 inches below the soil surface. Allow the stalk to grow for several weeks until it begins to turn brown. The bulb is now resting, and the withered stalk should be removed. Soon a new stalk will appear, and by late summer a second season of bloom should occur.

Easter lilies are not generally winter hardy in most parts of the Midwest. However, a winter mulch may give enough protection to see the plants through a mild winter. After the ground freezes in late autumn, apply 2–3 inches of mulch such as straw, chopped leaves, or shredded bark. Be sure to remove the mulch in spring as new growth appears. If the plant does survive, blooms will appear in the summer.

Gardening Questions

Q. For 2 years, our peas have done poorly. After they come up about 2 inches, they seem to wilt and get smaller. This year we dug up a few of them and found a tiny maggot or worm in the stem, which we thought was the reason the plants died. We tilled the plants up because they were getting smaller and smaller. Do you think a disease or the little maggot caused this? What can we do about it? We always had good peas other years.

A. Root maggots tunnel into roots and stems and cause the plants to wilt or die. They attack beans, peas, carrots, melons, spinach, cabbage, turnips, onions, and radishes. These pests are most destructive to early-season plantings.

Rotate your peas to a different part of the garden each year. Apply an appropriate insecticide to the soil at planting time according to the label rate to help prevent root maggots and stem borers.

Any time you find insect- or disease-infested plants, make sure you remove the plants from the garden instead of tilling them in to reduce the chance of reoccurrence.

Q. Last year my seedless grape vines leafed out well and set many grapes. I thought I was going to have a truckload of grapes. When the little grapes were about the size of peas, the leaves had a few yellowish brown spots on them. I sprayed them with an insecticide, but a few days later, the little grapes developed brown spots. The plants recovered and grew well, but the fruit was lost. What happened?

A. It sounds like black rot, which is characterized by light brown spots surrounded by a dark brown line on the grapes. The spots soon enlarge to discolor the entire grape in a couple of days. The grapes then shrivel but stay on the vine. Other signs of black rot are round brown spots on the leaves and sunken dark-purple lesions on the canes.

Black rot is a plant disease caused by a fungus, so insecticides do not affect it. It is most severe in a wet season. Since the fungus overwinters in infected plant material, the best line of defense is to remove all infected fruit and prune out infected canes and tendrils. Always plant grapes in sunny open areas, which allows air to move freely through the plants. Good weed control also enables plants to dry more quickly.

Fungicides are ineffective after the fruit has begun to shrivel. Next year, spray early in the season with a multipurpose fruit spray containing a fungicide labeled for control of black rot. Follow label instructions carefully.

Q. I planted asparagus roots in the spring. They grew about 3 feet tall or more. Do I cut them off this fall or let frost do the job? Do they set seed from the tops?

A. The answer to your question depends upon your asparagus each year. If the plants produce red berries during the season, they have set seed. The seeds can fall to the ground and germinate, but the seedling offspring is inferior to the original plant, so you don't really want to allow seed production.

If there are any disease or insect problems, remove the tops to eliminate over-wintering sites. After frost has killed the asparagus back, you may cut the foliage off and remove it from the garden. However, if the plants are healthy and no berries have formed, the tops can be left in place to trap leaves and snow, providing winter protection for the roots. In this case, cut the foliage back before the spears emerge in spring.

2. I'm having a problem keeping grass out of an asparagus bed I have been trying to start for several years. The grass takes over and chokes the asparagus in the spring. An old-timer told me that using fine salt like farmers used to buy in bags for household and livestock would work. Would it kill grass and weeds and not the asparagus I do have growing?

A. Apply a nonselective, postemergent herbicide at least 1 week before asparagus spears emerge in spring or immediately after plants have been cut back at the end of their growing season. Direct contact of these herbicides with any green plant tissue will injure or kill the plants.

Cut an edge around the garden each year to cut the creeping rhizomes of many grasses. A thick layer of mulch will also keep weeds under control.

The story about salt has been around for a long time. Some sources say it should be applied at a rate of 1 pound per square foot! It is not a recommended practice. Salt damages the soil structure and harms worms and beneficial insects in the soil as well as life touched by water runoff from the salt bed.

2. Where can you buy the seeds or whatever you start garlic from? I have looked wherever you buy spice starts or seeds and have never found any.

A. Garlic is commonly available from garden centers and nurseries but may not be found with the seeds, since the lumpy cloves do not lend themselves to a seed rack. Look near the onion sets next time you shop for garlic. (See pages 218–19 on how to grow garlic.)

Q. Every year there are more kinds of plants at the store. It used to be easy to remember why I liked one tomato or petunia instead of another, but now there are so many on the market, it's confusing. Does it really matter which one I grow? How do I pick the best one?

A. Each year, plant breeders make improvements upon existing plants. These are introduced to the market as cultivars, short for cultivated variety. The improvement may be something everyone will like, such as improved disease resistance, stronger stems, or a new flower color. On the other hand, what may be an improvement to some people can sometimes be a drawback to you. For example, some tomatoes are developed for the commercial market. A firmer, harder tomato will ship better, but most home gardeners prefer big, juicy tomatoes. So every new cultivar is not necessarily a better plant for you to grow.

It makes sense to keep up with recent introductions and choose the ones that appeal to you. Winter magazine issues usually preview the best new cultivars and highlight the All-America Selections (AAS) winners. Seed catalogs often showcase their new introductions in the beginning pages.

If you have always been happy with a particular cultivar of tomato, you might grow some of your old favorites and a few tomato plants of a new, intriguing cultivar. If the new cultivar doesn't work out for you, you'll still have tomatoes. If it performs well, you might phase out your old favorite the following year.

Q. My shady yard is perfect for ivy and vinca, but I want more color, and I'm tired of removing the fallen leaves out of the tangled vines. I think planting perennials would make fall cleanup easier. Since they will be dormant during the late fall and winter, I could probably rake or blow out the area. Do you have any suggestions?

A. Early bulbs receive enough spring sunshine through the leafless branches of deciduous trees to thrive in your yard. Plant crocus, scilla, lily of the valley, and early daffodil bulbs this fall. Spring color also is found in anemone, columbine, bleeding heart, and Virginia bluebell. In the summer, brighten a shady garden with astilbe, coral bells, goatsbeard (*Aruncus*), and meadow rue (*Thalictrum*).

Foliage also adds variety to the garden. In the shade, try dead nettle (*Lamium*), Solomon's seal (*Polygonatum*), or some of the many cultivars of hosta. Annuals such as impatiens, or caladium, a tender bulb, will add further color and variety, especially while you wait for your perennials to achieve full growth.

Q. For the first time in 8 years of growing impatiens from seed, I am having terrible luck. I usually have 75–80% germination, but this year I have 4 plants out of 75 seeds. They were from a well-known seed company, so they ought to have been quality seed. The sterilized potting mix grew a scum of green algae under my plastic wrap and eventually succumbed to that fuzzy white "mold" that precedes damping off. The seeds were still visible on the surface unsprouted. Did I possibly place them too close to the grow light, or was my soil mix contaminated?

A. Several possibilities come to mind. Is your sterilized potting mix from an unopened bag? If the bag is punctured or opened prior to planting, it may be infected with disease organisms.

Also, containers and tools used for seeds must be cleaned to prevent the spread of diseases. Rinse them in a solution of 1 part chlorine bleach and 10 parts water. Let containers and tools dry before using them.

The humid atmosphere created by covering the flat with plastic wrap is ideal for seeds, but it's also ideal for diseases. Some air circulation will benefit the seeds. Increase germination rates by using containers with drainage holes, carefully monitoring watering needs, and covering containers loosely with perforated clear plastic (see pages 40–41).

Q. My question is about annual statice (*Limonium sinuatum*). What should the soil pH be? I'd appreciate any information about statice.

A. *Limonium* is adaptable to a range of soil acidity but prefers slightly acid to near neutral (pH 6–6.8) soil. Sow the seeds indoors 8–10 weeks before the last frost date. Transplant the seedlings to light, well-drained soil in full sun. To avoid root rot, water established statice only when it is dry. Statice is beautiful in dried floral arrangements. Cut the flowers when they are fully opened and hang them upside down in a cool, dark place until they are dry.

Q. I am looking for information about the blackberry lily (*Belamcanda chinensis*). I found some on a pioneer homestead that is now farmed. They are growing well, but I would like to know how to care for them.

A. *Belamcanda* requires a sunny location with well-drained soil. Apply a layer of mulch in the winter to prevent frost heaving. Propagate them by allowing the self-sown seedlings to mature or by dividing them in the spring or early fall. Inspect the tubers for iris borers when dividing. If you let the plant go to seed, you may soon have more blackberry lilies than you want!

Q. Every year we add new mulch to our garden beds to keep the weeds down. We use a shredded hardwood bark mulch. Sometimes we see a yellow or beige foam on the mulch that eventually changes color, hardens, and dries. What is that stuff?

A. Did you think the dog ate something that it shouldn't have? That disgusting-looking pile is a slime mold called *Myxomycetes*, which is quite harmless. It grows in high humidity on organic matter like your bark mulch. Rainy fall and spring weather, as well as summer's high humidity, increases the occurrence. Remove the globs with a shovel if they offend you.

Q. I have heard conflicting reports about what to do with the foliage on spring-flowering bulbs. Some people say you have to leave it in place. Other people cut it off right after the plant blooms. What am I supposed to do with it? It's not very pretty!

A. The plants may be weakened if you cut, braid, or tie the foliage back after flowering. The foliage must remain unbroken to manufacture and store food for

next year's flower production. Gardeners that bend the foliage back and forth and rubber-band it into a neat ball may as well cut the foliage off, since they have broken the vessels that carry food down to the bulb structure. A more effective means of tidying the garden is to interplant bulbs with perennial plants and groundcovers. Their spring growth will hide the dying bulb foliage.

2. I have a question about my Venus flytrap. It has grown to a remarkable size of 4 feet. One flytrap has grown to about the size of a small dinner plate. I believe it has eaten our pet poodle, Scruffy. Is this something we should be alarmed about? We've heard that feeding it a mixture of soap and water will cause it to spit the puppy out. Is this true? We'd appreciate any help; we're expecting our first child in June.

P.S. We thought our cat ran off about four months ago, but we think now it

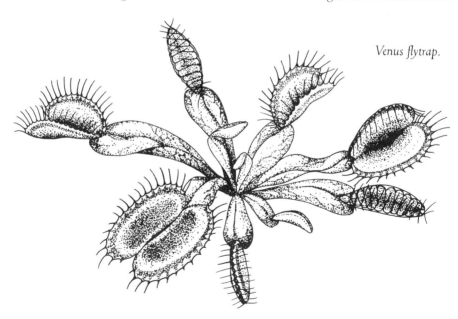

Venus flytrap.

was the first to go. The flytrap spit out a big hair ball a few weeks after the cat disappeared.

April Phule, Rimshot, Indiana

A. Dear April:

Have you been fertilizing with one of those miracle fertilizers? From time to time, they cause Venus flytraps to grow miraculously, much to the dismay of the plant owner, and his or her pet. To retrieve your poodle, try the Heimlich maneuver on the plant. Put your arms around the flytrap and push in and up with a sharp motion. Be careful to keep your hands hidden from the open flytrap. The plant will probably eject the poodle, but I'm afraid it is too late for your cat. Any cat remains produced from this maneuver may be unpleasant.

If you would like another pet, try a Chihuahua. Venus flytraps find their incessant yapping repugnant and will avoid them. If the constant noise becomes intolerable instead of repugnant, they may eat the Chihuahua, but you will probably be more relieved than distraught.

As far as the new baby goes, don't worry. There is nothing the plant finds palatable about children of any age.

MAY

May, marvelous May, brings a rush of excitement to gardeners. This is the gardening season at its finest. The landscape bursts with flowers, the air is fresh, and everything seems new again. This would be a good month to sit back and watch nature unfold before your eyes, but there is too much to do!

Lyndon B. Johnson said, "The best fertilizer for a piece of land is the footprints of its owner," and with that in mind, this is the month to cover every inch of your garden. Your fruit trees, vegetable garden, and landscape beds will all benefit from your attention as you plan, plant, mulch, and harvest.

Garden Calendar

HOME

Many indoor plants can be moved to a shady location outdoors after danger of frost is past. Plants will dry out more often outdoors, so keep a close eye on soil moisture. Sinking the pots in the soil will help slow down moisture loss.

Take cuttings of houseplants to increase a collection or share with friends. Root cuttings in a medium such as vermiculite, perlite, or potting soil rather than water.

YARD

Remove and destroy overwintering bagworms from landscape trees and shrubs.

Follow a spray schedule to keep the home orchard free of pests. While trees are in bloom, use fungicide sprays only, without the insecticide, to avoid injury to bees. Read and follow all label directions.

Apply herbicide to control broadleaf weeds in the lawn if they are a problem, but be particularly cautious to prevent spray drift onto garden plants. Never spray on a windy day.

Prune early spring–flowering trees and shrubs after flowers fade.

Apply fungicide sprays to roses to control diseases such as black spot.

Plant balled-and-burlapped or container nursery stock and water thoroughly.

Fertilize the lawn at the rate of 1 pound of actual nitrogen per 1,000 square feet.

GARDEN

Plant frost-tender plants after danger of frost is past for your area. This includes tomatoes, peppers, eggplants, vine crops, most annual flowers, and tender perennials.

Make successive plantings of beans and sweet corn to extend the season of harvest.

Thin seedlings of crops planted earlier to their proper spacing.

Harvest early plantings of radishes, spinach, and lettuce.

Harvest asparagus by cutting or snapping spears at or just below the soil level.

Harvest rhubarb by grasping the stalk and pulling it up and slightly to one side or cutting with a sharp knife.

Remove blossoms from newly set strawberry plants to allow better runner formation.

Remove unwanted sucker growth in raspberries when new shoots are about a foot tall.

To prevent bacterial wilt in cucumbers, control the cucumber beetle (the carrier of the bacterium), as soon as plants germinate or are transplanted (see pages 140–41).

Pinch chrysanthemums and flowering annuals to keep them compact and well-branched.

WILDFLOWERS CAN BE ALTERNATIVE TO LAWN

Many of today's busy homeowners would like to find a low-maintenance substitute for their lawns and think wildflower plantings may be the way to go.

Wildflowers can be a reasonably carefree planting once established, since they generally require little watering or fertilizing and no mowing. Does this labor-free yard sound too good to be true? Well, it does involve a considerable investment of time and work in planning, preparing the area, and getting your wildflowers off to a good, vigorous start. There are also a few down sides: many wildflowers escape the initial planting site and spread to areas where they may be undesirable. Moreover, the planting will have a much more casual appearance than a formal, traditional lawn. Some cities and neighborhood associations may actually have restrictions on such plantings.

A wildflower is a plant that is native to the area in which it grows and is thus well adapted to the growing conditions—temperature, rainfall, soil type, and soil chemistry—of the area. Some species of flowers may be native to a different locale but can adapt to local conditions so well that they are considered naturalized.

Many companies offer prepackaged wildflower seed mixtures, but some may not be appropriate for the Midwest. Such mixes may contain some species that are not hardy to your area, and some of the species in the mix may be much more vigorous and invasive than the others, so you may end up with just one or two dominant species. Gathering plants from the wild is not a viable alternative; it is harmful to endangered species and may even be illegal.

Choose seed mixes that are specially blended for your region or select individual species according to adaptability to your site and desired characteristics. Species that are recommended for the Midwest to grow in open, sunny locations include tickseed (*Coreopsis*), purple coneflower (*Echinacea*), black-eyed Susan (*Rudbeckia*), Indian blanket (*Gaillardia*), Shirley poppy (*Papaver*), cornflower (*Centaurea*), and rocket larkspur (*Delphinium*). Woodland wildflowers, such as Solomon's seal (*Polygonatum*), Jack-in-the-pulpit (*Arisaema*), cardinal flower (*Lobelia*), and bloodroot (*Sanguinaria*), don't adapt well to open sites, since they require the cool, moist shade provided in nature by forest trees.

If you're converting a lawn to wildflowers, you'll need to kill out the existing grass and weeds first. One method is to spread black plastic over the area to be killed. The black color will absorb heat, which eventually kills out the existing plants if left in place for several weeks. Alternatively, the lawn can be killed with a nonselective herbicide available at garden centers.

As always when establishing seedbeds, the soil should be carefully prepared. Choose an area that has good drainage and till to a depth of 6–8 inches. Remove the dead vegetation and level the soil with a rake.

Sow the wildflower seed evenly over the area and rake it in lightly to just cover the seed. You'll need to be able to provide moisture for at least the first 6 weeks, until the new plants have established root systems. Supplemental water during droughty periods is also helpful.

Weeds will probably be the most troublesome foe until the wildflowers fill in. Herbicides are not practical, since most of the chemical weed killers would also damage the wildflowers. Weeds can be hand pulled when they are still quite small, but they may be hard to distinguish from the young wildflower plants at this stage.

LANDSCAPES AREN'T JUST FOR LOOKING ANYMORE

Previous generations of gardeners used to make a sharp distinction between beauty and utility, but today's creative gardener can choose among dozens of plants that provide both beauty *and* a tasty harvest. The only rule is, there are no rules.

If properly planned, the landscape can provide food and ornament throughout the growing season. Some will provide ornamental flowers and edible fruits, while the fruit itself may be the ornamental characteristic on some plants. A whole range of plant sizes is available, from the 12-inch-tall strawberry to the 4-foot raspberry to the 60-foot black walnut.

Strawberries can begin the season by providing fruit in late May and June as well as providing attractive ground cover. Serviceberry (*Amelanchier*) and cherry trees can provide a focal point in the landscape and yield fruit in late June and July.

Summer brings currants, gooseberries, raspberries, blackberries, and some apples. Peaches, nectarines, apricots, and blueberries also come on during summer for those fortunate enough to have the right soil and weather conditions.

Late summer and early fall bring plums, grapes, elderberries, pears, most apples, Chinese chestnuts, and filberts (hazelnuts) into fruit. Some cultivars of strawberries and raspberries fruit in the fall.

By late fall, the more common nuts are ready for harvest, including walnuts, butternuts, and hickory nuts. Many other plants can also play a role in the edible landscape, including quinces, pawpaws, and persimmons.

Just as in the home orchard, the edible landscape must be carefully planned to provide for cross-pollination needs of those plants that require it, such as apples and plums. Most home fruit plantings require some measures to control pests. Disease-resistant cultivars can cut down on many preventive tasks.

As is the case with choosing any plant, one must determine the winter hardiness and soil requirements of the plants before making any purchase. The selection of adapted cultivars is just as important.

The need for maintenance and fruit production seem to be related. Most high-yielding, traditional orchard plants require a regular program of pruning, spraying, and soil amending. Gardeners who are unwilling or unable to invest a good deal of time into maintenance are bound to be disappointed. But busy or lazy gardeners can take heart: many plants that require relatively little maintenance can supply an edible product, though they may not be the fruits most typically found in the produce department. Crab apples, persimmons, quinces, and many nut trees are quite self-reliant once established.

BE CHOOSY WHEN SELECTING GROUND COVERS

For adding large patches of color and texture to the landscape while controlling erosion and weeds, a well-chosen ground cover just can't be beat. A wide variety of plant species can be used as ground covers, but whether they are 1 inch or 4 feet in height, they are all chosen because of their ability to spread to cover an area.

Ground covers are all perennial plants, meaning that they live for 3 or more years. They can be herbaceous plants (those that die back to the ground each year) or woody plants (those that retain some live above-ground portions through the winter).

Cool-season turfgrass, such as Kentucky bluegrass and fescue, is probably the most commonly used ground cover in the Midwest. But there are more than 100 different species of plants that can be useful as ground covers.

The key to successful use of ground covers is matching the plant to the existing site conditions and the desired functions you want it to perform. First consider what color, texture, size, and other attributes you want the plant to have. Also important is the level of maintenance you're willing to provide, including mowing, pest control, and pruning. The amount of traffic a particular area receives is crucial in determining an appropriate ground cover; if you have children or pets, it is a good idea to use ground covers that withstand some abuse.

Keep in mind that the same vigorous nature that makes a plant a good ground cover may also make it an aggressive plant that will escape the desired planting area. One of best examples is ground ivy, or creeping charley. This plant was originally introduced as a ground cover but is far more often considered an unwanted weed. What's worse, even reputable nurseries do not always volunteer that a plant might be invasive.

Also important is the cold hardiness zone for your area. Walls, buildings, other plants, sloping ground, and bodies of water can greatly affect the microclimate of the planting. Don't forget to assess the amount of light the site will receive. Most plant references will refer to a plant's adaptability to full sun, partial shade, or full shade.

Determine the soil pH and texture. Is the soil acidic, alkaline, or neutral? Is the soil well drained and loamy, or is it heavy, compacted, or otherwise poorly drained? Poor soils can be improved, but it can't be achieved overnight. Soil improvement should be considered a continuing program. Instead of fighting the existing conditions, try to select plants that can adapt to the situation.

Last and perhaps not least, assign a budget for your project. Cost can affect your choice of plants as well as the spacing. The number of plants needed per square foot will depend on the individual species and how fast you expect the plants to cover the area.

A picture says a thousand words, so check your local library or bookstore for references that include color pictures of the plants. Many books will also list plants grouped together by flower color, fruiting characteristics, or site adaptability.

Spring is generally the best time to establish a new ground cover; early fall is second best. Avoid planting in midsummer if possible, as the hot, dry conditions are very stressful for young plants with inadequate root systems.

Some ground covers may be available from seed, but they usually take at least a couple of years to provide good cover—by which time weeds may have gained the upper hand. Plants are more expensive but will fill in much faster. Also, many ground covers are only available as plants either because they do not produce seed or because of the variability among seedling plants. Check your local garden center for supply and price. If large quantities of plants are needed, you may find mail-order nurseries to be an economical alternative.

FRUIT TREES NEED COMPANY

If you're dreaming of picking tree-ripened fruits in your own backyard, you may need to plant more than one tree to insure fruit set. There are two types of fruit trees: self-fruitful and cross-pollinating.

Self-fruitful trees can pollinate other flowers on the same tree. However, pollination of self-fruitful trees is enhanced if more than one tree is in the area.

Most fruit trees require cross-pollination. These trees need pollen from another tree of a different cultivar. Pollen from a tree's own flowers or those of another tree of the same cultivar will not produce fruit.

When pollination is not successful, the flowers may drop immediately following the blooming period. In some cases, what appears to be a small fruit will form but then drop off after a few weeks.

Apples are one of the most popular home-grown fruits, and most cultivars require cross-pollination. Generally, early-blooming cultivars should be used as pollinators for other early-blooming types, and so on. Midseason bloomers can often act as pollinators for all others, since they will have some overlap with both early- and late-season cultivars. Early-blooming cultivars include 'Paula Red,' 'Macintosh,' 'Lodi,' 'Yellow Transparent,' and 'Spartan.' Midseason cultivars include 'Red Delicious,' 'Golden

Delicious,' 'Jonathan,' 'Winesap,' and 'Priscilla.' Late-season bloomers include 'Northern Spy,' 'Granny Smith,' and 'Rome Beauty.'

Most pears are not self-fruitful, so at least two cultivars are needed. Generally, any two cultivars will be compatible, with the exception of 'Seckel' and 'Bartlett,' which will not pollinate each other. 'Kieffer' and 'Duchess' will set fruit adequately without benefit of cross-pollination.

Plums are divided into the European group, which are best adapted to southern portions of the Midwest, and the Japanese group, which can be grown throughout the Midwest. Nearly all plums must be cross-pollinated, but 'Damson,' 'Stanley,' and 'Green Gage' are generally self-fruitful. European plums and Japanese plums cannot pollinate each other.

Tart cherries are self-fruitful, but sweet cherries are more complicated. The sweet cherry 'Stella' is self-fruitful, but other sweet cherries need to be cross-pollinated, and some can only be pollinated by certain other cultivars. Ask your favorite nursery to provide information on pollination needs before making any purchase.

Peaches, nectarines, and apricots are generally self-fruitful, but fruit set may be enhanced by having more than one tree.

In order for adequate cross-pollination to take place, trees should be within 50 feet of one another. Pollen is too heavy and sticky for wind to carry it, so bees must do the job. Protect those bees by omitting the insecticide from your orchard pesticide spray while trees are in bloom.

WARM SOIL KEY TO EARLY PLANTING

Avid gardeners know that the earlier they get their vegetable plants in the ground, the earlier the harvest. But rushing to plant warm-season crops, such as tomatoes, peppers, and melons, won't bring an early crop if the soil hasn't yet warmed.

Seeds of warm-season crops will not germinate in soil that is cooler than 50° F. Roots will not grow from transplants set into cold soil, either. Even if you protect the tops from late frosts, planting early won't gain you an advantage if the soil isn't warm. Premature planting might bring on a cold stress that affects performance for the rest of the summer.

If you've just got to have the first tomatoes on your block, warm the soil up ahead of time by laying plastic sheets on top of the soil. Clear plastic effectively warms the soil but must be removed before planting because it allows weeds to germinate and may eventually overheat the soil, which injures sensitive roots.

Black plastic can be left in place to act as a mulch through the growing season. Because light does not pass through the black plastic, weeds do not grow beneath the cover. Leaving the mulch in place will also help minimize the spread of soil-borne diseases by keeping soil from splashing onto the plants. To use black plastic as a mulch, dig trenches at the perimeter of the area to be covered. Lay the edges of the plastic in the trench and fill it in with loosened soil. Apply the plastic two to three weeks before you want to plant to allow time for the soil to warm below.

Hardening off young transplants before planting outside helps them adjust from the controlled environment indoors to the stresses they will encounter outdoors. Gradually expose the transplants to cool temperatures, bright sunlight, and wind for a few hours each day. After planting, be prepared to cover plants when frosts are expected. Baskets, boxes, paper hot caps, plastic milk jugs, and newspaper tents are just some of the materials that provide protection.

Occasionally, even the most prepared gardener will lose the battle to a late freeze. When temperatures drop very much below freezing, it is difficult to provide enough protection to see these tender plants through. But there will still be time to start again with new plants!

THE TOMATO: QUEEN OF THE HOME GARDEN

The tomato has consistently reigned as the most popular home garden vegetable for many years. Indeed, it's hard to beat the sweet flavor and juicy texture of a vine-ripened

POSSUM
IN THE
PAWPAW
TREE

tomato that you've grown yourself. Tomatoes are low in calories yet packed with nutrients—one medium tomato provides 20% of the U.S. recommended daily allowance of vitamin A and 40% of vitamin C, yet has only 35 calories.

Tomatoes are native to the Andes Mountain countries of South America, which includes Peru, Ecuador, Bolivia, and Chile. Animals are believed to be responsible for the spread of the seed northward to Central America. Explorers then brought the tomato back to their European homeland. Because the tomato belongs to the nightshade family, it was originally thought to be poisonous. Tomatoes were at first grown as an ornamental in American gardens such as Thomas Jefferson's at Monticello. The Puritan colonists thought the tomato fruit too sensuous in appearance and therefore evil. Thankfully, by the mid-1800s, the tomato had gained wide acceptance as a vegetable.

The tomato is a versatile vegetable, great for fresh eating as well as for cooking in sauces, soups, stews, and casseroles. There is also a wide selection of cultivars available, especially if you shop the seed catalogs from mail-order houses. Fruit sizes vary from the bite-size cherry types to the jumbo beefsteak types. Some cultivars are best for slicing, while others are ideal for processing. Traditional tomatoes are red, but now orange, yellow, white, and pink tomatoes can also be found. Most modern hybrid tomatoes have good resistance to diseases such as verticillium and fusarium wilt.

Tomatoes are often classified by their growth habit as determinate or indeterminate. Determinate plants grow foliage first, then the top and side buds produce flowers followed by fruit. The plant stops growing in size when the top bud flowers. Determinate plants produce all of their fruit at about the same time, making them a good choice if you're looking for large quantities of fruit for canning. Indeterminate plants continue to produce flowers, fruits, and foliage throughout the growing season on plants that can become quite tall. Indeterminate tomatoes are the choice for gardeners who want to spread their harvest over a longer period.

Tomatoes can be grown along the garden floor, but their fruits will be cleaner and less prone to disease if you train them along a stake or inside a cage. If you're short of backyard space, tomatoes can also be grown in containers such as whiskey barrels, bushel baskets, or hanging baskets.

By choosing a good range of cultivars, tomato plants can be selected to provide a bountiful harvest right up until frost takes the plants. Even then, the green tomatoes can be harvested and ripened indoors.

LEGGY TOMATOES

If you're like most overanxious gardeners, you probably started your tomato seeds too early. Particularly when tomatoes and other transplants are grown under the relatively low-light conditions experienced in most homes, they tend to get long and leggy as they stretch in search of light. Even many store-bought transplants get leggy if we buy them too long before we can plant them out, or they may be too leggy to begin with from overcrowding in the pack.

Most gardeners get around this problem by setting their tomato transplants deeper when they plant them out. Fortunately, we can usually get away with this on our tomatoes, since they will root along the stem. Other crops do not root quite so readily and should not be planted deeper.

If you must plant leggy tomatoes, try to plant them at an angle, so that the roots aren't planted too deeply. The deeper you place the roots, the cooler the soil will be, and tomato roots like warm soil. There will also be less oxygen supplied to deeply planted roots, and oxygen is essential for good root development. Remove any leaves that would otherwise be buried below the soil.

Although leggy tomatoes can be rescued, the best solution is to start out with good-sized plants. Smaller plants adjust to the shock of transplanting much more easily, since they have less foliage to keep supplied with water.

If you're shopping for transplants, avoid the plants that have already begun to flower or even set fruit. You want your plants to be in a vigorous growing stage. The leaves manufacture the food for the plant to produce a bumper crop, so you want the plant

to make good foliar growth before it begins fruiting. Look for short, stocky plants with a thick stem.

If your homegrown transplants turned out too leggy this year, make yourself a note to give them as much light as possible and to start your seeds a little later next year.

SWEET CORN ISN'T JUST FOR LARGE GARDENS

Nothing tastes better than home-grown corn fresh from the garden to the dinner plate. But because of its demand for space, sweet corn has traditionally been confined to larger gardens.

Sweet corn plants usually produce only one ear per stalk, possibly two. And because sweet corn is pollinated by wind rather than insects, a large block of plants is usually needed to insure good yields. Inadequate pollination results in poorly filled ears. If you have limited space, plant your corn in short blocks rather than long rows. Or try planting seed in hills; start with 3 seeds per hill and thin to 2 plants after germination. Shaking the plants to help distribute the pollen during bloom time may help insure adequate pollination.

Sweet corn will adapt to any well-drained soil. Corn is a warm-season crop and should be planted only after soils have had a chance to warm. Standard sweet corn seeds can be planted about 10 days before the average last frost date. The newer supersweet, or sugar enhanced, sweet corns are even more demanding of warm soils and should not be planted until soil temperatures have exceeded 60° F, so wait to plant these new corns at least until you're ready to plant tomatoes.

Start out with freshly purchased seed each year, since sweet corn seed is relatively short-lived, even under ideal storage conditions. If poor germination occurs, the missing plants will contribute to poor pollination. Replanting seed for skipped plants won't help, since the plants won't mature and produce pollen at the same time.

Sweet corn should not be planted near field corn, ornamental corn, or popcorn unless you can be sure they won't be in flower at the same time. Pollen from these corns will make sweet corn kernels starchy. Some of the supersweet corns must also be isolated from other sweet corns as well. If you're planting more than one cultivar of corn, stagger your planting dates or use early- and late-season cultivars to keep the different types of corn from being in bloom at the same time.

CONTAINER AND RAISED BED GARDENING CAN EASE THE PAIN

Many would-be gardeners might want to grow their own vegetables and flowers, but for various health reasons, they are not physically able. Traditional gardening requires a strong back and arms to work the soil, plant the crops, and harvest the rewards. Weeding, watering, and general garden care may also take quite a bit of bending and elbow grease.

If your mind says yes but your body says no, don't despair. Gardening in containers and raised beds can help you indulge your green thumb. Although gardening in containers is by no means trouble free, it can bring your garden to a height and size that will be workable for you. No heavy digging and little or no weeding will be required. The relatively new, soilless media are much lighter than garden soil, making containers easier to handle. Container gardening also enables apartment dwellers and others who lack garden space to participate in one of America's favorite pastimes.

There are numerous possibilities for containers: conventional clay or plastic pots are perhaps the most obvious choices, but many other materials work just as well. Old whiskey barrels, tires, bushel baskets, buckets, wash tubs, coolers, window boxes, hanging baskets, and homemade boxes are just a few suggestions; use your imagination to complete the list.

The most important characteristics in choosing a container are size and drainage. Containers must be large enough to support full-grown plants. Most plants need a minimum of 6–8 inches of rooting depth. Whatever the container, it must have a means for excess water to escape (usually through holes in the bottom). If excess water is

trapped in the soil, pores that should be holding air will be filled with water, and roots need oxygen just as much as we do.

Many vegetable and flower plants are quite adaptable to growing in containers. Shorter plants usually adapt better to the limited soil area, but even tall tomatoes can be containerized if given enough space. Fortunately, plant breeders have become sensitive to the needs of container and small-plot gardeners and have been developing new cultivars of both flowers and vegetables that are compact yet productive. Check your garden catalogs and garden suppliers for these new dwarf or mini-cultivars.

Container gardening does have its special problems, though. Containerized soil will need watering more often than a garden bed, every day or even twice a day. The best way to tell if it's time to water is by feeling the soil with your fingers. When the top inch or so of soil begins to dry, it's time to water. Watering so that some excess runs out of the drainage holes at the bottom will help insure that the entire root area is moistened. Peat moss is very difficult to wet once it becomes dry, so be sure to check the watering needs of soilless media frequently.

You'll have to pay greater attention to fertilizing as well. Soilless media carry little or no nutrients on their own, while potted soil will lose water-soluble nutrients as excess water drains out of the bottom of the container. Water-soluble fertilizers can be applied when watering, or timed-release fertilizers can be mixed in the soil. Follow label directions for application rates.

In addition to improving accessibility, gardening in raised beds also offers other advantages over traditional ground-level beds. Raised beds improve water drainage in heavy soils and can be planted earlier in spring, since they warm and dry earlier than do ground beds.

If your goal is to improve accessibility to the garden, you'll need to raise beds at least 2 feet, and you'll need some walls to retain the bed. Rocks, wood, or bricks can be used for the walls. The width and length of the bed are flexible, but make sure the middle of the bed can still be reached comfortably.

Fill the bed with a good-quality, loose soil mix that includes soil, peat moss, and a soil conditioner such as vermiculite, perlite, or coarse sand. Because water drains rather rapidly in raised beds, you'll probably have to water a little more often than in ground-level beds.

MULCHING CONTROLS WEEDS, CONSERVES SOIL MOISTURE

Mulch is one of the most versatile tools known to gardeners. Mulch is any material that will help prevent weeds, conserve soil moisture, and modify soil temperatures.

Mulching prevents most weed seeds from germinating by blocking light from the soil. Those weeds that do come through the mulch are usually easier to pull. Mulch slows down evaporation of water from the soil surface, which helps keep the supply of moisture more even. Organic mulches tend to cool the soil, while most plastic mulch tends to warm the soil.

Many materials can serve as garden mulch, the most common being hardwood bark, straw, plastic sheeting, and rocks, but many other materials work just as well. A good mulch is clean of weed seeds, insects, and other pests, easy to apply, and economical. So use your imagination to make use of materials around the home.

When using organic mulch, a 2–4-inch layer of mulch should be sufficient to conserve moisture and control weeds. Applying more than 4 inches may cut off the supply of air to the plant's root system.

You can use grass clippings for mulch in the garden, as long as the grass has not been treated with weed killers within the last month or two. Grass clippings break down rather quickly, but those who water their lawns in summer will have a continuous supply. Because grass clippings tend to pack down, apply no more than a 2–3-inch layer around garden plants.

Other common materials that can be used include newspaper, pine needles, and sawdust. Newspaper can be used either shredded or in sheets, but be sure to weight down the paper if sheets are used. A two-ply layer should provide adequate weed

control yet allow moisture to pass through. Modern inks used for printing should not pose any danger of heavy metals such as lead. However, when in doubt, avoid using the color sections.

Pine needles have a slight acidifying effect on soil, but this should not pose a problem if used in limited quantities. Sawdust, as well as some other organic mulches that are high in carbon, may cause a nitrogen deficiency because the microorganisms in the soil use up nitrogen as they break down the materials. Adding a little extra nitrogen fertilizer to the garden will make up for that which is used up by the microorganisms.

If organic mulch has been piled up for some time, it may start to compost or break down. The center of the pile will be very warm and may give off steam and possibly ammonia and other substances that can harm young plants. Mulch from such piles should be spread out and allowed to cool before you apply it directly to tender garden flowers or vegetables.

Black plastic mulches also work well in combating weeds and conserving soil moisture, but they cause the soil to heat up rather than cool. This warming effect is a great advantage in the spring to get a head start on the season but is less desirable in hot, sunny weather. Most plantings should have sufficient foliage cover to shade the plastic, but if not, a shallow layer of organic mulch might help cool the soil. Plastic mulch should not be used around perennial plants, including shrubs, trees, flowers, and ground covers, due to the lack of permeability to water.

The most recent development in mulches is fabric mulch, which is most commonly used in the landscaping business. The fabric is made of woven or spun plastic cloth, allowing water and air to penetrate. Unfortunately, these fabrics also allow some light to penetrate as well, which gives weeds a chance to germinate and break through the barrier. The fabric is best used where another, perhaps decorative mulch will be used on top to prevent light from reaching the seeds. Plants may develop roots between the fabric and the decorative mulch, leaving the plant susceptible to drought damage. Thus, fabric mulch is probably of limited usefulness around the home grounds.

As temperatures warm up in late spring, many home gardeners take some of their houseplants outdoors. Most indoor plants will flourish outdoors if they're given proper attention.

Wait until after the danger of frost is past for your area before moving plants outdoors. Most houseplant species originate in the tropics and are sensitive to temperatures below 55° F. Be prepared to bring the plants back in or otherwise protect them when nights are cool.

Although a given plant may require full sun indoors, outdoors it should be given no more than a half day of morning sun; afternoon sun will probably be too strong. Overexposing the tender leaves to the strong summer sun will result in a sunburn, turning the leaves yellow or white and eventually brown. Most houseplants will do just fine in a shady northern exposure.

Plants will be exposed to stronger winds, which results in increased water needs. Also, most plants will grow faster outdoors, contributing to a greater need for both water and fertilizer. Sinking the pot into the soil will help cut down on moisture loss.

Keep an eye on the plants for disease and especially insects. Many houseplant pests are picked up while the plants are outdoors for the summer. Give the plants a thorough inspection and cleaning before returning them indoors in the fall. An insecticidal soap or other pesticide spray for houseplants may be needed to avoid contaminating other indoor plants. Make sure the product is labeled for the specific pest you're trying to control and for your particular type of plant. And don't be surprised if your plants drop many leaves when you bring them back indoors next fall. Many plants will drop their leaves in response to the lower light indoors.

Gardening Questions

Q. I read about a last frost date in the paper, but everyone seems to plant their annuals and vegetables before that date around here. Is that wise? It doesn't seem to frost much in May. Maybe I wasn't reading about *my* frost date. How do I find out what it is where I live?

A. Researchers keep records on weather patterns and have developed maps that predict, on the average, when you may expect the last 32° F freeze of the spring and the first frost of the fall. At the time of your frost date, you have a 50% chance of a freeze. Planting before that date just means the odds are greater that the plants will suffer from a freeze.

Protect a small number of plants with floating row covers, upside-down bushel baskets, or other protection, but it isn't wise to risk large, expensive plantings when the odds of a freeze are against you. However, gambling with petunias and peppers may provide an outlet for reformed high rollers, since it is one of the few socially accepted forms of gambling.

Information on your local average last date of spring freeze should be available from your county extension agent (see Appendix C), local radio or television station, and library.

Q. What do I plant to attract butterflies to my garden? I've noticed they seem to like purple coneflower.

A. Butterflies are attracted to flowers by their color and prefer yellow, orange, red, and purple. The coneflower (*Echinacea purpurea*) is perfect for a butterfly, since the flat top allows it to land and feed. Site your butterfly garden in a sunny area sheltered from the wind.

Add azalea, asters, verbena, pinks (*Dianthus* species), and liatris to the garden to attract more butterflies. I guarantee you'll find them on a butterfly bush (*Buddleia davidii*). Black-eyed Susan (*Rudbeckia*), yarrow (*Achillea*), butterfly plant (*Asclepias tuberosa*), and sunflower are other butterfly favorites.

Attracting butterflies means attracting caterpillars, and they consume large quantities of foliage. For example, the spectacular swallowtail butterflies might make quite a dent in your carrots, parsley, or fennel. You need to be willing to sacrifice pesticide use, allow the caterpillars to dine upon your garden plants, and grow some weeds for the earlier stages of their life cycle. Butterflies like to lay eggs on clover, thistle, and milkweed, so allow a few to grow in your garden and watch the butterflies flutter by.

Q. How do you get iris that used to bloom to bloom again?

A. Divide iris every 3–5 years, or they will quit blooming. In late summer or early fall, place a spade or fork under the clumps and lift them entirely. Use a sharp knife to separate the rhizomes so that each one has a green growing point coming from it. Be sure to leave as many roots on each rhizome as possible. Cut the leaves to ⅓ of the original height. Discard the old center divisions and any rhizomes that are soft or rotted.

Plant the iris 18–24 inches apart just below the surface of the ground. Spread the roots underneath the rhizome and cover them with soil. Leave the surface of the rhizome exposed to the sun's rays.

Apply a low-nitrogen fertilizer, such as 5-10-10 or 5-10-5, in the early spring and just after flowering. Place the fertilizer around, not on, the rhizome, then water it thoroughly.

Q. I have two peony plants that seldom bloom. The plants have never grown any larger since I planted them 12 years ago. Someone said there should be ants on peony plants. I have the house sprayed for spiders and wasps. Maybe the spray also killed the ants. Is that the problem?

A. Many people believe ants open the buds, but they don't actually affect the peony. They are looking for their next meal, which is a sweet secretion from the peony buds.

Usually peonies do not bloom because they are planted too deeply. Cover the

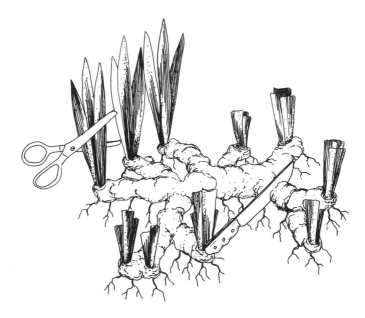

Divide and replant iris rhizomes to renew bloom.

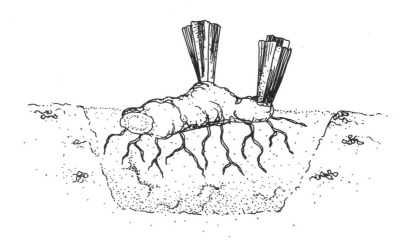

uppermost buds (eyes) with only 1–2 inches of soil. Lift the plants in the fall or spring and reset them at the proper depth.

Other possibilities include excess nitrogen fertilizer, which encourages foliage growth at the expense of flower production, or insufficient sunlight. Peonies require at least a half day of full sun.

Q. Can I get larger flowers from my peonies if I pick off the side buds? After the flowers die off, can the bushes be cut back to just above ground level?

A. Pinch off the side buds when they begin to form to produce fewer, larger flowers. The blooms may require stronger supports, since they will be heavier.

After flowering, you must leave the foliage in place to manufacture food for next season's flowers. Cut the spent blossoms off, however, to keep the plant from putting energy into seed production. The dark green, glossy foliage of a healthy peony can be an asset to the garden. Removing all peony foliage from the garden bed after the plants have been killed back by frost will reduce the occurrence of disease.

Q. My peonies aren't blooming the way they used to. Some of the leaves wilt, the stalks fall down, and the buds never open. I've noticed that about 2 inches from the ground the stalk turns brown. There are no insects present. What's wrong?

A. You have written a perfect description of botrytis blight, which is caused by a fungus. In addition to the symptoms you describe, a gray mold usually covers the base of the stalk. Wind and insects carry the mold spores and can further infect flowers and leaves.

Sanitary measures offer the most effective means of control. Begin with a thorough cleanup of old, infected stems and leaves and other plant debris in the fall. Pull the soil away from the crown without injuring the buds.

In the spring, remove and destroy any wilted or rotted shoots as soon as you detect them. If mulch or another covering is used for winter protection, remove it in the spring before the new shoots emerge from the soil.

Although improving air circulation and penetration of sunlight to peony plants often solves the problem, chemical control may be necessary. When the new shoots appear in spring, spray with a fungicide labeled for botrytis blight and follow label instructions. Thoroughly soak the surrounding soil. Repeat the procedure a week later and again when the shoots are 3–6 inches tall.

Q. I bought a potted plant. On the label stuck in the pot was the name prairie rose lisianthus. Then below that name was Eustoma. Which is the right name? The label says how to plant it but doesn't say if it lives through the winter. It is really pretty, and I haven't seen it in any other place. I have looked in my flower books and can't find anything by those names. I would like to keep it alive though the winter if possible.

A. *Eustoma*, the correct botanical name, is an annual flower that is native to the Southwest. The plant is often labeled lisianthus or prairie gentian.

You may try lifting the entire plant, potting it, and bringing it indoors for the winter. Cut it back to ⅓ of the original height. After potting, water it thoroughly and begin monthly fertilization about one week later.

Initially, place the plant in a well-lit location to help it adapt to indoor conditions. It will probably be unattractive during the winter, but it can be cut back again in the spring and planted outdoors after all danger of frost has passed.

Seeds, which are available from many mail-order catalogs, germinate very slowly and do best if started in the fall and overwintered in a cold frame. Lisianthus seeds can be tricky, so you may choose to purchase transplants at a garden center. Lisianthus is becoming more commonly available, so it should be easier to replace it next spring.

Q. I would like to raise aubrieta along our stone wall. I planted 4 last year. Some leaves started to turn brown on the edges, and the lower leaves dried up. One plant was especially vigorous until we had a 3-inch rain. Then it just gradually turned brown and dried up. What does it take to raise aubrieta?

A. *Aubrieta*, or false rock-cress, performs best in full sun and in well-drained soil of average fertility. The plants probably had too much moisture around the roots. Increase the drainage by incorporating organic matter, such as peat moss or compost, into the soil where you plant aubrieta.

Other perennials that grow well along a stone wall include basket of gold (*Aurinia saxatilis*), some of the creeping sedums, and creeping phlox.

Q. I would like to know what I should do when planting petunias next year to keep them from becoming so leggy and long stemmed. They are brittle and break easily.

A. Most flowering annuals respond to pinching, which means removing 1–2 inches from the growing tip and leaving 3 or 4 leaves. Plants that are pinched produce more flowers during the growing season, even though the earliest blooms are often lost. Petunias can be especially leggy, so pinch them several times throughout the summer to increase branching. Another option is to plant compact cultivars of petunias. The 'Carpet' series is recommended for bedding use. These petunias, which have smaller flowers and bloom early, remain compact and can withstand rain well. Look for this series and other compact cultivars in seed catalogs or at a local garden center.

Q. My spring tulips and jonquils need dividing. I planted them about 10 years ago, and in the most recent years, they have produced plenty of foliage but few blossoms. I dug up a clump, and there were lots of little bulbs attached to each big bulb. When should I divide them?

Can I divide an Oriental poppy? If so, when should that be done?

A. Divide tulips and daffodils any time during their dormant period, that is, after the green tops have died down. Ideally, transplanting is done immediately after the top growth dies. Lift the bulbs with a garden fork or sharp spade. Space them 3 inches apart for small bulbs and 5–7 inches for large bulbs. Large bulbs may flower the following year; small bulbs will require 2 or more years to reach flowering size.

Divide Oriental poppies in the fall. Lift the plant with a spade and cut it into sections so that each division has several buds or shoots and a healthy root system.

2. What can I do to make my lilac bush produce some blooms? The bush is about 5 years old. The foliage is beautiful, but it has only had a few flowers, and that was 2 years ago.

A. "Why doesn't my ——— bloom?" is the most common question that gardeners ask. The following information applies to most flowering plants, whether they are grown for the fruit or the flowers, both indoors and out.

Age—Many woody plants have a vegetative phase of growth, called the juvenile stage, in which the plant does not flower. Juvenility may last 2–3 years on some flowering shrubs or 5–10 years on certain trees. Plants with a juvenile phase include crab apples, flowering cherries, wisteria, and some nut trees.

Pruning—Pruning a spring-flowering tree or shrub in the winter or early spring will remove its flower buds, which form in the late summer and fall. Prune spring-flowering plants just after they blossom.

If Mother Nature prunes your woody spring-flowering plant for you by killing it back to the ground in the winter, there will be no flowers. Some form of winter protection may be necessary if the plant is marginally hardy.

Light—Consider a plant's light requirements when choosing its location. A plant that requires full sun will flower poorly, if at all, in the shade. The flowering of some plants, including poinsettias, chrysanthemums, and gardenias, is controlled by the number of hours of light and darkness they receive each day.

Temperature—Some plants, including fruit trees, spring-flowering bulbs, and ornamental landscape plants, require cold temperatures to induce flowering. A mild winter may not provide an adequate chilling period. Temperatures can also be too cold. Plants may survive the winter only to have their buds damaged by late-spring frosts.

Nutrition—Excessive nitrogen fertilizer promotes an overabundance of leafy growth at the expense of flower formation. A balanced fertilizer, such as 12-12-12 or 6-10-4, ensures that your plants receive nutrition in the correct amounts.

Remember these 5 possibilities when your plants fail to bloom. A little detective work can usually pinpoint the trouble. In the case of your lilac, the most likely causes are inadequate light or too much nitrogen.

2. Each year some of the new growth on my pear trees turns black and wilts. This year it is worse than ever. What is the problem, and how do I fix it?

A. Fireblight causes young twigs and flower blossoms to wilt, blacken, and die. Often the tips of blighted twigs become crooked, resembling a shepherd's staff. Fireblight affects apples, pears, and certain ornamentals, including crab apples, hawthorns (*Crataegus*), and firethorns (*Pyracantha*).

This disease is caused by a bacterium that overwinters in cankers on the branches, and in the spring, droplets of amber-colored ooze form from the cankers. Insects and splattering rain carry the bacterium from the droplets to blossoms and twigs. Fireblight is most damaging in years when spring temperatures are above normal with frequent rains.

Reduce the impact of the disease by pruning out the infected twigs. Cut 8–12 inches below the diseased tissue and sterilize the cutting tools between each cut. A 70%-denatured alcohol solution or a 10%-bleach solution will remove the bacterium from the pruners.

The most effective chemical control of fireblight is an antibacterial spray labeled for fireblight. The spray will not kill bacteria already present; it can only prevent new infection. Carefully timed, repeated applications are necessary. Gain further control by applying a dormant oil spray in the winter.

New growth is most susceptible to fireblight, so avoid overfertilizing or excessive pruning and remove any suckers that develop on the trunk or main limbs. In the future, choose apple and pear cultivars resistant to fireblight.

Q. What is happening to our grapevine leaves? They are all distorted this year.

A. Distorted grapevine leaves are often caused by aphids. Check for small, soft-bodied insects on the undersides of the leaves. The leaves and fruit may be covered with a shiny, sticky substance, and a black sootlike substance may be seen in places.

Aphids are tolerable until their population builds up and damages the plant. A strong spray of water will dislodge them from the grape plant and may solve the problem if you hose them off regularly. Insecticidal soaps and certain insecticides are labeled for aphid control. Follow all label instructions carefully.

Another possibility is herbicide drift. Grapes are especially sensitive to certain weed killers, to which they react with curled, cupped leaves with twisted petioles (the part between the base of the leaf and the branch). To prevent damage from herbicide drift, avoid applications on windy days and increase the droplet size.

Q. I have trouble with my tomato plants. When I put them in cages or tie them to a stake, they fall over at the top of the cage or at the last tie on the stake and break off. Should I trim them? They look healthy, but I'm about ready to go back to straw mulch and just let them wander.

A. Untrained tomatoes have their drawbacks, too. The sprawling plants take up more room, have more disease and insect problems, and harbor a bumper crop of slugs!

The solution is a bigger cage or taller stake. To grow staked tomatoes, try an 8-foot stake inserted 1–2 feet into the ground and prune the plant regularly.

Cages may be preferable because caged plants require less pruning and thus are more productive. Caged tomatoes usually have less sunscald injury, since the abundant foliage protects the fruits. Build wire cages of concrete reinforcement wire, 4½ feet in diameter and 4 feet tall. Make sure the mesh pattern is large enough to allow you to put your hand through to pick the tomatoes. Hook the two cut ends of the mesh together to form a cylinder, and remove the bottom

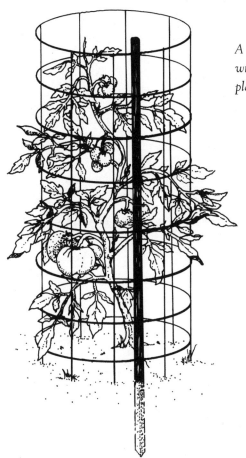

A tomato cage of concrete reinforcement wire will support the most vigorous plant.

rung of wire to form prongs to push into the ground for support. Support the cage by driving 1 or 2 stakes into the ground 1 foot and wiring them to the cage.

2. We have nut grass that has taken over our yard. Can we use crabgrass preventer to rid our yard of it? If we can, when do we use it? I have dug up a lot of it, but there is just too much to try anymore.

Could it be possible that we got it in some grass seed my husband bought a year ago? We never had this much before he seeded the yard.

A. Nut grass, or yellow nut sedge, is difficult to control. It reproduces by seeds, underground stems, and tubers. Pulling the weeds by hand is ineffective, as you have discovered, since any remaining part of the tuber will send up more shoots.

Some crabgrass herbicides are labeled for nut sedge and are usually applied several times. Read the product label carefully.

If you graded the lawn and reseeded, the nut sedge seed could have blown in and become established, or underground stems and tubers may have been pulled up into the top layer of soil, where they could sprout. Reputable grass seed producers are very careful to keep weeds out of their mixes, and the seed was probably not introduced that way.

JUNE

June brings out our plant parenting skills as we witness our gardens' teenage season. Annual flowering plants have developed their roots and are beginning to blossom. Most landscapes are decked out with fine foliage and flowers, and the vegetables are eager to produce their lush crops. It seems so easy to garden this month, but don't be lulled into complacency. Bacterial wilt, chlorosis, and other garden hazards lurk around the corner. Early detection of problems in the garden is the difference between delight and disaster. Keep your eyes open for symptoms of drought, diseases, and insects as you admire your accomplishments.

Garden Calendar

HOME

Indoor plants will require more frequent watering and fertilizing as they increase growth in the summer.

Cut garden flowers for indoor beauty. Recut the stems again just before placing in water. Add a floral preservative and change the solution frequently.

YARD

Remove faded flowers and seedpods on lilacs and other spring-flowering shrubs.

Prune spring-flowering shrubs after blooms fade.

Water newly planted trees and shrubs every 7–10 days when rain is lacking.

Propagate deciduous shrubs, such as forsythia, lilac, pyracantha, and weigela, by stem tip cuttings.

Thin any excess fruit on trees or prop up heavy branches to avoid breaking. Most fruit should be spaced 6–8 inches apart on a branch.

Continue applications of home orchard fruit sprays to insure problem-free fruit.

Keep lawn mowed regularly, maintaining height at about ½ inch higher than usual to help protect the crown of the plant from heat stress.

When watering lawns, apply 1–1½ inches of water in a single application per week. Frequent, light sprinklings will encourage roots to stay shallow, making them more susceptible to drought.

GARDEN

Keep weeds controlled. They're easier to pull when they are still young.

Mulch to control weeds and conserve soil moisture after soil has warmed. Many materials, such as straw, chopped corncobs, bark chips, shredded paper, and grass clippings, can be used.

Supplement natural rainfall to supply a total of 1–1½ inches of water per week to the garden.

Discontinue harvest of asparagus and rhubarb around mid-June to allow foliage to develop and store food reserves for next year's harvest. Fertilize and water when dry to promote healthy growth.

Harvest spring plantings of broccoli, cabbage, and peas.

Remove cool-season plants, such as radish, spinach, and lettuce, as they bolt during hot summer weather.

Continue planting carrots, beans, and sweet corn for successive harvests.

For staked tomatoes, remove suckers while they are 1–1½ inches long to allow easier training.

Blanch cauliflower when heads start to form (see pages 78–79).

Protect ripening strawberries from birds by using netting.

Start seeds of cabbage, brussels sprouts, broccoli, and cauliflower for fall garden transplants.

Remove spent blooms on flowering annuals and perennials.

Remove tops of spring-flowering bulbs only after they have yellowed and withered.

Continue planting gladiolus for a succession of bloom.

Plan now for your Halloween pumpkin (see pages 146–47).

Start strawberry harvest, checking frequently for ripe berries.

OFF WITH THEIR HEADS!

Summer is not the preferred time to prune landscape trees and shrubs, but it is a great time to prune many annual flowers. Plants such as petunias, impatiens, zinnias, and marigolds tend to get leggy and produce fewer blooms by midsummer. Pinching these plants back about halfway will encourage more branching and, in turn, more flowers.

Although chrysanthemums do not bloom this early, they should be pinched now to encourage branching and more blooms. Pinching mums will also help prevent premature summer blooming.

The foliage of spring-flowering bulbs can be cut down and removed from the garden after the green leaves fade to yellow. Removing the foliage too early will lessen the food reserves that the plant is able to manufacture and store. These food reserves are needed for the plants to make a good showing next spring. Flowering annuals can be interplanted among the bulbs in the spring to help mask the untidy appearance of the bulb foliage after their flowers fade.

Removing the faded blossoms from flowering annuals and perennials, which is often referred to as dead-heading, will help encourage more blooms by preventing seedpods from competing for the plant's food supplies and will keep the plants looking better. Many faded flowers can simply be pinched off, while some will need to be cut off with a knife, scissors, or pruning shears. Remove the clippings to the compost pile or the trash to avoid insects and fungal organisms that will be attracted to the decaying plant material.

HOW TO WATER THE GARDEN

One thing is certain about gardening: you'll never know whether you can depend on Mother Nature to water your garden. Most garden plants need 1–1½ inches of water per week to maintain healthy leaves, flowers, and fruit. When nature does not provide enough, it's up to the gardener to supply the rest.

When you do have to water, it's best to water thoroughly and then put the hose away for the rest of the week. The worst thing you can do to your garden is sprinkle lightly every day. Light sprinklings only wet the upper layer of soil, which encourages the roots of the plant to stay shallow. That top layer of soil then dries out quickly, so that shallow-rooted plants will be more susceptible to drying. This advice goes for lawns as well as gardens.

Oxygen is just as important to plants as water, and overwatering forces valuable oxygen out of the soil. When heavy rains fall or thorough irrigation is applied, don't water again until the soil begins to dry. Obviously, you don't want the soil to become so dry that plants begin to wilt. But it is very important to allow air to occupy some of the pore spaces in the soil.

Newly set plants need to be watered more frequently until they have a chance to establish new roots. Young vegetable or flower transplants may need to be watered every day or two, especially if the weather is windy or sunny and hot. But as the new plants become established, try to cut back on watering.

TRICKLE IRRIGATION EASES WATERING CHORES

If you find moving watering hoses around the garden a dreaded chore, why not install a semipermanent trickle irrigation system? Trickle irrigation makes more efficient use of water, which means savings on your water bill. In some areas, such a system can end up paying for itself.

A trickle irrigation system applies water directly to the plant's root zone. It doesn't waste water on foliage or between the rows, where only the weeds will benefit. Very little water is lost to the air from evaporation. Not only are plants well watered; because the foliage stays dry, plants often have fewer disease problems. Another advantage is that you can often work in the garden after, or even during, watering.

The components of a trickle system can be found in most hardware or garden stores—plastic pipe, fittings, flow regulators, and hoses or tubes to deliver the water. Design your system to fit your particular gardening needs. Buy enough hose to service each row. Trickle irrigation kits are available that have all of the necessary components.

When the system is in place, all you have to do is turn on the faucet when needed. For the epitome of trouble-free watering, you can eliminate even that chore by using a timer and a solenoid valve to automatically turn the water on and off. Some companies offer a moisture-sensing probe that activates and shuts off the system as it detects appropriate soil moisture levels.

Because the trickle system can be left in place throughout the gardening season, plan to dedicate one faucet just to the system. If you must use the faucet for other purposes, attach either a Y-shaped connector or an easily removed "quick connector" attachment.

PREMATURE FRUIT DROP

Don't worry if some small fruits fall from your fruit trees—most trees begin to set more fruit than needed for a full crop.

Only 1 bloom in 20 is needed for a good crop on a full-blossoming apple tree. Although the fruit drop in June can be alarming, it's just nature's way of thinning the crop so the remaining fruit can reach full size.

Most fruit trees have at least two waves of fruit drop. The first occurs shortly after bloom. This drop is usually caused by a lack of pollination or incomplete pollination.

The second drop, which occurs 3–4 weeks later, is usually bigger and more dramatic because the fruits are larger, usually ½–1 inch in diameter. This second drop is called June drop because it usually takes place in early June. Competition among the

fruits for water and nutrients is thought to be the cause of June drop. Fruits that contain the fewest or weakest seeds are usually the first to drop.

Although June drop may appear devastating, many trees do not shed enough fruit naturally for good production of the remaining fruit. For best quality, some hand thinning is recommended before the fruit is halfway to maturity.

Appropriate final spacing varies with the type of fruit. Apples should be thinned to about 6–8 inches between each fruit. Peach, plum, and nectarine fruits should be spaced about 4–5 inches apart. Apricots need only 2–4 inches between fruit, while cherries rarely require thinning.

If you simply cannot bring yourself to remove the excess fruit, be prepared to prop up heavily loaded branches. Excessive fruiting can cause serious limb breakage. Fruits will be smaller and of poorer quality, since there won't be enough food reserves to go around. In most cases, it's best to sacrifice fruit early on for the benefit of the rest of the crop.

BACTERIAL WILT DEALS FATAL BLOW TO CUKES AND MELONS

If you've ever grown cucumbers or muskmelons, you've probably experienced the frustration of bacterial wilt. Bacterial wilt is a particularly exasperating disease, since it seems to strike overnight, usually killing the plants just as they're beginning to set fruit. The quality of fruits produced on plants that manage to survive the infection is likely to be decreased. Bacterial wilt may affect other vine crops, although watermelons, squashes, and pumpkins are seldom affected.

Bacterial wilt kills the plants by clogging up the plant's plumbing system, so that water taken up by the roots cannot reach the foliage. Individual leaves or runners may wilt first, but often the entire plant seems to succumb all at once. To check whether your plants are wilting because of the bacterial infection rather than some other cause, cut through the stem of an infected plant and squeeze a bead of cloudy, sticky sap from the cut ends. When the two cut ends are placed back together and then pulled slowly apart, the viscous sap forms thin strands. The viscosity of the sap is caused by the bacterium.

The most frustrating aspect of this disease is that by the time you notice the problem, it's too late to control it. Bacterial wilt has an accomplice in the cucumber beetle, which comes in both striped and spotted forms. The beetle not only causes damage by directly feeding on the plant but also infects the plant with the bacterium as it feeds. So the key to preventing bacterial wilt from striking your plants is to control the beetles before they have a chance to infect the plants.

Check with your local garden supplier for a product that it is labeled for controlling cucumber beetles on your crop. Whatever control you use, the time to start is early, when seedlings push up or when transplants are set. Infection can occur any time during the growing season, so controls must be continued throughout the season on a regular basis. Spraying underneath the foliage as well as from the top will reach all the beetles, which often gather in clusters on the undersides of the leaves. Early-season control can be achieved by using floating row covers of lightweight fabric that allows light to penetrate. The cover prevents the insects from landing on the plants, but it also prevents bees from reaching the flowers. Bees are needed for pollination, so be sure to remove covers as soon as flowering begins.

Next year, consider planting cucumbers that are resistant to the bacterial wilt, such as 'County Fair 83' and 'Saladin.'

IRON-STARVED LEAVES TURN YELLOW

Yellowing foliage is as common a symptom in plants as headaches are to humans. There can be a number of causes resulting in the same symptom. Low light, cold or heat stress, under- and overwatering, and inadequate nutrition are the major causes. Yellowing of foliage that is normally green is known as chlorosis.

Chlorosis is a lack of chlorophyll, the pigment responsible for healthy plants' green

color. When chlorophyll is not present, the plant usually turns yellow. A major cause of chlorosis in some midwestern landscape plants is a deficiency of iron or manganese. Both are plant micronutrients, meaning they are needed in small quantities by plants. Pin oak, rhododendron, river birch, holly, and sweet gum are particularly susceptible to iron chlorosis.

Iron and manganese deficiencies usually are not caused by an actual lack of these nutrients in the soil but rather by soil that is too alkaline. As soil pH becomes more alkaline, iron and manganese are chemically tied to the soil, making them unavailable for plant uptake.

Iron deficiency causes interveinal chlorosis—a yellowing of the tissue between the veins—while the veins remain green. This striking contrast becomes apparent on the youngest foliage first. In extreme cases, the tissue may turn brown and plants may be stunted.

Manganese deficiency symptoms are similar to those of iron. However, if manganese-deficient plants are treated with iron, they become even more chlorotic. Silver and red maples are especially sensitive to manganese deficiency.

Iron and manganese chlorosis can be corrected in several ways. Iron or manganese can be sprayed on the foliage, but such treatments generally give only temporary relief. And of course, you'll need sprayer equipment that can reach the entire plant.

Nutrients can be injected directly into the trunk of the tree. Injections are very effective, but they are expensive and create wounds that can provide entry for insect and disease organisms.

Adding nutrients to the soil near the plant is yet another option. Specially formulated nutrients known as chelates enable the plant to take up the nutrients in spite of the alkaline soil. These materials can be expensive and slow to work.

For a longer-lasting solution, make the soil more acidic to free up the existing nutrients. Relatively small areas can be treated by applying acidic organic matter, such as peat moss, to the soil. Larger areas are more practically treated by adding elemental sulfur, iron sulfate, or aluminum sulfate to the soil. The amount needed depends on the size of the area, the current soil pH, and soil type. These materials are relatively slow-acting, and the soil will have a tendency to become alkaline again, so it can be a never ending battle.

The best solution is to choose plants that are adapted to your location. Avoid chlorosis-sensitive plants if your soil is alkaline.

POISON IVY: A VARIABLE PEST

Perhaps you've heard the old saying "Leaves of three, let it be!" Excellent advice for those who are sensitive to poison ivy.

Known botanically as *Toxicodendron radicans*, poison ivy can sometimes be hard to identify. It is generally a woody plant with 3 leaflets; that is, each individual leaf is divided into 3 leaf-like structures. But that's where the generalizing ends. Poison ivy can be a vine growing up the side of a tree or building. It can also grow as a self-supported shrub. The edges of the leaflets can be smooth, toothed, or lobed. Leaves can be variable even on the same plant!

The flowers are no help in identification, since they are greenish and small and are not generally noticeable. Late in summer and fall, white-gray, waxy berries will ripen. Poison ivy often has outstanding red fall foliage.

Poison ivy does have some look-alikes, making identification even more confusing. Boston ivy, *Parthenocissus tricuspidata*, is often mistaken for poison ivy. When Boston ivy is young, the foliage is 3-parted. As the plant matures, the leaves are then lobed much like maple leaves. Other plants may also have 3 leaflets, so if there is any doubt, it is best to proceed with caution.

The offending chemical in poison ivy is contained in oil throughout the plant, including leaves, stems, fruit, roots, and flowers, and is present year-round. For those who are sensitive to the oil, handling tools, pets, clothing, or other items that have been in contact with the plant may be enough to cause a skin reaction. People become more sensitive to the oil the more they are in contact with it. People who have always

believed themselves to be immune can become sensitive if repeatedly exposed to the oil. According to the American Medical Association's *Handbook of Poisonous Plants,* if you suspect you've been in contact with poison ivy, wash the area with plain water immediately. (Contact your physician for information on how to treat a reaction to poison ivy.)

The plant can spread quickly and is thus difficult to control. Apparently birds can eat the berries without harm, but in so doing, they spread the plants by seed. Once established, the woodiness of the plant makes it difficult to control. Repeated cutting of the plant back to the ground may eventually starve it. However, each time you cut, you are potentially exposing yourself to the oil. Small plants can be dug up and discarded. However, if any portion of the root system is left behind, the plant will probably resprout.

Several herbicides are available for control of poison ivy. Any herbicide that will kill poison ivy will also kill any desirable plants, so if the poison ivy is growing among shrubs and trees, chemical controls must be applied directly to the poison ivy plant and not to any of the other plants. In some cases, it may be worth sacrificing some desirable plants to eliminate the poison ivy. Some of the products that are commonly available for poison ivy control include brush killers and nonselective herbicides. Repeated applications may be necessary to completely eliminate the plant. Be extremely cautious when applying such chemicals and always read the label directions before applying any pesticide.

No matter what control method you use, be careful to avoid exposing your skin to the plant. Wear gloves, long pants, socks and shoes, and a long-sleeved shirt. Burning is the worst possible way to get rid of poison ivy; the smoke contains particles that can cause serious injury to the eyes, skin, and respiratory tract.

GERANIUMS REPEL MOSQUITOES??

By now, you've probably seen several advertisements for a "miraculous new" plant that keeps those pesty mosquitoes away. And this is the time of year when you wish for just such a miracle. Well, keep in mind that if it sounds too good to be true, it probably is! And sure enough, the claims about a plant for repelling the winged monsters have not been supported by published research.

The plant in question is often called Citrosa and is touted as a new discovery. In fact, this so-called mosquito repellent is none other than a citrus-scented geranium. These geraniums do have a highly fragrant oil in the foliage, but the aroma is mostly released when the foliage is bruised, broken, or otherwise disturbed. You would need a lot of plants around a deck or porch to have any effect on the mosquitoes. And since they are sold for anywhere from $6 to $12 each, even a minimal reduction in mosquito bites is pretty expensive.

The "mosquito repellent plant" appeals to those of us who want to cut back on pesticides. But when it comes to effective mosquito control, we haven't found a way to completely avoid using chemicals. The best way to avoid mosquitoes around the home is to stay inside a screened area at dawn or dusk. If you are outdoors in mosquito territory, wear a hat, long sleeves, and full-length pants. If you're opposed to applying repellent to your skin, apply it to your clothing instead.

Insect repellents, including citronella oil, generally must be tasted by the insect in order to be effective. A mosquito is not repelled by a product's odor as much as it is by its taste when it tries to feed.

Maybe these plants have value as novelty items in the garden. They are attractive, and the aroma they produce pleases some people. But be sure to keep some conventional repellent handy so you can stay outdoors long enough to enjoy the plants!

STORING LEFTOVER GARDEN SEED

If you didn't use up all of the garden seed you bought this year, you might be able to use it in next year's garden, depending on what the crop is. Seeds of some vegetables, such as corn, parsley, and onions, are not very long-lived and probably should not be saved. Other seeds, including beans, carrots, lettuce, peas, and radishes, will remain viable for 3–5 years.

The way the seeds are stored will dramatically affect how well they will germinate next year. The best method for storing leftover seeds at home is to place them in airtight containers and keep them in a cool, dark area, such as the refrigerator (but not the freezer). A layer of powdered milk or uncooked rice beneath a paper towel at the bottom of the container will absorb any excess moisture.

To be sure last year's seeds are worth planting, you can perform a test on them to determine their viability. Place 10 seeds between moistened paper towels and put them in a warm area, making sure they do not dry out. By the end of a week or so, count the number of seeds that sprout. If fewer than 5 of the 10 germinate, you should buy fresh seed. If more than 6 germinate, it is probably worthwhile to use the old seed, but you might want to sow it just a little thicker than usual to make up for any that don't come up.

Some seed companies are now offering minipackages of seeds, which is a good solution for small gardens. Then you won't have to agonize about throwing out leftover seed.

PLAN NOW FOR YOUR HALLOWEEN PUMPKIN

It may seem either too late or too early to be talking about growing Halloween jack-o'-lanterns, but mid-June or so is the best time to plant for a Halloween harvest. If you planted your pumpkins back in May along with the tomatoes and other warm-season crops, you'll probably have pumpkins ready to harvest by September.

What do you do with the pumpkins until Halloween? With ideal storage conditions, many pumpkin cultivars can be successfully stored 2–3 months, but home growers rarely have such ideal conditions. Most homes don't have a cool, dry place to store the pumpkins until carving time, so they may get a bit soft by the time you're ready to use them. It's much wiser to have the pumpkins mature closer to Halloween. The key to timing your pumpkin crop is to choose a planting date based on the number of days to maturity for the cultivar that you are growing. There are early-, mid-, and late-season cultivars of pumpkin, ranging from about 90 to 120 days to maturity.

To determine the best time to plant your pumpkins, check the seed packet for the number of days to maturity. Then count backwards from a week or two before Halloween. For example, the 'Big Max' pumpkin requires 120 days to mature, which is about 17 weeks. So, counting backwards from mid-October, the proper planting time is about June 20.

Pumpkins should be harvested before frost hits, so you might want to move your harvest date up and try to store them until carving time if frost is likely before mid-October in your area (see page 213).

PROPAGATING TREES AND SHRUBS FROM CUTTINGS

If you'd like to have a few more of those prize lilacs in your yard, you can spare your wallet by propagating them yourself. Most ornamental shrubs and trees can be easily propagated by stem cuttings.

Cuttings taken from the succulent, new growth that occurred this spring are referred to as softwood cuttings. These cuttings usually root faster and more easily than cuttings taken from harder wood later in the season. However, softwood cuttings wilt more readily and thus require close attention to water and relative humidity.

Take a cutting just below a node, the area where the leaf joins the stem. A 4–6-inch length is ideal. Remove the lower leaves and insert the cut end into a moist rooting medium such as vermiculite, perlite, or potting soil. Placing cuttings directly into water is not recommended because it deprives the developing roots of oxygen. The resulting root system is weak and spindly and does not adapt well to a soil environment.

Powdered hormone, which promotes faster rooting, is available at most garden-supply stores. Dip the cut end into the powder, tap lightly to remove excess powder, and insert into the rooting medium.

High relative humidity can be maintained by enclosing the rooting container in a plastic bag, but be sure to poke a few holes through the plastic to allow air circulation.

Place your cuttings in bright but indirect light while they are rooting. Check the medium frequently for watering needs. When roots are about 1 inch long, the cuttings are ready to be potted up in a good-quality soil mix. Move the potted cuttings to a bright, sunny location, such as a south-facing window.

New plants grown from cuttings might not be ready to face summer stress, so nurse the plants indoors until next spring.

GIVE ASPARAGUS AND RHUBARB A BREAK

Asparagus and rhubarb may be the earliest garden crops to be harvested; they're also among the first crops to stop being harvested. Because they are perennials, asparagus and rhubarb must be given a chance to rebuild food reserves so that a healthy crop can be produced again next year.

A good rule of thumb is to stop harvesting asparagus about the middle of June, allowing the spears to produce large, fernlike growth. When the plants send up mostly spindly shoots, it's time to stop harvesting.

There's no better time to clean up the asparagus bed than when all spears have been removed prior to letting the plants grow out for the summer. You can use a hoe, or even a herbicide, to get tough weeds under control while the bed is free of spears.

Mid-June is also a good time to give rhubarb a chance to renew its food reserves. Of course, if you get a strong urge for a rhubarb pie later in the summer, you won't hurt the plant by sneaking a few stalks here and there. But the stalks get tougher and stringier as summer progresses.

To help the foliage manufacture the food reserves needed for the plants to come back healthy the following year, apply a nitrogen fertilizer to both asparagus and rhubarb plantings. Nitrogen is the most important nutrient to add at this time and can be applied as composted animal manure or a commercially prepared fertilizer such as ammonium nitrate. Apply about 2–3 inches of dried manure or about ⅓ pound of ammonium nitrate per 100 square feet.

Gardeners often wonder whether the yellowing asparagus fronds should be cut off in the fall or left over the winter. If you've had problems with diseases or insects, it is probably best to remove the foliage to prevent overwintering sites for these problems. If plants have been healthy, leaving the dead foliage in place will help collect leaves and fallen snow for additional insulation through the winter.

Gardening Questions

Q. Our mums grow 28–36 inches tall, and after they bloom, they fall over. How can we keep them short, like they were the year we bought them?

A. In order to have shorter, well-branched plants, remove the growing points once or twice during early growth. Pinch them back when the plants are about 6 inches tall (about mid-June) to induce branching. When the branches are 6–8 inches long (about mid-July), remove their tips to induce more branching. This procedure may seem drastic, but the results will be bushy, well-shaped plants that flower abundantly.

    Many old garden sayings have a grain of truth to them. The axiom "Pinch mums until the fourth of July" may help you remember how to care for your mums.

Q. I would like to know how to control hard-shell potato beetles. Our garden is crawling with yellow and black striped beetles. They are devouring our potato plants. I have tried everything anyone has suggested and just can't get rid of them.

A. The adults and larvae of the Colorado potato beetle feed on leaves of potato, tomato, eggplant, and pepper plants. They cause reduced growth or death of the plant. Damage can be reduced by fall tillage, crop rotation, and elimination of volunteer potato plants and plant debris. Cultural practices alone usually will not prevent an infestation from reaching damaging levels.

There is a form of a bacterial disease, *Bacillus thuringiensis* (Bt), that controls potato beetles. Bt attacks the digestive system of its host. This is only effective on young larvae, so timing is critical. Follow the label instructions carefully.

Q. Possibly the most disgusting insects I have ever seen are on my tomato plants. They are huge, green worms with white stripes and a black horn.

A. Those lovely beasts are tomato hornworms or tobacco hornworms. Their ugliness is matched only by their ability to eat enormous quantities of the fruit and foliage of tomatoes, peppers, and eggplants. Handpicking is an effective means of control *if* you can bring yourself to touch them. If not, scrape them into a bucket of soapy water or control them with a form of Bt labeled for caterpillars. If the number of hornworms is out of control, you may have to resort to an insecticidal dust labeled for hornworms.

If the hornworms are covered with white sacs, do not apply an insecticide. The sacs are egg cases of a parasitic wasp. When the eggs hatch, the young wasps will feed on, and eventually kill, the hornworm. When the wasps mature, they will lay more eggs and destroy more hornworms. Wise gardeners will not harm such valuable allies.

Q. We have raspberries that were planted a few years ago. They had a great abundance of greenery and blossoms, but as the berries formed, they fell apart in our hands.

We fertilized with chicken manure and straw mulch. I know it's not the fault of the cultivar because we have friends 5 miles away who have the same cultivar and get large, firm berries.

We have 7 beehives, and the blossoms were swarming with bees, so I'm sure they were adequately pollinated.

A. Soft, crumbly berries may be caused by anthracnose or a number of viruses. Anthracnose first appears in the spring when the young canes are about 6 inches high. Small, purple, slightly raised spots are found scattered over the length of the canes. These lesions soon enlarge, become sunken, and turn gray with purple borders. Apply an appropriate fungicide to keep anthracnose from spreading.

If none of the anthracnose symptoms are present, the problem is probably caused by a virus. Viruses may be spread by a number of insects or by nematodes, and symptoms may vary on different plants and cultivars.

There are no cures or controls for viruses. The plants should be removed and destroyed as soon as possible. Always purchase disease-free plants from a reputable company.

Q. I had a perfectly healthy burning bush until about the middle of June. Then it started to lose its leaves. I know it is due to spider mites because I can see the mites and their webbing on the leaves. I've sprayed with an insecticide with no results. This has happened at the same time 2 years in a row.

A. Mites are not true insects but are closely related to spiders and so they are not affected by many insecticides. They are most destructive during hot, dry weather. To prevent mite infestations, begin with a dormant oil spray applied in early spring, before the buds are open and when the temperatures are above 45° F.

For mite infestations that occur during the growing season, you can achieve some control by simply spraying the plants with a strong stream of water. Insecticidal soaps and miticides are available for spider mite control. Check the label carefully to make sure mites are controlled by the product.

Q. I have two wisterias, a tree and a vine. They are both more than 7 years old, and we have trimmed them back. They grow well, are healthy and green, but they still haven't bloomed. How can I get them to bloom?

A. Wisterias pass through a juvenile, nonblooming phase, and vines started from seed may require 15 years to bloom! Encourage mature plants to bloom with proper fertilization and pruning. Too much shade, water, fertilization, or pruning

will produce lustrous foliage at the expense of flower production. Excess nitrogen causes leafy growth. Use a balanced, low-analysis fertilizer, such as 6-10-4, in early summer to help promote flower bud formation for the next season.

Since flower buds are formed the year before bloom, it is important to prune correctly. Prune back vigorous shoots in the summer. Flower buds are produced on spurs that grow from the side shoots, so do not drastically prune the side shoots.

Q. I am trying to raise hostas. They grow well, but insects eat them. Some of the leaves are full of holes. What can I do?

A. Hostas are a slug's favorite meal. You'll rarely see them, since they feed at night. To determine if they are the culprit, place a wooden board near the plants. In the morning, look for slugs on the bottom of the board. Kill them by scraping them off the board into a bucket of soapy water.

Many gardeners control slugs by sinking a cup of beer into the ground so the top of the cup is even with the soil level. Slugs are attracted to the brew and then drown when they are unable to get out of the cup. Some people believe the slug is too tipsy to get out, but actually nonalcoholic beer is just as attractive and effective on slugs. Poisonous slug pellets are available but should be used with care, since they also appeal to birds and pets.

Q. What vines or plants can I use to mask dead tree stumps that are 5 inches above the ground and 18 inches in diameter? They are unattractive in my flower beds, but there is really no reason to have them removed, since I do not need the space they take up.

A. Purple wintercreeper (*Euonymus fortunei* 'Colorata'), periwinkle (*Vinca minor*), or English ivy (*Hedera helix*) will send out long stems that cover the stumps. Since these plants are evergreens, they will provide cover throughout the year. Periwinkle has the added bonus of flowers in the spring. Another possibility is a low-growing juniper, which would eventually reach across the stumps and hide them.

A low-growing perennial, such as spotted dead nettle (*Lamium maculatum*), creeping baby's breath (*Gypsophila repens*), or cranesbill (*Geranium sanguineum*), will provide excellent camouflage during the growing season but leave the stumps exposed in winter.

Q. I'd like to give away some starts from my Jackman clematis vine. Should this be done in the summer or fall, and how do I make starts?

A. Softwood cuttings taken in June are usually successful. Take a 4–5-inch tip cutting from a healthy, normal shoot. You can treat it with a rooting compound, available at most garden centers, to help initiate rooting. Place it in a medium such as sand, peat, vermiculite, or a mixture of these ingredients. Maintain an even moisture until the cuttings have taken root.

JULY

It's hot! Most of us would be happy to just sit back and enjoy the fruits of our labor, but maintenance is the key this month, which a Kipling poem drives home:

> Then seek your job with thankfulness and work till further orders,
> If it's only netting strawberries or killing slugs on borders;
> And when your back stops aching and your hands begin to harden,
> You will find yourself a partner in the Glory of the Garden.

The strawberry harvest will end, but bugs, slugs, and poor pollination will whip most gardeners into shape. Plants, as well as gardeners, also need protection from heat stress and inadequate moisture. During the cool days of spring, it was hard to justify a few hours of relaxation, but no one can fault us now for spending the heat of the day admiring our gardens from a shady retreat. Just as long as we continue our garden maintenance when it cools down!

Garden Calendar

HOME

Keep an eye on houseplants that have been set outdoors. Because of the hot summer breezes, they need more water than they did indoors.

YARD

Keep newly established plants well watered during dry weather. New plants should receive 1–1½ inches of water every 7–10 days.

Apply a mulch around young plants to help conserve soil moisture and control weeds.

Pinch off faded rose blossoms. Continue rose spray program to control insects and diseases.

Remove water sprouts (sprouts from the trunk) and suckers from fruit trees.

Many trees are plagued by "lawn-mower blight." Be careful to avoid nicking tree trunks while mowing or trimming.

Bluegrass is a cool-season plant and is under great stress during hot, dry summers. If water is not applied, the bluegrass will become dormant and turn brown until more favorable conditions arrive in autumn.

GARDEN

Supplement natural rainfall, if any, to supply 1–1½ inches of water per week in a single application.

Harvest crops such as tomatoes, squash, okra, peppers, beans, and cucumbers frequently to encourage further production.

Complete succession planting of bush beans and sweet corn.

Harvest summer squash while small and tender for best quality.

Harvest sweet corn when silks begin to dry and kernels exude a milky (rather than watery or doughy) juice when punctured.

Broccoli will form edible side shoots after the main head is removed.

Make sure potato tubers, carrot shoulders, and onion bulbs are covered with soil to prevent development of green color and off flavors. Applying a layer of mulch will help keep them covered.

Allow blossoms on newly planted everbearing strawberry plants to develop for a fall crop.

Renovate June-bearing strawberry plants immediately after last harvest (see pages 166–68).

Fertilize strawberries with ½ a pound of actual nitrogen per 100 feet of row.

Harvest raspberries when fully colored and easily separated from stem. After harvesting is complete, prune out the fruiting canes to make room for new growth.

You can safely remove the foliage of spring-flowering bulbs after it fades. This is also a good time to lift the bulbs for transplanting or propagation.

Remove faded blossoms from flowering annuals and perennials to prevent seed formation.

Pinch leggy annuals and perennials to promote bushier growth.

Condition flowers cut from the garden for arranging by removing lower leaves, placing cut stem ends in warm water, and storing overnight in a cool location.

Dry summers are not unusual in the Midwest. Gardeners really have a battle to maintain healthy plants when extreme high temperatures are accompanied by low relative humidity and lack of rain.

Most gardeners are accustomed to watering flower beds and vegetable gardens. These plants require approximately 1–1½ inches of water per week to maintain healthy flowers, foliage, roots, and fruits. In times of drought, established plants may tolerate 10–14 days between waterings, but problems such as fruit cracking and blossom-end rot will increase (see pages 161–62). Watering is most critical during pollination and fruit set for most vegetable crops. Use a mulch where possible to conserve what moisture there is.

The best way to apply the water is by thoroughly soaking the soil with the prescribed amount of water in one application. Frequent shallow watering encourages shallow roots, which are more likely to succumb when the top layer of soil dries out. Deep watering will encourage deeper root growth, and the roots will then be better able to withstand the drought. Sandy soil and containerized plants will need more frequent irrigation.

While many homeowners regularly water their lawns to keep them green throughout the summer, others prefer to allow cool-season bluegrass to become dormant in the summer by withholding irrigation. In "normal" years, this strategy works just fine. But during severe drought, dormant lawns may begin to die if some water is not applied. Dormant bluegrass can generally last about 4–6 weeks without water. To minimize water usage while keeping crowns alive, apply ½–¾ inch of water every 2–3 weeks. The grass will then green up with the return of normal precipitation and more favorable temperatures.

Leaf scorch, a browning along the edges of the leaves on trees and shrubs, is very common in dry summers. While minor cases of leaf scorch are not terribly harmful to plants, prolonged lack of moisture can spell disaster for landscape plants. Young and

newly established plants are most susceptible to the dry conditions, but even established plants may reach a critical point during prolonged drought.

During prolonged drought, branch dieback combined with eventual root death can occur, making plants more susceptible to winter injury. Plants that were already under stress from other factors may succumb to severely dry soils.

Since next year's growth will be determined by buds that form this fall, drought damage may become apparent next year, even if plants show no sign of stress now. Flower buds for many spring-blooming plants will also be developing this autumn.

Watering of landscape and fruit plants should be aimed at where the roots naturally occur. While these woody plants do have some roots that grow very deep, most of the feeder roots that are responsible for water uptake are in the top 18 inches of soil. Most of these feeder roots are concentrated near the dripline of the plant and beyond, not close to the trunk. Allow water to thoroughly soak the target area by applying water at a slow enough rate to allow penetration rather than wasting water by runoff. Don't apply the water any faster than 1 inch per hour. As with annual plants, a mulch will help prevent moisture loss due to evaporation.

The time it takes to apply the proper amount of water depends on how much water pressure you have, the amount of space you need to cover, air temperature, and wind speed. Use an empty tin can or a rain gauge to determine when you've watered enough.

The ideal time to water is before 8:00 A.M. because it makes maximum use of water while allowing foliage to dry. Watering during midday—when temperatures are high, sunshine is strong, and winds are brisk—wastes water. Watering in the evening or at night is convenient for many, but since foliage is unlikely to dry overnight, an environment is created that promotes the growth of fungi and bacteria.

Household gray water—that leftover from the bath or washing dishes—can be used within limits if fresh water is not available or in short supply. Gray water does have a high level of salts from detergents, which can eventually build up to a harmful level in the soil. If the water came from a water softener, it has a particularly high level of sodium, which over time can cause soils to compact and become impervious to water. Use gray water only as a last resort and use it as sparingly as possible to avoid salt buildup. Never use gray water on edible crops or on containerized plants. Use the bypass on your water softener, if possible, when watering any plants.

Of course, many communities impose restrictions on water use during droughts, so ideal watering practices may not be possible. But considering how much time, effort, and money you have put into your garden, it is certainly better to water when permitted than not water at all.

TOMATO TROUBLES

Tomatoes continue to be the most popular plant in midwestern vegetable gardens despite the sizeable list of problems they are susceptible to. Many of these problems are related to environmental factors, such as temperature and moisture, rather than insects or disease. The good news is that these environmentally caused problems are not infectious, and many of them can be prevented.

The most common noninfectious tomato affliction in the Midwest is known as blossom-end rot, so named for the black, leathery scar that occurs on the blossom end of the fruit. Blossom-end rot tends to occur most frequently when there are extremes in soil moisture, which lead to a calcium deficiency in the developing fruit. It is thought to be a result of the calcium's not being taken up fast enough to keep up with the spurts of rapid fruit growth that occur when rain or irrigation follows a dry period. Most soils in the Midwest have plenty of calcium, with the exception of very sandy or highly organic soils. Maintaining a more even level of moisture by irrigating and mulching will help prevent blossom-end rot.

Another common problem is blossom drop. Tomatoes are fairly picky about air temperature when it comes to setting fruit. Tomato pollen becomes ineffective when temperatures are below 55° F or above 90° F. Most early-season cultivars are tolerant of cool temperatures but may have problems with hot weather. If tomato flowers are not pollinated, they drop off the plant.

Tomatoes may crack open when excessive growth is brought on by rainy periods following a dry spell. To reduce the incidence of fruit cracking, water when rainfall is inadequate and apply mulch to conserve soil moisture.

"Catfacing" refers to deformed, misshapen fruit and occurs when days are cool and cloudy during fruit set. The blossom tends to stick to the side of the developing fruit, resulting in puckering.

Sunscald is most common on immature green fruits that are exposed to excessive sunlight, particularly during hot weather. It appears as a yellow or white patch on the side of the fruit facing the sun. Often the tissue blisters and may eventually form a shrunken, grayish white spot with a papery surface. Sunscald is often a problem on tomatoes that do not have good foliage cover—which can be caused by insect or disease damage or by letting the plants sprawl unsupported and open. Supporting tomatoes in a cage helps keep the fruit covered.

The good news is that because all of these problems are noninfectious, they will not spread to other plants. Most can be avoided by maintaining a steady supply of soil moisture.

THE BITTER TRUTH ABOUT CUCUMBERS

Cucumbers have long been on the list of gardeners' favorite vegetables. The cucumber is native to India, where it has been cultivated for nearly 3,000 years. Cucumbers arrived in America with Columbus, where he grew them in an experimental garden in 1493. By 1806, eight named varieties could be found growing in colonial gardens.

There are two types of cucumbers: slicers and picklers. Slicers are eaten fresh from the garden and are usually longer than picklers, though their length can vary from 4 to 12 inches depending on the cultivar. Pickling cucumbers can be eaten fresh but are usually grown for preserving as pickles.

Most cucumbers produce separate male and female flowers on the same plant. Pollination by bees or hand-pollination transfers the pollen from the male flowers to the female. Some new cultivars produce plants that bear only female flowers and are referred to as gynoecious. Gynoecious plants can bear higher, more concentrated yields, but a normal plant with male flowers must be nearby to provide a source of pollen. When gardeners purchase a gynoecious cultivar, a few "pollinator" seeds will be included in the packet.

Although many gardeners have heard of "burpless" cucumbers, there seems to be some confusion as to what the "burpless" refers to. Most cucumber plants contain a bitter compound, called cucurbitacins, that can be present in the fruit. For some cucumber eaters, the bitter taste can be accompanied by digestive discomfort. Some of the newer cultivars of cucumbers do not have the bitter compound, and thus no bitter flavor and no "burp."

Bitterness in cucumbers tends to be more prominent when plants are under stress from low moisture, high temperatures, or poor nutrition. Cutting off the stem end of

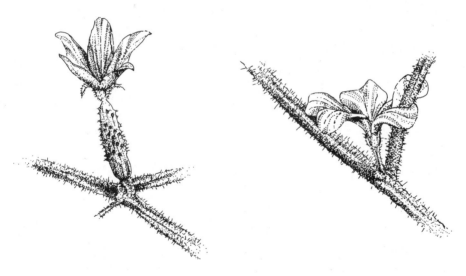

Cucumber flowers: left: the female flower with the young fruit at the base; right: the male flower supplies the pollen.

the fruit and removing the skin will remove much of the bitterness in most cases. But your best bet is to plant "burpless" cultivars and provide good growing conditions when possible.

WHY FRUIT TREES MAY FAIL TO BEAR

So you decided to plant a home orchard last year, but much to your disappointment, no fruits have appeared this year. You may have to wait several more years to realize your first harvest.

Ideally, a fruit tree will begin to bear once it has become old enough to produce flowers. Most dwarf fruit trees take at least 3 years from the time of planting before they begin to flower freely. Standard-size trees can take 7 years or longer to bloom.

Certain cultivars also vary in the number of years to bearing, particularly in the case of apples and pears. Trees that have a spreading growth habit, such as 'Jonathan' apples, tend to come into bearing earlier than those with an upright growth habit, such as 'Red Delicious.' The type of rootstock the tree is grafted on also affects the bearing age of apples and pears. A particular cultivar that is grafted onto a dwarfing rootstock will begin fruiting at a much earlier age than that same cultivar grafted onto a standard rootstock.

Other factors may also inhibit flowering in fruit trees. Most begin developing their buds in mid-June to July of the previous year. Unfavorable growing conditions in the summer can prevent or greatly reduce the production of the following year's flower buds. Plants with inadequate sunlight tend to be slow coming into bearing. Drought stress can also cause the loss of flower buds.

Even once the tree has begun to flower, there are a number of factors that may prevent the formation of fruits. Severe cold temperatures in winter—below –20° F—can kill flower buds of peaches, nectarines, apricots, and sweet cherries. Flower buds of all fruit trees can be killed by late frosts and freezes after buds have begun growth.

Assuming flower buds have formed and survived, there is yet another requirement for fruit production: pollination. Many fruit trees produce few or no fruit unless they receive pollen from another cultivar within the same species. This is true for most apples, pears, plums, and sweet cherries. Most peaches, sour cherries, and apricots are self-fruitful and can set a good load of fruit without cross-pollination (see pages 111–12).

Honeybees are needed to transfer pollen from one flower to another, so what affects the bees will affect pollination and thus fruit set. Bee activity is greatly reduced in cold, rainy, gusty weather. Some insecticides are highly toxic to bees, and their use on fruit trees should be omitted while the trees are in full bloom.

IMPROPER USE OF PESTICIDES
CAN BE HARMFUL TO PLANTS

Pesticides are developed to help protect plants from such enemies as insects, diseases, and weeds. But when they are improperly applied, they can hurt the plants they are meant to help.

When pesticides are applied at too high a dose or in combination with certain other chemicals, plants can be injured or killed. Even the weather can cause pesticides to be harmful.

The symptoms of pesticide injury can be easily confused with other problems. Foliage may appear burned or bleached on the edges of the leaves, or in spots, or over the entire leaf. Some chemicals will cause abnormal growth, such as distorted leaves or stunting. Usually the new growth is most affected by pesticides, but damage can occur elsewhere on the plant.

To avoid pesticide damage on your plants, be sure to read the label thoroughly on any product—preferably before you buy, but certainly before you apply the chemical. This includes all of the fine print, too. Make sure you apply only the recommended rate—no more, no less. Make sure the plants you want to treat, as well as the pests you want to control, are listed on the label.

Don't spray plants during hot, sunny weather when temperatures are above 90° F. Also, be sure that plants are not wilting from lack of water when you apply pesticides, as dry plants are more susceptible to spray damage. Avoid spraying in very humid weather or late in the day when the spray will remain wet for long periods of time.

Check the package label before you mix different pesticides together. While many chemicals are compatible with each other, some others combine to form a more damaging mixture.

Some formulations of pesticides are safer to work with than other types. Powders that can be mixed with water are generally safer than concentrated liquids. All aerosol sprays can cause plant damage if held too close to plants during spraying. Whatever the pesticide, never endanger your health by using it too close to harvest. Products vary considerably in how soon you can harvest after applying a pesticide, so be sure to read the label.

Whenever a question arises as to how to apply the product, be sure to reread the label. Don't rely on your memory from last year's spray job. And remember that once you apply the pesticide, it is too late—read the label before you head to the garden.

RENOVATING THE STRAWBERRY PATCH

The strawberry harvest may be over, but that doesn't mean it's time to forget the strawberry patch. Postharvest care is an important part of keeping your patch healthy. With yearly renovation, strawberry plants can remain productive for 10 years or longer.

Begin renovating the strawberry bed immediately after the last harvest. Mow or trim off the leaves near the base of the plant, being careful not to injure the crown. Removing the foliage helps keep diseases under control.

Strawberry plants produce numerous runners—long, horizontal stems that trail along the ground—that give rise to miniature plants. As these new plants grow, they fill in the space between the original plants. Thin matted rows to 8–18 inches wide by

Crowded strawberry plantings should be renovated.

Mow the tops of the strawberry plants.

Remove excess plants, allowing room for new plants to be produced from the runners.

tilling or hoeing the plants you want to remove. Within the row, thin plants to one every 6–8 inches, removing the older plants and leaving the younger, more vigorous ones. Giving the plants a little room to grow reduces the competition for water, light, and nutrients and also improves air circulation.

Renovation is also a good time to fertilize the patch. Apply a balanced garden fertilizer, such as 12-12-12, at a rate of 3–4 pounds per 100 feet of row. Place the fertilizer in bands alongside the crowns, scratch it into the soil with a rake, and water the planting.

Try to get weed problems under control, either by hand pulling or by shallow cultivation with a hoe or tiller. Apply a mulch after cultivation to prevent new weeds from getting started.

Continue to weed and water through the rest of the growing season. Flower buds for next year's crop begin developing in mid- to late August, so this is a critical time to keep the plants healthy.

POTATOES GROW TOMATOES?

Some midwestern gardeners may have witnessed a new phenomenon in their potato patch. At least it's new to them. Potato plants can appear to produce little green fruits about the size of large cherry tomatoes.

These berries are actually the fruits of the potato plant. It's not surprising that they look like tomatoes, since both plants are in the nightshade family.

Most gardeners never see these fruit form on potatoes. Cool temperatures during long days tend to promote fruiting in potatoes. Some cultivars seem more prone to fruit formation than others, so some potatoes may be fruiting while others growing nearby may not.

Plant breeders tend to locate potato fields in cooler climates, such as Idaho and Wisconsin, to facilitate hybridization and fruit production. The seeds that form inside the fruit as it ripens are then grown to maturity so that breeders can evaluate the new plant.

For production of the tubers that we eat, a particular hybrid that has disease resistance or high yields is propagated through pieces of the underground tubers. This type of propagation assures that the desired qualities of the hybrid will be preserved, since hybrid plants rarely reproduce true from seed.

Gardeners could harvest the seed from the fruit as it matures and raise the seeds for next year's garden as a novelty. The resulting plants may not be as desirable as those grown from the tubers this year. Also, one would need to start the seeds indoors early in the year, as plants are much slower to develop from seed than from tubers.

Potato fruits are likely to contain high levels of solanine, a substance that is toxic to humans, particularly children. Potato fruits should not be eaten, no matter how much they look like tomatoes!

SQUASHKINS AND CUCUMELONS

If you grow a zucchini squash next to a giant pumpkin, do you end up with squashkins? Will planting cucumbers next to watermelons yield cucumelons?

These plants probably can't pollinate one another, so in this case the answer is no. Plants of different species rarely cross-pollinate in nature. However, cross-pollination can take place among the winter squash, pumpkins, and gourds. But the results of such a cross would not be evident in this year's fruit.

How can this be? Let us first look at the anatomy of these vine crops. The fruit of any plant is actually a mature ovary, botanically speaking. The seed inside is similar to a child, while the fruit is analogous to the mother. The seed, or child, has characteristics of both parents. The fruit remains whatever the mother plant was to begin with. In other words, if cross-pollination did take place, the seed, not the fruit, would be the result of that cross.

The seed would have to harvested, stored, and planted out the following year to determine if cross-pollination had an effect. Then the resulting fruit on those plants might look like a combination of both parents. (Corn is the exception to the rule; cross-pollination can affect this year's corn crop.)

If you do turn up some unexpectedly odd-looking fruits in your squash patch, it is possible that the seed packet contained a few seeds that were of questionable parentage. However, it is more likely that a "volunteer" squash from last year's garden is the culprit.

GLADIOLUS FOR SUMMER FLOWERS

If you're looking for a versatile cut flower that can be easily grown at home, the gladiolus is just the ticket.

The gladiolus gets its name from the Latin word *gladius,* meaning "sword." Indeed, "glads," as they are named for short, do produce their large showy blossoms along a long pointed stalk with sword-shaped leaves. It's hard to beat the wide choice of colors that glads offer, including red, pink, yellow, white, purple, lavender, and bicolors.

Each flower spike is made up of several florets, which are lined up in double rows. Taller cultivars will probably need staking to prevent the weight of the flowers from bending or breaking the stems. Plants usually stay in bloom up to 2 weeks, but if you stagger your plantings through late spring and early summer, you can have glads in bloom from June through September.

Glad buds will open beginning at the bottom of the spike. Cut the flower spikes after at least 3 of the florets have opened. The rest of the florets will open in the next few days as the lower florets fade. The best time to cut glads is in the early morning or late evening, when temperatures are coolest and flower stems are full of water. Leave as much foliage as possible remaining on the plant so that the corm will receive food reserves for next year.

Glads are grown from bulblike structures called corms, which must be dug up and replanted each year, since they are not usually winter hardy in the Midwest. When foliage begins to turn yellow in the fall, dig up the corms and allow them to air dry for 2–4 weeks. Then pack the corms in a box of dry vermiculite or peat moss and store them in a cool, dry location.

Many garden supply stores run clearance sales on summer-flowering bulbs at this time. You can get some real bargain prices, but it is pretty late in the year for planting, and these older corms would not store well over the winter. Depending on the cultivar, glads take from 60 to 120 days from planting to produce flowers. But if the price is right, it may be worth the gamble of hoping for a late frost this autumn.

EDIBLE FLOWERS FOR THE GOURMET GARDENER

A floral garnish can add color and elegance to a dinner party that your guests will never forget. Many garden flowers can be used as an edible garnish or to lend flavor and color to a cooked dish.

Blossoms of borage, chrysanthemum, cornflower, and dianthus can be floated in a bowl of soup or punch. Violet, miniature rose, lavender, and honeysuckle blooms add a sweet flavor to salads or desserts. Daylily and squash blossoms can be stir-fried or batter-dipped and deep-fried. Nasturtiums and mustard flowers impart a spicy flavor to casseroles. Bright yellow calendula flowers make an economical substitute for saffron.

Go easy on the flowers, though, especially for your first trial. Eating too many blossoms can lead to an upset stomach, diarrhea, and cramps. You might want to start out using flowers as a garnish and sample the flavors before trying more daring culinary delights. The flavor can be strong and/or different from what your palate is used to.

Pick flowers in the early morning or late afternoon, when water content is at its peak. Choose only those blossoms that are free of insects, disease, or other damage. Do not harvest from plants that were treated with pesticides unless the product was labeled for use on *edible* flowers. Gently wash the blooms in water to remove dirt and allow them to drain on paper towels. Once harvested, flowers will not keep long, even when refrigerated, so plan to harvest within a few hours of serving.

Gardening Questions

Q. Why do my peppers flower but not set fruit?

A. Pepper flowers drop off the plant in high temperatures, low humidity, and drying winds. Healthy transplants usually flower and set ample fruit before midsummer weather is detrimental.

Plant peppers only when the soil has warmed to 65° F. To make sure the soil is warm, cover the bed with black plastic a week before planting. The plastic serves double duty as a mulch if you plant the peppers in slits cut into the plastic. When summer arrives, the plastic should be covered with organic mulch or removed to avoid overheating the pepper plants.

Q. This past year our 'Kentucky Wonder' pole beans had a lot of stuff on them I call rust. Our early ones weren't quite as bad as our later ones. I was wondering what I might do to prevent this problem.

A. "Rust" is exactly the correct term. It is caused by a fungus that attacks bean plants when growing conditions are cool and moist. Late-planted, heavily fertilized beans are most likely to sustain severe rust damage. Each year, initial infections are established by spores that overwinter in the soil among bean residue or by airborne spores that blow in from other rust-infected beans.

The most obvious symptom of bean rust is the presence of pustules containing rust-colored spores. Late in the summer, these spores are replaced by overwintering spores, which are dark brown or black.

Remove bean residue and discontinue planting beans in a problem area for 3–4 years to help reduce the number of overwintering spores, which cause the initial infection each summer. The fungus does not attack any weeds or crops other than beans. A fungicide labeled for rust on beans may be necessary. Fungicides will not cure those plants already infected but will keep the fungus from spreading further.

Q. My cucumber, melon, and squash vines look fine for a while, then they all wilt and die. There are holes in the stems where the wilting starts. What should I do to prevent this? We like every kind of summer and winter squash.

A. Squash vine borer is the likely culprit. These insects cause sudden wilting by tunneling into stems. At the base of the plant, you will see their entrance holes filled with tan, sawdust-like material.

Insecticides are ineffective after the borer is inside, so it is important to prevent their attack. Plant debris can harbor overwintering borers, so keep the garden clean. Bt (*Bacillus thuringiensis*) will control borers if it is applied as the borers enter the stems in early summer. Repeated applications of an appropriate insecticide in June and July are another means of prevention.

Once the borers are established, the only treatment is to slit the affected stems and destroy the borer. If the cut portion of the plant is then covered with soil, new roots may form and the plant might survive. At the end of the season, remove and destroy plant debris.

In the future, you may want to choose a resistant squash. Butternut and hubbard are reported to be less susceptible to borers.

Q. Why do my vining geraniums (*Pelargonium peltatum*) get brown spots on their leaves and turn yellow?

A. Brown spots on all annual geraniums (*Pelargonium* species) may be caused by rust, alternaria leaf spot, or bacterial leaf spot. A proper diagnosis is difficult without seeing the affected leaves. Alternaria leaf spot causes leaves to turn black, but since yours turn yellow, this diagnosis is not likely.

Rust is characterized by yellow spots with brown centers on the undersides of the leaves. It is caused by a fungus that develops and spreads in wet conditions. Avoid wetting the foliage when watering and always water early in the day so foliage can dry quickly if it does get wet.

Rust may be controlled by using an appropriately labeled fungicide at 10-day

intervals. The fungicide will protect new foliage but will not remove the fungus from diseased leaves. These should be picked off.

Another possible culprit is bacterial leaf spot, which causes dark, circular spots. Eventually, the leaves wilt and die. When an infected stem is sliced open, a thick, yellow fluid may ooze from the cut. Bacterial leaf spot is a very common disease of geraniums. It develops quickly during warm, moist weather and spreads in splashing water droplets or on tools. Control involves removing and destroying infected plants. To avoid spreading the disease to healthy plants, water carefully, without splashing water on the foliage.

If the geraniums were growing in a container, change the soil and wash the container before planting new annuals in it. If they were growing in a landscape bed, avoid planting geraniums in that area for several years to reduce the risk of infection.

Q. I have a problem with my old-fashioned phlox; they haven't bloomed the last 2 years. I water them all summer long. What should I do to get them to bloom? Also, they are covered with a white powder. They used to be big and tall. Should I fertilize them or move them to a different place?

A. Several factors contribute to vigorous blooming of phlox (*Phlox paniculata*). The plants should be in full sun if possible. Remove the spent blossoms to encourage repeat blooming and divide the plants every 3–4 years in the spring or fall.

The white powder is powdery mildew, and phlox and lilacs are especially susceptible to this fungus. Appropriate fungicides will help but require repeated applications during the growing season and year after year. Since full sunlight and good circulation reduce the severity of powdery mildew, the wisest choice is to move the phlox to a sunny site and give it plenty of space.

Q. I have a rose garden with a total of 22 plants. My big problem is Japanese beetles. I didn't have any early in the year, but the garden was infested in July. I have tried traps, but they seem to just bring more beetles.

A. Japanese beetle larvae develop underground and emerge in late June or early July as adult beetles, becoming most active in July and August. They feed upon many different species of plants, but you are raising one of their favorite foods in quantity.

A mild infestation of Japanese beetles can be controlled by picking them off and dropping them in a bucket of soapy water. Severe infestations require the application of an appropriate insecticide.

Traps rely upon a sex attractant and a floral scent to lure the beetles. However, since the traps attract many more beetles to the area than they catch, they are an ineffective means of control. Ideally, you want your neighbors to hang Japanese beetle traps, luring the beetles out of your yard and into theirs!

Q. I would like to know what kind of bug or mite is attacking my black oak trees. Small branches are dying, and some of the little branches fall off, even without a wind storm.

A. Oaks provide a home and food for dozens of insects, but few seriously damage the plant. The twig girdler is a borer that may be responsible for the twigs you have seen on the ground. Unless the pests significantly threaten the trees on which they feed, no chemical control measures are recommended. Sanitation is the best form of control. Collect and burn or bury the fallen twigs. If the infestation is unusually heavy, an insecticide labeled for twig girdlers will reduce the pest populations, but applications to a large tree are expensive and generally unnecessary. Young trees with heavy infestations may be worth treatment.

Q. My rhubarb plant sends up seed stalks in the summer. What causes it? Should I remove them?

A. The formation of seed stalks, or bolting, usually takes place when the days become long and hot. Bolting can also be caused by extreme cold or drought and is more common in older plants. The cultivar 'Valentine' seems to bolt less than

many of the green-stalked varieties. Plants have a natural tendency to reproduce and will do so at the expense of their roots and general strength. Remove the seed stalks as soon as they form so the plant will remain vigorous and produce well next year.

Q. I have a 10-year-old hydrangea bush that has never bloomed. It was given to me as a gift years ago, and I planted it outdoors. How can I get it to bloom?

A. You probably are referring to the bigleaf hydrangea, *Hydrangea macrophylla*, which, if it bloomed, would have large globes of flowers in blue or pink, depending upon the soil pH. It is a popular florist plant and is not reliably hardy beyond zone 7. The roots overwinter each year, but the tops are killed back to the ground. This causes a problem, since flowers are produced on the previous year's growth.

Improper pruning is another cause of flower failure. Late-fall or early-spring pruning removes the branches bearing flower buds. If no flowering has occurred, remove only the dead wood in late spring. Provide a layer of mulch each fall and hope for a mild winter.

Other hydrangea cultivars are more reliable, including *Hydrangea arborescens* 'Annabelle' and 'Grandiflora'; *H. paniculata* 'Grandiflora,' called the PeeGee hydrangea; and *H. quercifolia*, the oakleaf hydrangea.

Q. I have pecan trees that are more than 10 years old and about 20 feet tall. How do I get them to bloom?

A. Pecans have inconspicuous blooms that hang in strands from the branch, so you may have missed noticing them. If there are no nuts, you may need to plant another pecan cultivar in the area to maximize pollination and fruiting. If there really are no flowers, the trees may be too shaded. Pecans require full sun.

Q. We would like to know how to sprout peach, cherry, and hawthorn seeds. We have tried different methods with no success.

A. Cherries and peaches are not commercially propagated by seed because they do not breed true. For fruit production, purchase a grafted plant from a local nursery or a mail-order fruit nursery.

If you would like to raise them from seed for novelty, provide cold (40° F), moist conditions for 3–4 months. Place them in moist peat moss or vermiculite in the refrigerator for the winter and plant them next spring. For greater germination rates, soak cherry seeds in water for 24 hours before cooling them.

Hawthorns do reproduce true from seed but have a pronounced seed dormancy. Store the seed in moist peat moss for 3–4 months at 70–80° F, followed by 5 months at 40° F, or simply plant them outdoors in early summer for germination the following spring. It may take 2–3 years for some seeds to germinate.

2. I am writing to comment on the best way to get rid of moles: the dog. We could not fix this problem until our dog dug up half a dozen or more of them and solved the problem. They never came back. Of course, there will be some dug-up spots on the lawn for a time, but they soon disappear.

A. They are effective. We have three dogs (totaling 270 pounds), no moles, and some large craters in the yard!

Our mutt seems to have the best nose and is the most successful mole hunter. We can point to an area where we see mole runs and she'll dig there for us. Sometimes she is wiser than we and refuses, so we assume there has been no recent mole activity in that area. The only problem is the dogs cannot distinguish between crabgrass and my favorite daylily! Wherever the mole has gone, they go, too.

If an animal has shown interest in wildlife, you can attach it to a long leash in the area of the mole activity on mole-active days. Moles are most active during the spring and fall on damp days or following rain showers. Daily peak activity takes place during the morning hours. When using the "predator" method of mole control, have a shovel and grass seed on hand to repair the damage to the lawn.

Q. Our small, decorative pond is filled with green water. This green water is not what we imagined when we installed the pond in our yard last year. The fish and plants appear healthy.

A. Chemicals exist for treating algae-filled water, but they only temporarily fix the problem. A pond turns green when it is out of balance. Excess fish food, fish wastes, and decaying plant material make the water rich in nutrients. Usually, plants remove those nutrients, but when there are too few plants, or too much debris or waste, algae will form.

Submerged plants, or oxygenators, will reduce algae by competing for nutrients. Buy oxygenators at a garden center with a pond department, or a fish store. They are usually sold in bunches, and you will need at least 1 bunch per 3 square feet of water surface.

The addition of other plants will help, too. As water lilies and other pond plants spread to cover more water surface, less sunlight is available for algae growth.

Make sure that fertilizers do not run off the lawn into the pond and that fish are not overfed so that the water doesn't become a nutrient-rich soup for algae. Expect some greening of the water if you change the water and each spring before the plants are actively growing. With patience and the addition of plant material, the water should become clearer.

AUGUST

In August, gardening seems relatively easy; the vegetable harvest continues, and the annuals and perennials seem self-sufficient. It appears to be a good time to take a vacation, but every gardener knows that turning your back on the garden is sure to bring on a drought or rampant weed growth.

Although setting sprinklers and pulling weeds sounds mundane, there are other garden activities with more appeal. Planting fall vegetables, propagating raspberries, and saving seeds will make you glad you stayed active in the garden this month.

Garden Calendar

HOME

Cut flowers from the garden to bring a little color indoors or to dry for everlasting arrangements.

Take cuttings from plants such as impatiens, coleus, geraniums, and wax begonias to overwinter indoors. Root the cuttings in a medium such as moist vermiculite, perlite, peat moss, or potting soil rather than water.

Order spring-flowering bulbs for fall planting.

YARD

Check trees and shrubs that have been planted in recent years for girdling damage by guy wires, burlap, or ropes.

Remove and destroy bagworms, fall webworms, and tent caterpillars.

Don't fertilize woody plants now. It stimulates late growth that will not have time to harden off before winter.

Pears are best ripened off the tree, so don't wait for the fruit to turn yellowish on the tree.

Established lawns can be fertilized beginning in late August if moisture is adequate. Have soil tested for fall fertilization requirements if it has been more than 3–4 years since the last test.

Seed new lawns or bare spots in established lawns in late August or September.

GARDEN

Keep the garden well watered during dry weather and free of weeds, insects, and disease.

Complete fall garden planting by direct seeding carrots, beets, kohlrabi, and kale early this month. Lettuce, spinach, radishes, and green onions can be planted later.

Harvest watermelon when several factors indicate ripeness: the underside ground spot turns from whitish to creamy yellow; the tendril closest to the melon turns brown and shrivels; the rind loses its gloss and appears dull; and the melon yields a dull thudding sound rather than a ringing sound when thumped.

Harvest onions and garlic after the tops yellow and fall over, then cure them in a warm, dry, well-ventilated area. The necks should be free of moisture when fully cured, in about a week's time.

Harvest potatoes after the tops yellow and die. Potatoes also need to be cured before storage.

Prune out and destroy raspberry and blackberry canes that bore fruit this year. They will not produce again next year, but they may harbor insect and disease organisms.

Spade or till soil for fall bulb planting and add a moderate amount of fertilizer.

HARVEST WINTER SQUASH IN SUMMER

Winter squash is so named because it is harvested at the mature stage, when flavor is rich and the rind is tough, making it suitable for winter storage. Summer squash is harvested in the immature stage, when the rind is still very tender and seeds have not yet developed.

Usually, winter squash begins maturing in late August or September. How can you tell if your squash is ready? There are many different types of winter squash, and each has its own signs of maturity. In general, look for a color change on the rind. For example, butternut squash changes from a light beige to a deep tan color when ripe. Many winter squash will develop an orange blush in spots. Acorn squash is a good example, with a deep, glossy, green rind that develops a yellow spot facing the ground. When the yellow spot changes to orange, the fruit is ready to pick.

Spaghetti squash changes from a creamy white to a bright yellow at maturity. The delicata squash, which has green streaks across a white background, is ready when the white changes to a beige and an orange blush appears.

You'll probably want to eat the early-maturing fruits right away, since it's been such a long wait since last year's crop. But when you're ready to start storing squash for winter use, choose a cool, dark, dry location. Winter squash can be stored from 2 to 6 months if kept at about 55° F.

SAVING SEEDS FROM THE GARDEN

Collecting seeds from garden plants to plant next year may seem like a good way to save money, but you may be in for a surprise. Some seeds can be saved from year to year with good results, particularly the old-fashioned cultivars. But modern hybrid cultivars rarely breed true from collected seed.

To get that disease-resistant tomato or that frilly double petunia, two or more plants that have desirable characteristics were crossbred. The seed from a hybrid plant will produce varying results due to recombination of different genes. Thus, the resulting plants may not be as productive, attractive, disease-resistant, or flavorful. Each seedling could be quite different from the parents and from each other.

As long as you're prepared to accept this variability, it can be fun to experiment. You never know when you might actually stumble across an improvement!

Some gardeners are tempted to propagate fruit trees from seed—either from fruits grown in the backyard or from purchased fruit. If you're interested in serious fruit production, resist the temptation. Most fruit trees are grafted by splicing a piece of the desired fruiting cultivar onto a seedling rootstock that is disease resistant, hardy,

vigorous, and perhaps dwarfing. Trees grown from seeds of grafted plants will not only produce inferior fruit but could be huge, unmanageable trees for the home landscape.

Saving seeds from your garden plants can be an interesting adventure. As long as you proceed with this in mind, you won't be disappointed with the results.

PLANT NOW FOR FALL HARVEST

Fall is an excellent time to grow many vegetable crops in the Midwest, as the gardener can take advantage of cooler temperatures and more plentiful moisture. Many tradition-ally spring-planted crops, such as radishes, lettuce, and spinach, tend to bolt and become bitter in response to long, hot summer days. Fall gardening helps extend your garden-ing season, so that you can continue to harvest produce after earlier crops have faded.

Some vegetables, such as broccoli, cauliflower, and brussels sprouts, are better adapted to fall gardening because they produce best quality and flavor when they can mature during cooler weather. For many crops, insects and diseases are not as much of a problem in fall plantings.

Since days are getting shorter, use fast-maturing cultivars whenever possible to ensure a harvest before killing frost occurs. Check with your local garden centers for available plants and seed. If you order seeds by mail, keep the fall garden in mind while planning your spring and summer gardening needs. Seeds of the cultivars you want may be out of stock by late summer.

To prepare your garden for a fall crop, remove all previous crop residues and any weeds. Till or spade at least 6–8 inches deep. A general-analysis fertilizer, such as 12-12-12, may be mixed into the soil at the rate of 1–2 pounds per 100 square feet of bed area.

Although cooler temperatures and plentiful rain should be just around the corner, late-summer plantings often suffer from hot soil and inadequate moisture. Soils may form a hard crust over the seeds, which can interfere with seed germination, particu-larly in heavy soils. Use a light mulch of vermiculite, compost, or peat moss over the seed row to prevent a crust from forming. Seeds of lettuce, peas, and spinach will not germinate well when soil temperature reaches 85° F and above. Shading the soil and mulching lightly over the seed row will help keep the temperature more favorable for germination. Planting the seeds somewhat deeper than for spring plantings may also be beneficial, since temperatures will be slightly cooler and moisture more plentiful.

Do not allow seedlings and young transplants to dry out excessively. Apply 1 inch of water in a single application each week to thoroughly moisten the soil if rainfall is inadequate. Young seedlings may need to be watered more often during the first few weeks of growth. Young transplants may benefit from light shade until their new roots become established.

Some vegetables that are already growing in the garden will continue to produce well into the fall but are damaged by even a light frost. Others are considered semi-hardy and will withstand a light frost without protection, while yet others are hardy enough to withstand several hard frosts.

Midwestern gardeners often enjoy several more weeks of good growing after the first frost. You can extend the fall growing season for tender crops by protecting them through early, light frosts. Cover growing beds with blankets or throw cloths supported by stakes or wire to prevent injury to the plants. Small plants can be protected with such items as paper caps, milk jugs, plastic water-holding walls, and other commercially available products. The season can be extended even further by planting crops in a cold frame or hot bed.

BRUSSELS SPROUTS BEST AS FALL CROP

The brussels sprout is a member of the mustard family of plants and is closely related to broccoli, cauliflower, kohlrabi, and cabbage. In fact, one could think of this plant as producing numerous miniature heads of cabbage in the axil of the leaves (where they attach to the stem) instead of making one large head at the top. Botanists date the brussels sprout's cultivation in Europe at least back to the 1500s and place its origin

in northern Europe. But the plant gets its name from Brussels, Belgium, because that was the first area believed to have a great deal of the plant in cultivation. Brussels sprouts spread from Belgium to France, England, and America some time between 1800 and 1850.

Brussels sprouts require a long, cool growing season (about 90 days), which makes them more suitable for a fall crop in much of the Midwest. The plant can withstand considerable freezing, with best production occurring during sunny days and cool nights. Spring crops tend to produce soft, open heads due to overly warm temperatures. While the plants can adapt to a variety of soil types, good drainage is essential.

Assuming a transplanting date of mid- to late August, you should begin harvesting most cultivars some time in October. Sprouts begin to form near the base of the plant and continue to produce for several weeks on up the plant. To have more sprouts ready at the same time, you can cut out the growing tip of the plant when the plants are about 15–20 inches tall. This practice is especially helpful in northern areas, where hard freezes may come on early.

Keeping the plants picked frequently will help insure high-quality sprouts. If left on the plant too long, they turn yellow and tough and become more strongly flavored. The sprouts are easily twisted off from the stem when they are about 1–1½ inches in diameter.

COVER CROPS OR GREEN MANURE— WHAT'S IN A NAME?

Although many gardeners use the terms interchangeably, there are some distinctions between green manure and cover crops. Technically, a cover crop is a plant that is grown to hold soil in place and suppress weeds. A green manure is a plant raised as a source of organic matter to improve soil structure and nutrition.

Many plants can provide the benefits of both cover crops and green manure, which may explain the confusion of the two terms. Cover crops are generally sown in the fall after crops are harvested to protect against soil erosion. The plant residue is then turned under and mixed with the soil in the spring. Green manure is usually started during the growing season either in place of, or in between rows of, vegetable crops.

The type of plant you grow will depend on the desired function and on availability. Winter rye, buckwheat, hairy vetch, and winter wheat are ideal for use as cover crops and are among the most commonly available through garden centers and mail-order catalogs. Clover, alfalfa, and oats make excellent green manure but may be more difficult to find.

The amount of seed to plant will vary with the species, but in general, winter cover crops are seeded at a higher rate (2–3 pounds per 1,000 square feet) than summer green manure (½–1 pound per 1,000 square feet). Till or spade the soil and scatter the seed over the area to be covered at a depth corresponding to the size of the seed. Large seeds should be covered with ¼–½ inch of soil or compost. Small seeds can be left on the surface and lightly raked. Apply a thin layer of loose straw to protect the area from wind and runoff from heavy rains.

Fertilizing is generally not necessary, especially for established garden beds. Some members of the legume family of plants, most notably alfalfa and hairy vetch, actually provide a home for certain soil-borne nitrogen-fixing bacteria known as *Rhizobium*. The bacteria colonize in nodules of the legume's roots and convert atmospheric nitrogen to nitrates and nitrites that can be taken up by plants.

The root growth of green manure crops will help loosen heavy clay or otherwise compacted soils. The manure crop can be turned under in the fall to further improve aeration, water-holding capacity, and nutrient levels. For areas that are susceptible to erosion by wind and water, the green manure can be left in place until spring, providing the added benefits of a cover crop.

Turn the manure or cover crop over several weeks before planting in the spring to allow the vegetation a chance to break down a bit. Then till the soil again just before planting the garden.

Include cover crops and green manure as a regular feature of your soil improvement routine. You'll reap the benefits for years to come.

DIVIDING PERENNIALS

Late summer or early autumn is the best time to divide perennials that bloom in spring and summer. Generally, perennials should be divided to rejuvenate an old, overgrown planting or to increase the number of plants in the garden. Plants such as peonies, irises, hostas, and daylilies are among the most common garden perennials that are easily divided.

Making divisions is a simple task but should be done with care to avoid injury. Dig the plants, preferably with a spading fork, and lift as much of the roots as possible. Then use a large, sharp knife or hatchet to cut the larger roots into smaller pieces. Each new piece should be large enough to ensure successful foliage and flower production next year.

Replant the new pieces in the desired location and be sure to plant at the proper depth. With peonies, this is where most gardeners go wrong. Planting too deeply may

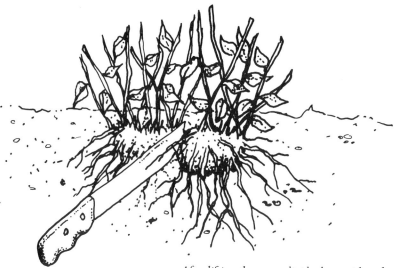

After lifting the roots, divide them with a sharp knife.

188

prevent flowering. Set peony roots so that the buds, or eyes, are only 1–2 inches below the surface of the soil. Each root piece should have at least 3 good buds.

Division of daylilies is recommended every 7–10 years or so to keep plantings vigorous. Older plantings become more difficult to divide and reestablish due to their extensive rhizomes (underground stems). Daylilies are usually divided into single fans or clumps for propagation purposes.

Iris may quit blooming as plantings become overly crowded. The rhizomes are easily lifted and cut into smaller sections to create new plantings (see page 123).

Hostas seldom require division but can easily be propagated by dividing young plants. Older plants become tough and do not reestablish as readily.

Not only do you end up with healthier perennials from division; you also get free plants! If you have no room for them in your own garden, friends and neighbors won't turn them down.

PRUNING AND PROPAGATING RASPBERRIES

All raspberries need to be pruned regularly, ideally twice each year. Summer pruning is best done late in the season.

The canes of the raspberry plant are biennial, that is, they produce foliage the first year and flowers and fruit the second year. The canes die after the fruit is harvested.

Summer pruning is generally done to remove the old fruiting canes. The particular pruning technique will depend on which type of raspberries you're raising. Summer-bearing red and yellow raspberries should be pruned to remove all old fruiting canes completely down to the ground.

Everbearing raspberries produce a summer crop on the canes that fruited the previous fall. Remove these canes only after the summer crop is harvested. Some growers prefer to sacrifice the summer crop for ease of spring care and to create a larger fall crop. In this case, no summer pruning is required; all canes are mowed off in spring.

Black and purple raspberries benefit from two types of pruning. As with other

raspberries, remove the fruiting canes after the harvest is complete. Then tip prune the top 3–4 inches of the 1-year-old canes to encourage more branching, which should result in more berries.

While you're pruning, you'll probably notice that your raspberry plants are propagating like bunny rabbits! Red raspberries tend to produce small plants growing nearby that come from the roots of the mother plant. These suckers can be divided from the mother plant with a sharp spade and replanted in the desired location (could be your neighbor's yard!).

Black and purple raspberries often have canes that are so long that the tips bend over and make contact with the soil; they may form new roots if the soil is moist. Covering the tips with 2–4 inches of soil will help encourage rooting. Next spring, the rooted tips can be severed from the mother plant with a sharp spade and replanted. This method of propagation is known as layering.

Older raspberry plantings are often infected with virus. Propagating from virus-infected plants will pass the virus on to the new planting. Check your plants for signs of disease (yellowing, spots, wilting) before propagating.

TIME TO START YOUR NEW LAWN

Late summer to early fall is the best time of year to establish a new lawn. Whether from seed or sod, fall-planted lawns should have all the right growing conditions to get off to a good start. Early-fall weather usually brings moderately cool temperatures and plenty of moisture, which is needed to get a cool-season lawn established. Cool-season grass species include bluegrass, perennial rye, and turf-type fescue.

It is essential to clean the area of weeds before you lay your new lawn. It's also a good idea to have your soil tested for a new site. That way you'll know exactly how much of which fertilizer materials to apply.

Ideally, the soil should be a well-drained loam with a firm, level surface before you seed or sod. If soil improvement is needed, add the necessary amendments. Good-quality topsoil or peat moss, manure, or other organic material should help improve heavy soils.

If your plan of attack is to seed your new lawn, be sure to start off with good seed of a known origin. You'll be living with your lawn for some time, so don't skimp on quality. Seed must be applied evenly across the surface. Using a lawn seeder, apply half of the seed in one direction and the rest at a right angle to that direction. Rake the seed lightly to provide good contact between seed and soil. A light mulch, about 1 bale of straw per 500 square feet, will help keep the seed in place and conserve moisture. Water as needed to keep the area evenly moist until the new grass is well established.

Sod can provide a new lawn in a hurry but, of course, is more expensive than starting from seed. Sod must be laid as soon as possible after it is harvested—within 24 hours—if it is to thrive. Try to stagger the end pieces, rather than lining them up evenly, to prevent the formation of lines across the lawn. The edges of the sod should be touching each other but not overlapping. Roll the sod after it is in place to provide good contact with the soil, and water thoroughly.

HERB PROPAGATION

Herb gardeners can snip fresh herbs throughout the winter by propagating their outdoor plants now.

There are several approaches to overwintering plants. One easy method is to dig up a plant, or a portion of one, and pot it up. Plants such as chives, lemon balm, mint, burnet, and sweet woodruff can be lifted and divided into sections to create more plants. Dividing is a fairly foolproof method of propagation because both roots and shoots are already formed. Leggy plants should be pruned back about halfway to encourage new growth.

Many herbs can be propagated by cuttings for rooting indoors. This method works especially well for plants that are too large to move in their entirety. Plants such as basil, oregano, lavender, rosemary, thyme, and sage will root easily from shoot tip cuttings.

To propagate by layering, cover the stem with soil and sever from the mother plant when roots have been established.

Take the cutting just below a node on the stem (where the leaves attach) because this is where root formation is more abundant. Remove the lower leaves and insert the cut end of the stem into a moist medium such as vermiculite, sand, or perlite. Cover the container with plastic to help increase relative humidity, and place the pot in a warm, shaded location.

Some herbs, including mint, lemon balm, and thyme propagate easily by layering. Bend a stem to the ground, remove the leaves from that stem section, cover the section with soil, and water it gently. The new plant will be nourished by the mother plant until it is ready to survive on its own. Leave about 6 inches of the upper portion of the stem above ground and upright. If necessary, stake the stems to hold them in place, or put a rock or other heavy object on top of the mound. Cut a wound just below a node on the stem portion to be buried to help stimulate faster rooting. Once rooted, the new plant can be severed from the mother plant and potted for indoor growing.

Herbs can be grown indoors but will need a well-lit location, especially when they are first brought inside. Even a sunny window may not match the light intensity of a lightly shaded outdoor location. Indoors, a sunny southern exposure would be ideal. Supplemental or artificial lighting may be needed. Special light bulbs for plant growing can be purchased, but the same results can be achieved by using a combination of warm white and cool white fluorescent lights.

Most herbs thrive in infertile soil and do not require extra fertilizer in the garden. However, if planted in the soilless potting mixtures that are commonly used today, some fertilizer may be necessary. A balanced, low-analysis fertilizer, such as 5-10-5 or 6-10-4, should be sufficient. Read the product label for specific instructions for application.

Although herbs differ in their moisture needs, your finger can be a guide. Water when the top inch of soil feels dry when pinched. Apply enough water so that some drains from the bottom of the pot, thus washing away any excess salts.

POTPOURRI: A FRAGRANT MEMORY

You can keep the fragrance of summer blooms year-round through the age-old craft of potpourri. Potpourri is any combination of flowers and herbs that imparts a pleasant scent.

The name "potpourri" is of French origin and literally translates to "rotten pot." Potpourri was originally used to mask the harsh smells of moldy, damp rooms and the like. Today, potpourri is widely used to lend fragrance to closets, drawers, pillows, or the bath.

Most potpourri is made of dried flower petals and buds as the base. Fragrances from oils, spices, fruits, or herbs may also be added. A fixative is needed to blend the different aromas and to help them last longer.

Your garden can probably supply you with most of the needed materials. Roses, carnations, lavender, and chamomile are just a few of the floral favorites for potpourri. Foliage from plants such as mint, scented geraniums, lavender, and many other herbs can be blended along with the flowers.

All America Rose Selections offers the following recipe for custom potpourri that can't miss. Take 1 quart (4 ounces) of dried rose petals, which are prepared by gently pulling petals away from the flower and spreading them in a shallow layer on paper towels or screens to dry, and mix them with 1 ounce of chopped fixative (not powdered), such as orris root, benzoin, or patchouli. (It will take at least 2 quarts of fresh rose petals to get 1 quart of dry petals.) Then add the secondary scent from spices, herbs, or dried fruit peels at the rate of 1 ounce per quart of petal mixture. If an oil fragrance is desired, add 3 drops of essential oil per quart and mix well with your hands or a wooden spoon. Allow the mixture to cool in a dark place until all of the scents have had a chance to blend. Then place it in a bowl, sachet, envelope, or other suitable container. If the fragrance fades after a while, you can renew the potpourri by adding a few more drops of essential oil.

BRIGHTEN YOUR GARDEN WITH SUNFLOWERS

Nothing beats sunflowers for adding a splash of color to both the flower bed and the vegetable garden. Sunflowers are native to America and have adapted to conditions in every state in the continental United States. It is believed that wild sunflowers once covered thousands of square miles of what is now the western United States.

Sunflower remnants have been found in North American archeological sites dating to as early as 3000 B.C. Native Americans used sunflowers for food, medicine, and dyes. The seeds were roasted and ground into flour for baking breads. Various tribes considered the plant a pain reliever, a disinfectant, and even an antidote for snake bites. A yellow dye was extracted from the brightly colored flower petals, while a purple dye was made by soaking the purple seeds. These dyes were then used to decorate baskets and human skin.

Spanish explorers are credited with bringing the seeds of these lively flowers to Europe. The first published record of the sunflower, by a Belgian herbalist, appeared in 1568. By the early 1600s, the sunflower had become common in many of England's gardens.

Today, most sunflowers are classified for growing as ornamentals or for seed production, although for the home gardener, many cultivars can perform both functions. Sunflowers are widely known for their large flower heads, which bloom on 5–6-foot plants. In the past, these huge plants were mostly confined to large gardens or grown as landscape oddities. But today's selection offers many dwarf and intermediate flower and plant sizes, making sunflowers suitable for any size garden. For the small garden, try the charming cultivars 'Sunspot' and 'Teddy Bear.'

The seeds are ready to harvest when the backs of the flower heads turn from green to a light yellow and the bracts (leaflike structures) surrounding the individual seeds turn brown. Generally, seeds will be ready to harvest about 30–45 days after flowering, depending on the weather.

The heads should be hung upside down inside a paper or cloth bag to catch the seeds that fall out. Cutting the heads with a portion of the stem attached will make

them easier to hang. Allow them to dry in a well-ventilated area for a few weeks. After the seeds are fully dry, they can be prepared for eating in one of several ways. For salted seeds, soak them in a strong salt-water solution overnight. Then drain the water, spread the seeds on a cookie sheet, and roast them at 200° F for about 3 hours, or until the seeds are crisp. Or mix the dry seeds with butter and salt and then spread on cookie sheets. Roast them at 250° F for about 1 hour. Shake or stir the seeds occasionally. After cooling, place the seeds in an airtight container and store them in the refrigerator. Seeds for feeding birds or other animals can simply be dried and stored in paper sacks until ready to use.

PLANTS HAVE ALLERGIES, TOO!

People aren't alone in experiencing unpleasant reactions to plants. Some plants are quite sensitive to substances produced by certain other plants. The relationship between plants in which one produces a substance that inhibits the growth of sensitive plants growing nearby is called allelopathy.

The black walnut tree is the most common example of a plant that is toxic to other plants. Black walnuts produce a chemical called juglone, which occurs naturally in all parts of the tree but especially in buds, nut hulls, and roots. Plants that are sensitive to juglone exhibit symptoms such as foliar yellowing, wilting, and possibly death. Unless one is aware of the toxicity of juglone, it is easy to blame such symptoms on disease. Unfortunately, there is no cure once plants are affected.

Plants vary in their sensitivity to juglone. Many plants commonly grown in the Midwest are quite sensitive to it, including tomatoes, cabbage, apples, peonies, alfalfa, and some species of pine, spruce, and maple. Beans, corn, cherries, hawthorns, viburnums, poison ivy, and soybeans have been observed to be tolerant of juglone.

Gardens should be located away from black walnut trees to avoid damage to sensitive plants. Keep in mind that the tree's roots reach beyond the dripline of the tree's canopy and can remain active for several years after the tree is removed. Raised beds can help protect sensitive plants if black walnut trees are unavoidable. But care must be taken to keep leaves, nuts, and twigs out of the raised beds. Black walnut leaves, bark, and wood chips should not be used as mulch or compost in the landscape or garden, even if sensitive plants are not currently being grown. Small amounts of juglone may still be released even after several years.

Gardening Questions

Q. Is there a way to keep raccoons out of sweet corn? Lights and radios on all night kept them out in past years but not this year. They have completely ruined my crop, even before the corn was mature.

A. One of the most effective methods is to place an electric fence, or "hot wire," around the corn planting. Two wires, placed 8 and 18 inches above the ground, should keep the raccoons at bay.

   Live trapping is another alternative. Raccoons can be suspicious of the trap, so wire the trap door open for 2–3 days and bait it daily. The animals will learn to come and go from the trap and will be in for a surprise when the wires are removed. Effective baits include corn, fish, fish-flavored cat food, and bacon. Attract the raccoons' attention with a ball of aluminum foil or other shiny object in the trap. Contact the Department of Natural Resources for disposal instructions. In some areas, they can tell you where to relocate the animal so that it will not pose a problem to anyone else.

Q. I have been growing tomatoes for 20 years, and my problem is production. I have more vine than I need but not that many tomatoes. What's wrong?

A. Full sunlight is a key ingredient in tomato production. A minimum of 6 hours of direct sunlight daily is necessary for optimum fruiting.

Cultivar selection is another way to control the yield. Determinate tomato plants grow to a height determined by their genetic makeup and should not be pruned. Pruning will remove the central leader, which will produce fruit if left intact. Determinate plants, including plum tomatoes, ripen their fruit within a couple of weeks' time, making them ideal for canning.

Indeterminate tomato plants increase in size throughout the growing season. Pruning will produce more side shoots, giving larger quantities of smaller fruits. These ripen over a longer period of time. Recommended cultivars for high yield include 'Celebrity,' 'Jetstar,' and 'Early Girl.'

Finally, excess nitrogen encourages the plant to produce more leaves and fewer tomatoes. Before planting, use a balanced, low-analysis fertilizer according to label rates or following soil test recommendations. Try using a starter solution to water in your transplants. An excellent starter solution can be made by dissolving 1–2 tablespoons of high-phosphorus fertilizer, such as 5-10-5, in one gallon of water. Then side-dress the plants with nitrogen after they are already bearing fruit.

Q. We set out sweet Spanish onions, and when they got big, the bulbs came out of the ground. Should I pile dirt up around them so they don't get green?

A. Hill soil around the onions or apply a 2–4-inch layer of mulch to keep sunlight from reaching the bulb. Avoid heavy, wet material around the neck of the plant because it increases the chance of rot. Taper the mulch or soil off near the neck so it does not invite infection.

Q. I have been having a very hard time planting oriental poppies and keeping them growing. The ground is good and brown, and I fertilize it with cow manure. I planted some last fall, and they all rotted. Do you have any suggestions that would help?

A. Oriental poppies have fleshy roots and demand a well-drained root environment. Plant them in a location that does not allow water to stand on the surface and in a soil that has been generously amended with organic matter, such as sphagnum peat moss or straw.

Sow seeds of oriental poppies on top of the soil and do not cover them, since they must have sunlight to germinate. Expect them to die back after they bloom, since poppies often go dormant in the heat of summer. Allow the seed heads to ripen and open to increase your planting next year.

Q. I would really like to grow lupines, but mine die each year. First the leaves curl and turn yellow. Then they just die. They are growing in partial shade.

A. Lupines are one of the more difficult perennials to grow in the Midwest. They prefer cool, moist, acidic soils and cool summers. Lupines are susceptible to powdery mildew, rusts, lupine aphid, and plant bugs. None of these pests are usually serious alone, but a combination of insect, disease, and cultural problems can spell death for the plant.

Other plants can provide vertical accent in the garden, including liatris, cardinal flower (*Lobelia cardinalis*), sage (*Salvia*), speedwell (*Veronica*), and astilbe. Your options are to struggle along with lupines, substitute another plant, or move to a different climate!

Q. Every year my husband grows lovely baby's breath. But after it dries, it becomes too brittle to use in the many dried arrangements that I make as a hobby. Do you have any ideas?

A. Treating baby's breath with glycerin creates a soft, pliable material. Harvest the stems when 60–70% of the blossoms have opened. Place the stem ends in a mixture of glycerin and water. One part glycerin to 10 parts water will keep the baby's breath white, while 1 part glycerin to 4 parts water will turn the baby's breath beige.

Allow the stems to stand in the solution for 3–4 days in a dark, cool place. Then hang the branches upside down for 2–3 weeks.

You can order glycerin through a pharmacy. Although it is expensive, it does not evaporate rapidly, so a glycerin solution can be rejuvenated by adding more water. You can also add leafy tree branches to your arrangements by treating them with the solution.

Water-soluble absorption dyes may be added to the solution to tint the baby's breath if desired. A florist or craft store should be able to order these for you.

Q. I have a lot of pawpaw trees. They bloom well and the fruit sets, only to fall off when they are maybe ¼ of an inch long. What is wrong, and what can I do? Some of them have grown from seed, and some I have transplanted.

A. If this has only happened once or twice, it may be that a late frost has killed the developing fruits. If this is a recurring problem, then pollination is failing.

The pollination of the pawpaw is a subject of debate. Each pawpaw flower requires pollination from another flower, but botanists aren't sure how the pollen is transported. Pollination may take place through honeybees, a certain beetle species, or carrion flies, which leads to the belief that hanging a dead animal in the tree will attract pollinators. The method of procuring and hanging that animal in a pawpaw tree is left up to the imagination, but it may be an effective means of attracting carrion flies! And disgusting your neighbors!

There is another difficulty with pollination. On any given tree, the female organs are no longer receptive when the pollen is shed. Planting more than one tree will greatly increase the chance of successful pollination.

These problems with pollination keep the pawpaw from becoming a major food crop. Researchers are currently working on identifying the pollinators.

Q. We live in a new subdivision and are trying to establish a foundation planting of yews, but they keep dying. First they turn yellow, then brown. We water them regularly, so that's not the problem.

A. Yews are intolerant of wet feet, or poor drainage. Quite often, the rich topsoil is removed from a new development before the lots are sold to builders. The builders compact the remaining soil with their equipment and bring up subsoil when they excavate for the basement.

This does not provide a happy home for a yew. The compacted soil does not allow water to percolate through the soil; instead, it remains around the root zone of the yew.

To correct the situation, water only when necessary and make sure all down-spouts take water away from that planting bed. If you replace some of the yews, amend the soil in the bed with organic matter and plant the replacements up higher than normal, so that the top inch of the root ball is above soil level. Apply 3–4 inches of mulch. On the other hand, consider replacing the yews with another evergreen that is not so finicky about drainage.

Q. The cracks in my driveway produce a bumper crop of weeds, so I use a soil ster-ilant. I have a row of trees about 20 feet away from the driveway. Large branches are starting to die off. Could this be from the soil sterilant, or do they just have a disease or something?

A. There could be another problem with the trees, but you are right to suspect the soil sterilant first. These products are nonselective and provide long-term control of all vegetation in treated areas, but they can easily go awry.

Many users are unaware of the extent of the neighboring trees' root systems. Most tree roots are small and found in the top foot of soil, extending beyond the dripline of the tree. Any roots in an area treated with soil sterilant will be killed. Tree roots do grow under driveways, so they are susceptible.

Q. While visiting relatives in Georgia, I noticed that their lawns seemed to look green and lush, even during hot, dry weather, while my lawn always looks so brown and dull during the summer. Can we grow that kind of grass here?

A. Warm-season grasses, including zoysia and Bermuda grass, are popular turf grass choices for the South because they tolerate summer stress. These grasses may be useful in southern portions of the Midwest but have some drawbacks.

Zoysia and Bermuda grass will thrive in hot, dry weather, while bluegrass and other cool-season grasses must be watered regularly to keep them green. But the warm-season grasses do not tolerate cool weather and so can be expected to be dormant and brown from early fall until midspring in most of the Midwest. Zoysia, and especially Bermuda grass, can be quite aggressive in sunny, warm locations and can quickly spread to areas where they are not wanted.

If possible, observe an existing warm-season lawn in your area for a year before planting one on your property to help you decide if it's right for you. Once established, these grasses can be difficult to remove, should you have a change of heart.

2. Does pampas grass grow here? I have seen it on my trips to Florida, and it is just beautiful. Which ornamental grasses do well here?

A. True pampas grass (*Cortaderia selloana*) is not hardy in the Midwest. A good substitute is sometimes called hardy pampas grass (*Erianthus ravennae*), which reaches a height of 12–15 feet. Chinese silver grass (*Miscanthus sinensis*) is a smaller ornamental grass that reaches a height of 6–10 feet and produces showy flower heads that persist through the winter. A finer-textured form of this grass is maiden grass (*Miscanthus sinensis* 'Gracillimus'), with very narrow, arching leaf blades that give the clump a fountain-like appearance. These *Miscanthus* cultivars are often more in scale with a residential setting than the enormous *Erianthus*. Other *Miscanthus* cultivars include those with white vertical variegation, yellow horizontal variegation, purple seed heads, or attractive fall color. They range in height from 2 to 10 feet.

Ornamental grasses have piqued the interest of both gardeners and breeders. There are currently more than 50 cultivars of *Miscanthus* on the market, and they have confusingly similar common names. I urge you to use the Latin names as you delve into the world of grasses. Latin can be a mouthful, but it will help you properly identify your collection.

You may want to include some smaller grasses in your garden. Fountain grass (*Pennisetum alopecuroides*) reaches 3–4 feet and is attractive in masses. A dwarf cultivar, 'Hameln,' or dwarf fountain grass, grows from 2 to 3 feet. Bring blue shades into the garden with fescue cultivars (*Festuca*) or blue wild rye (*Elymus arenarius*).

Most ornamental grasses require full sun, but the *Carex* genus features many shade lovers. Most are reminiscent of a mop in shape, and some are variegated with white, cream, or yellow.

Generally, grasses require little maintenance or pampering. Do not cut the tops off in autumn if you want to enjoy the winter interest that grasses provide. The tan, dried material is attractive until a heavy snow or ice storm breaks it down, which is usually by February in my garden. After the blades are broken, cut the grasses back to within a few inches of the ground. Make sure you tend to this garden task before April. Once the grasses begin to grow again in the spring, it is impossible to sort the old, dead blades out.

A garden devoted solely to grasses is interesting only to a collector. Mix ornamental grasses throughout your landscape by using them as accents, specimens, in perennial borders, and in masses.

Q. We suspect the birds ate some of the walnuts off our trees when they were small. Would it help if we put bird feeders out by the walnut trees?

A. I doubt birds are eating the walnuts, since the shells are difficult to break open. Squirrels may eat walnuts, but they usually wait until they are ripe. Instead, the early nut drop is probably caused by a lack of pollination. If a flower is not pollinated, it forms a small fruit that falls off.

Q. I use a dehumidifier in my basement during the summer months. Can the water from this be used on houseplants or outside flowers?

A. Dehumidifiers basically produce distilled water, and there is no harm in using it on ornamental plants. The water will be free of fluoride and chlorine, which are commonly found in tap water and cause tip burn on sensitive houseplants. Keep the dehumidifier clean and empty it daily to reduce bacterial growth in the water.

Q. I have heard of insecticidal soaps and wonder if I can make my own with water and dish soap?

A. Some gardeners mix 1–3 teaspoons of mild household soap per 1 gallon of water, but the safest route is to use only those products that have been tested for the strength of the dilution and safety for plants and gardeners. While it is true that some soaps will kill insects, some will also harm the plants they are meant to protect. Commercial insecticidal soap formulations are registered with the Environmental Protection Agency for control of certain insect pests. They have been found to be effective against insects with sucking mouthparts, including scale, aphids, whiteflies, and mealy bugs. They are safe to nontarget organisms, including people, which is the major advantage of insecticidal soaps.

Soaps are derived from plant or animal oils. Because each type of soap has a different chemical structure, each has different insecticidal properties. Several other soap products have been promoted as insecticides, including laundry or dish soaps. Some mixtures are effective, but if you are at all unsure, you should use products registered with the EPA.

SEPTEMBER

September is the month of the harvest moon, and throughout the ages, the harvest has been an occasion for song and celebration. As we gather in our crops and prepare them for storage or preserving, we feel grateful for the abundance. Since your garden may produce more than you need, you might want to donate some of your crops to a local shelter or soup kitchen.

September's cool weather and adequate moisture are ideal for fall vegetable production, but keep an eye out for the first frost and have protective covers poised for action. The weather also makes this a great time to plant trees.

Garden Calendar

HOME

Store leftover garden seed in a cool, dry place. A sealable jar with a layer of silica gel or powdered milk in the bottom works well.

Prepare storage areas for overwintering tender flower bulbs and garden produce.

Bring houseplants that were moved outside for the summer indoors before night temperatures fall below 55° F.

Dig and repot herbs or take cuttings for growing indoors over winter.

Thanksgiving (or Christmas) cactus can be forced into bloom in time for the holidays. Provide 15 hours of complete darkness each day for approximately eight weeks. Keep temperature at about 60–65° F. Temperatures of about 55° F will cause flower buds to set without the dark treatment.

YARD

Harvest apples, pears, grapes, everbearing strawberries, and raspberries. For most fruits, flavor is the best indicator of ripeness, although color change can also be a good indicator.

Fall is a good time to plant many container-grown or balled-and-burlapped nursery stock.

Clean up fallen fruits, twigs, and leaves around fruit trees to reduce disease and insect carryover.

To promote your lawn's recovery from summer stress, apply high-nitrogen fertilizer at the rate of 1 pound actual nitrogen per 1,000 square feet.

Vertical thinning or power raking of the lawn will help control thatch buildup if needed.

Early fall is a good time to apply broadleaf weed killers. Be sure to follow all label directions and choose a calm day to prevent spray drift.

Reseed bare spots or new lawns using a good-quality seed mixture.

GARDEN

Dig onions and garlic after tops fall over naturally and necks begin to dry.

Harvest tender crops, such as tomatoes, peppers, eggplant, melons, and sweet potatoes, before frost or cover plants with blankets, tarps, or newspaper to protect them from light frost.

Mature green tomatoes can be ripened indoors. Individually wrap fruits in newspaper or leave them on the vine, pulling the entire plant out of the garden. Store in a cool location, about 55–60° F.

Harvest winter squash when mature—when skin is tough, with deep, solid color—but before hard frost. Some cultivars will show an orange blush when mature (see pages 182–83).

Thin fall crops that were planted earlier, such as lettuce and carrots.

Plant radishes, sets for green onions, lettuce, and spinach for fall harvest.

Plant, transplant, or divide peonies, daylilies, iris, and phlox if necessary.

Save tender plants such as coleus, wax begonias, impatiens, or fuchsias for indoor growing over the winter. Dig plants and cut them back about halfway, or take cuttings of shoot tips and root them in moist vermiculite, soil mix, or perlite.

Plant spring-flowering bulbs beginning in September. Planting too early can cause bulbs to sprout top growth before winter. However, allow at least 4–6 weeks before the ground freezes for good root formation.

Dig tender perennials, such as cannas, caladiums, tuberous begonias, and gladiolus, before frost. Remove and discard tops, allow underground structures to air dry, and store in dry peat moss or vermiculite.

Cut flowers such as strawflower, statice, baby's breath, and celosia for drying and hang upside down in a dry, well-ventilated area.

HARVEST YOUR ROSES?

Even though rose flowers may be fading from the limelight, the time is right for harvesting your roses—rose hips, that is. Rose hips are those small red fruits that form when you allow rose flowers to mature on the plant rather than snip them off as they fade. These fruits not only have ornamental value but are a bountiful source of vitamin C.

Just about any type of rose will produce a hip if flowers are allowed to mature on the plant. But some roses produce particularly large hips, making them more convenient for eating or processing. *Rosa rugosa*, an old-fashioned rose grown particularly for its fragrance, produces hips as large as crab apples. Other roses recommended for their hips include dog rose (*Rosa canina*), sweet briar (*Rosa eglanteria*), *Rosa acicularis*, cinnamon rose (*Rosa cinnamomea*), and *Rosa moyesii*.

Gather rose hips when they are completely ripe but not overripe. The hips should turn from orange to red but not yet dark red. Make your harvest only from plants that have not been sprayed or dusted with fungicides or insecticides.

Rose hips can be eaten raw if you have a taste for the very tart and don't mind battling the many seeds. Or they can be used to flavor teas, jellies, jams, or other cooked products.

The American Rose Society also recommends rose syrup, potpourri, and rose vinegar from rose petals; and rose hip wine, honey of roses, and rose and caraway cookies. You can write to the society for recipes or other information on roses at P.O. Box 30,000, Shreveport, Louisiana 71130.

HARVESTING GRAPES

One of the toughest things about growing your own grapes is beating the birds to the harvest! Netting can be placed over a grape arbor to keep the birds away from the fruits. But don't be too hasty in cutting the fruits to one-up the birds. Make sure your grapes are ripe before you harvest.

Although color change is important in determining when to harvest grapes, it should not be the only consideration. Most berries change from green to blue, red, or white (depending on the cultivar) as they approach maturity. But most grape cultivars color up long before they flavor up. When fully ripe, the natural bloom, or whitish coating, on the berries should become more noticeable. The color of the seeds changes from green to brown.

One of the other factors to consider in determining harvest time is the size and firmness of the berry. It's helpful to be familiar with your cultivar's individual characteristics. Most grapes should become slightly less firm to the touch.

The best sign of ripeness is the grape's sweetness, and of course the most reliable method for home growers to test this is to taste them! Unlike some other fruits, once the grapes are cut from the vine, they will not ripen any further.

Grapes don't require direct sunlight on the fruits to ripen and develop good color. Rather, it is the amount of light that reaches the plant's leaves that governs the quality of the fruit. The leaves manufacture the sugars that are then translocated to the fruit.

To protect your ripening crop from hungry birds, you can place bags over individual fruit clusters when the grapes are about half grown. Use a sturdy brown paper bag that will allow enough room for the bunch to develop, and tie it securely to the grape cane. Bagging might also help protect the fruits from inclement weather, as excessive rains close to harvest time can cause the grapes' skins to split. Of course, bagging is not very practical for larger plantings, in which case netting is the best alternative.

Once you've harvested your grapes, you can store them for as long as 8 weeks, depending on the cultivar and storage conditions. Ideally, grapes should be stored at 32° F with 85% relative humidity. If you have an abundance of grapes, there are some good alternatives to eating them fresh. Grapes are excellent for making jellies, jams, juice, and wine.

PEARS BEST RIPENED OFF THE TREE

One advantage to growing your own fruit is that you can get tree-ripened freshness, a real rarity in the supermarket. But, unlike other fruits, pears will reach their best quality when ripened off the tree.

When left to ripen on the tree, most cultivars of pears leave something to be desired in terms of texture and flavor. Tree-ripened pears often turn soft and brown at the core and have an excessively grainy texture.

There are several indicators to know when to harvest pears. The most obvious sign is a color change. Pick pears when their color changes from dark to light or yellowish green but before they are fully yellow. The fruit should be relatively firm. The small dots on the skin should turn from whitish to corky brown.

The sweetness of the fruits should also increase with maturity, so be sure to sample the fruit regularly. Mature fruit will separate easily from the branch by lifting and twisting. When you taste the fruit, check the seeds inside; the seed coats should be brown. Fruit on heavily loaded trees usually matures a little more slowly.

Pears can be further ripened by storing them at 60–70° F with high relative humidity (80–85%). Mature pears should ripen within a few days. All ripening fruit gives off a gas called ethylene, which stimulates further ripening. Pears will ripen even faster if stored with other ripening fruit in a closed container.

If longer-term storage is desired, chill the pears to 32–35° F as soon as possible after harvesting. Perforated plastic bags can be used to keep relative humidity high. Be

careful not to bruise or puncture the fruit, as injuries provide an entry for decay organisms. Although different cultivars of pears vary in their maximum storage time, most can be held from 2 to 4 months under ideal conditions.

DIG THOSE POTATOES

Although the potato originated in the Andes of South America, most of today's crop is grown in Europe and the former Soviet Union. White is the most popular potato, but other colors, particularly red, blue, pink, and yellow, are available. The potato has good nutritional value and is less fattening than most people think. One medium-size potato (about ⅓ pound) has only 100 calories yet supplies 35% of the U.S. recommended daily allowance of vitamin C, 6% protein, and 10% iron, as well as other vitamins and minerals. The edible portion of the plant is an underground modified stem structure called a tuber; the eyes are the buds, which sprout shoots.

Potatoes can be dug before maturity for new potatoes throughout the summer and early fall. Harvest mature potatoes for storage after the tops have yellowed and begun to dry. Do not leave the tubers in the ground after the plants die back, as they may rot or resprout new stems if the weather is warm and moist. Lift the tubers with a potato fork or garden spade, taking care to avoid injuring the tubers. Sort through the tubers at digging time; those with cuts, bruises, or diseases should be discarded or used immediately. Cure the potatoes for 1–2 weeks at 65–70° F and 85–90% relative humidity to allow the skin to toughen and wounds to heal.

After curing, store the tubers at 40–45° F with 90% relative humidity in complete darkness. Potatoes can be stored from 2 to 9 months, depending on the cultivar and storage conditions. Late-season cultivars, such as 'Kennebec' and 'Katahdin,' tend to store the longest. Prolonged exposure to temperatures below 40° F causes the starch of the potato to convert to sugar, resulting in a peculiar sweet flavor. This conversion can sometimes be reversed by storing the tubers at 70° F for a week before using them. Prolonged temperatures above 45° F lead to sprouting.

Because the tuber is a modified stem structure that contains chlorophyll, potatoes will turn green when exposed to light. Exposure to light also leads to production of a toxic alkaloid called solanine. The amount of solanine produced increases with the length of exposure and the intensity of the light. Potatoes will turn green and accumulate solanine if grown too close to the soil surface and/or stored even with the least exposure to light. Although it is the solanine, and not chlorophyll, that is toxic, most of the solanine is concentrated near the skin of the tuber, so that peeling the green portion away should remove most of the toxin. Sprouting eyes or buds also are high in solanine. Do not rely on cooking to destroy solanine.

EARLY PUMPKINS

It seems that pumpkins always mature much earlier than we would like. Unfortunately, the conditions needed to store the pumpkins until Halloween are pretty hard to find this time of year. For optimum storage, pumpkins need cool, dry conditions with temperatures of 50–60° F and a relative humidity of about 50–70%.

Pumpkins that are bruised or otherwise damaged will rot faster, so store only the best-quality harvest. Pumpkins should be harvested with a portion of the stem attached. But don't carry the pumpkin by the stem—they're not as sturdy as you might think. Handle the pumpkins carefully to prevent wounds to the rind, and cure them in a warm, humid area for about 10 days so that the rinds have a chance to fully harden.

Under ideal storage conditions, pumpkins can be held for 2–3 months. However, considering the usual storage conditions found in the home, one month of storage is probably more typical. Just in case the pumpkins you harvest now are not in shape for Halloween, you may want to keep your eyes open for a farm stand or other pumpkin sales.

VEGETABLE SPAGHETTI

Vegetable and pasta lovers unite! Spaghetti squash allows you to eat your pasta and

your vegetables at the same time. The stringy flesh of this winter squash has a flavor that ranges from slightly sweet, like an acorn squash, to that of starchy flour pasta with a crunch.

The spaghetti squash grows, much like other winter squash, on large vines that produce several fruits per plant. The oblong fruits reach 8–12 inches long. Spaghetti squash generally needs about 100 days to mature after seeding. Harvest the fruit when the skin turns from creamy pale green to a bright yellow color.

Cook the squash by baking at 350° F for about 1½ hours. Pierce the skin before baking to allow steam to escape. You can also boil the squash until the outer shell softens, usually 20–30 minutes.

After cooking, split the squash in half and discard the center pulp and seeds. Rake out the stringy strands with a fork and serve with tomato sauce, lemon pepper, butter, or cheese sauce. Because the skin of the spaghetti squash is a bit thinner than that of other winter squash, it generally does not store well for long periods. However, you can cook the squash, remove the shell, and freeze the strands for later use.

PEANUTS FOR MIDWESTERN GARDENS

Peanuts have long been a popular backyard garden crop in the southern United States, much to the envy of northern gardeners. But since some garden seed catalogs make peanuts available all over the country, peanuts—also known as goober peas—are making their way north.

Peanuts do require a long, warm growing season, about 120 days. Bright yellow flowers begin to form about 7 weeks after planting. After the flowers fade, a small peg is formed, which grows down until it enters the soil. Then the nuts begin to form underground.

As the peanuts mature, the foliage begins to turn yellow. Peanut plants flower throughout the season, so nuts at many different stages of development will be found on the plant; there is thus no one good time to harvest the entire crop. If plants are harvested late in the season, many of the early-formed pods may rot or sprout underground.

But if plants are harvested early, much of the production potential will be lost. It's best to aim for the middle and harvest as the plants begin to show signs of maturation.

Harvest peanuts by carefully lifting the entire plant out of the ground; the nuts should still be attached to the plant. The nuts need to be cured or dried before processing. Allow them to air dry outdoors several days while still in the shell. Nuts can be left attached to the plants for ease of handling. Then stack the plants and store in a warm, dry, well-ventilated area for 2–3 weeks. When fully dried, the peanuts can be stripped from the plants.

Nuts will store longer if left in the shell unroasted and placed in a cool, dry area. Shelled nuts should be kept in the refrigerator to prolong their usefulness. The skins can be removed by boiling the nuts in water, a process called blanching, or by roasting them in the oven.

GARDENERS PREPARE TO AVOID FROST

Experienced gardeners are always prepared for an early frost. Of course, just as soon as we think we've got the weather figured out, it's likely to change. But for gardeners who are prepared, an early frost does not need to halt the gardening season.

Most years, a frost is usually followed by several weeks of good growing weather. Gardeners can take advantage of these extra weeks by protecting their plants through the early, light frosts.

Plants vary in their susceptibility to cold temperatures. Tender crops, such as tomatoes, peppers, melons, and okra, cannot withstand frost unless they're protected by some insulation. Cool-season crops, such as cabbage, broccoli, brussels sprouts, and kohlrabi, will tolerate frost or even a light freeze. Other crops, such as beets, carrots, lettuce, and potatoes, will stand a light frost.

Mulching is a good way to protect very small gardens. Use several layers of newspaper, straw, or chopped cornstalks. For those with large gardens, it may be more practical to protect only a few plants of each crop. Blankets, tarps, or floating row covers can be placed over rows of vegetables to supply insulation. Cloches, paper tents, hot

caps, and plastic walls of water are more expensive approaches to frost protection but are very effective. In cases of light frost, sometimes only the upper and outer foliage is damaged, and the plants can still continue production.

If covering the plants is not feasible, pick as much produce as possible if frost is predicted. Some crops can be further ripened indoors if they are not fully mature. Most green tomatoes can be ripened to full red indoors. Light is not necessary to ripen tomatoes. In fact, direct sun may promote decay of the fruit due to excessive heating. Ripening is mostly affected by temperature; the warmer the temperature, the faster the ripening. To store tomatoes for later use, wrap the fruits individually in newspaper and store them at 55° F. Your tomatoes will gradually ripen in several weeks.

The following chart lists most commonly grown vegetables and indicates their tolerance to frost.

Cold Temperature Tolerance of Vegetables

Tender (damaged by light frost)	Semihardy (tolerate light frost)	Hardy (tolerate hard frost)
Beans	Beets	Broccoli
Cucumbers	Carrots	Brussels sprouts
Eggplants	Cauliflower	Cabbage
Muskmelons	Celery	Collards
New Zealand Spinach	Chard	Kale
Okra	Chinese Cabbage	Kohlrabi
Peppers	Endive	Mustard Greens
Pumpkins	Lettuce	Onions
Squash	Parsnips	Parsley
Sweet Corn	Potatoes	Peas
Sweet Potatoes		Radishes
Tomatoes		Spinach
Watermelons		Turnips

Because spring is the time for new growth, most people think of planting trees and shrubs then. But cool temperatures and adequate rainfall make fall a good time to plant as well. The soil may be warmer and less damp than in the spring, and you may have more time to get the job done in the fall.

Fall-planted stock does demand extra attention. Plants may not have enough time to establish a good root system before winter hits. Cold winter winds and sunshine cause plants to lose water from their branches, and the roots must be able to replace it if plants are to survive. Evergreens, particularly broad-leaved evergreens, are more susceptible to winter desiccation because their leaves have more surface from which to lose water than bare trees.

Select balled-and-burlapped or container-grown plants rather than bare-rooted stock. Bare-root plants should only be planted in late winter or early spring, while the plants are still dormant.

Avoid planting large trees in the fall. They can be risky to transplant in any season but particularly when foliage is present. Leave the large trees to spring and get a professional to do the moving. They have the proper equipment and expertise to help ensure a safe move.

Some plants do not adapt well to fall planting because they are unusually susceptible to winter damage. Magnolias, dogwoods, tulip trees, sweet gums, red maples, birches, hawthorns, poplars, cherries, plums, and many of the oaks are among the plants that are best saved for spring planting. However, one can often justify the risk by finding exceptional bargains in the fall. Many garden centers are motivated to sell the stock because of the expense of keeping the plants through the winter.

Plant trees and shrubs early enough in the fall for the plant to develop a good root system. Soil temperatures should be well above 55° F at a depth of 6 inches at planting time. This condition usually exists until early to late October, depending on your location. Of course, weather conditions vary from year to year and with microclimates around the home landscape.

Prepare a good-sized hole, set the plant at the same depth it grew in the nursery, and water thoroughly. Continue watering until the ground is frozen to supply about 1 inch of water per week, even after deciduous plants have lost their leaves. Apply a mulch over the root zone to conserve soil moisture. Wrap the trunks of thin-barked, young trees in late November to prevent frost cracks, sunscald, and animal damage.

Ground covers and small, shallow-rooted shrubs may be heaved out of the ground, and a 2–4-inch layer of mulch can help prevent this by keeping the soil frozen. Apply materials such as compost, wood chips, or straw in late fall, after the ground is frozen.

PLANT GARLIC THIS FALL

Although garlic is thought to have originated in Asia, it has become an integral ingredient in most every country's cuisine. There is evidence that garlic was grown by the ancient Egyptians before 2100 B.C. China and India are the leading producers of garlic today, followed closely by the United States.

Garlic is usually grown for the flavorful bulbs that grow underground, although the green tops are used much like green onions in some countries. The flowers of the garlic plant are sterile and do not produce seed. New plants are grown from the individual sections of the bulb, which are known as cloves.

Garlic for planting should be purchased from a reliable garden center or mail-order catalog. The storage temperature of the dormant garlic affects the bulbing of the future plants. Temperatures above 77° F may inhibit bulb formation, so using garlic from the grocery store is ill advised for planting purposes. Garlic that has been stored at about 40° F for several months is ideal for starting a new planting.

Garlic can adapt to a wide range of soil types, but it must have a well-drained soil. Garlic can be planted in either the fall or early spring. Bulb formation is optimum as days are getting longer in late spring. Generally, most gardeners find it easier to get the garlic planted in fall, since early spring soils are usually too wet for planting.

A light application of fertilizer, such as ½ pound of 12-12-12 fertilizer per 100 square feet, should be adequate for most soils. Work the fertilizer into the top 4–5 inches of soil.

Separate the cloves of your "seed" bulb just before planting. The larger cloves tend to yield larger bulbs down the road. Discard the small center cloves. Plant the cloves 2–3 inches deep with the tip of the clove pointing upright. Cloves that are planted upside down will generally produce poor growth or none at all.

Fall-planted garlic should mature in July or August as the tops begin to fall down and dry. Snip off the tops and allow the bulbs to air dry for about 1 week out of direct sunlight. Garlic bulbs that you intend to eat can be stored for several weeks at room temperature. For longer storage, keep the bulbs cold, as close to 32° F as possible. If you want to use some of the bulbs for planting the next crop, store them at 40–50° F.

FIRE UP FOR HOT PEPPERS

Chilly weekends call for relaxing with a good football game and a steaming bowl of hot chili. And thanks to peppers, known as *Capsicum* in botanical circles, our chili can be as hot as we can stand it.

The Spaniards brought the pepper plant back to Europe from South America in the 1500s. They hoped to use this new pungent flavor as a substitute for the highly prized black pepper, and so named the vegetable so that people would associate it with the precious spice. As the pepper traveled to other European countries, it acquired other names, such as the Hungarian "paprika" and the British "Ginnie pepper." Today, several types of hot peppers are cultivated commercially, including jalapeño, cayenne, tabasco, and chile.

The element in peppers that causes the hotness is not actually related to the taste. The source of the notorious fiery sensation is a group of naturally occurring chemicals called capsaicins. The effects of the capsaicins have been described as delivering rapid bites to the back of the palate or a slow burn on the tongue and midpalate. Different

combinations of the individual capsaicins produce varying degrees of hotness, resulting in the various pepper strains.

Capsaicin content is dependent on many factors, including plant genetics, climate, geographic location, and stage of ripeness. Warm-weather regions generally produce hotter peppers than cooler areas. Warm nights in particular seem to be responsible for the higher capsaicin content. Peppers generally begin to produce capsaicins about 4 weeks after planting, and then the levels of capsaicins increase with age.

Flavor in peppers is thought to be associated with the pigments that give the fruit its color. Generally, the deeper the color, the stronger the flavor. Most peppers begin their development in some shade of green and then change color to red, orange, yellow, or purple as they ripen.

Peppers are a good source of vitamins, especially vitamin C, with the highest levels found in green fruits. The vitamin content drops off with maturity and processing, such as cooking, canning, and drying.

Peppers can be stored for later use either by freezing or drying. Chop peppers and separate the flesh from the seeds before placing it in freezer-safe containers. Peppers can be tied or threaded for drying in a warm, airy location. Strings of dried peppers can last for years and provide an attractive Southwestern touch to your decor.

Prolonged contact with hot peppers can burn your skin. Use plastic gloves when working with quantities of peppers and always avoid contact with your eyes.

BRINGING HOUSEPLANTS BACK INDOORS

Many houseplants thrive during the long, bright summer days, especially when properly moved outdoors. But these plants may have some trouble adjusting to indoor conditions when it's time to come in from the cold.

Many of our common indoor plants are native to tropical or subtropical climates and cannot tolerate cold temperatures. These plants should be brought back inside before the outdoor night temperature drops to 55° F. If days are warm but night temperatures are cold, you might consider bringing the plants indoors for the night and putting them back out in the morning.

Many plants will drop leaves in response to the lower light conditions inside most homes. Gradually exposing the plants to lower light intensity before permanently moving them indoors should help lessen the shock. But some leaf drop is unavoidable.

Plant growth will probably slow down considerably, so less water and fertilizer will be needed. The best moisture meter is your finger. For most plants, you should allow the soil to dry slightly between waterings. Reduce your fertilizer applications or discontinue fertilization entirely if plants seem to be in a resting period.

Be sure to inspect your plants closely for signs of insect attack. Pests such as spider mites and aphids are very prolific outdoors and may increase their population rapidly once they are brought indoors. What's worse, these pests can spread to other plants very quickly.

Often a sharp spray from the garden hose will remove insect pests from houseplant foliage. Insecticidal soaps also work well, particularly on soft-bodied insects, such as aphids. Several treatments may be necessary to ensure that the pests are gone. Start checking your plants now so that control measures will have time to work before you bring the plants indoors.

SOME LANDSCAPE TREES SHOULD BE WEEDED OUT

Nobody likes to see a big, seemingly healthy tree cut down in its prime. But if you look at your yard as a valuable crop, it makes good sense to remove the "weed" trees.

Some of the more valuable trees in your yard may get crowded out by other, less desirable plants. "Less desirable" can mean many different things, including weak-wooded, badly damaged, or simply an excessive number of trees. Removing the "weed" tree in the latter case gives the more valuable plants the room to grow and reduces competition for light, water, and nutrients.

Some trees may have relatively healthy-looking foliage, but a closer look reveals

some cause for concern. Trees with rotten centers or large dead limbs should be removed entirely to prevent injury to people or property. Mushrooms sprouting from the bark indicate rotting wood underneath, since mushrooms require dead, decaying organic material to grow on. Trees that have been weakened by rotting are prime candidates to come down in a violent storm.

Sometimes making a choice of which tree to take out can be difficult if all the plants involved are equally valuable and healthy. But it may be necessary to sacrifice a healthy tree to ensure the continued health of those that will be allowed to remain.

Thinning trees doesn't have to mean cutting them down. If a tree is of particular value—be it economic or sentimental—it is possible to move trees to a new location. The cost of such a move can be prohibitive for larger trees, but some experienced tree services and landscape firms do have the necessary equipment.

If you have a tree that is too large to move or otherwise needs to be cut down, don't try to fell the tree yourself. Removing even a small tree can be hazardous when space is tight or utility lines are nearby. Get a qualified expert with the proper tools and equipment to remove the tree.

EVERGREEN NEEDLES DON'T LAST FOREVER

Evergreens may provide green color all year long, but that doesn't mean that the individual needles live forever. Evergreens shed their needles to make room for new growth. But they also retain some foliage year-round instead of shedding all of the leaves at once.

Evergreen needles have varying life spans, depending on the species. Arborvitae and pine needles live for 2 years, while spruce needles live 3–10 years. Needle drop occurs gradually, with a small number of needles falling at one time.

Some species of evergreens have a more noticeable leaf drop than others. In autumn, arborvitaes and white pines will drop their 2-year-old needles all at once, causing alarm among some gardeners. The older needles of yew shrubs will turn yellow and drop in late spring or early summer. Rhododendrons drop their 2–3-year-old leaves in late summer and early fall. There's no need to worry as long as the leaf loss is not excessive and is restricted to old growth.

Gardening Questions

2. Each year I plant new seed potatoes, but when I harvest at the end of the season, there are discolorations in the tubers. Why?

A. Dark spots in potato tubers can be caused by a wide range of problems, including infections and environmental problems. Exposure to extremely high or low temperatures, early frost, or alternating extremes of soil moisture will cause internal discoloration.

   A virus or bacterium could also be the cause. The bacterium that causes bacterial soft rot is found in almost every soil, but it infects only damaged potatoes or those growing in wet soil. To prevent a virus, you must control the aphids that spread it. Follow proper growing and harvesting techniques to reduce the likelihood of spots caused by any of these factors. Keep potato plants healthy by planting only certified seed pieces, provide even moisture throughout the growing season, and harvest carefully to avoid damaging the tubers.

2. I have American hazelnut and Hall's hardy almond trees, which are just starting to produce. When should the nuts be picked, and how should they be prepared for eating?

A. When the outer shell of the almond splits open in the fall, harvest the nuts by striking the branches with poles or hitting limbs with a rubber mallet so that the nuts fall onto large sheets spread on the ground. Dry them in the hulls in a single layer for 1–2 days. Then remove the hulls and dry the almonds for another week in the sun. Keep squirrels away with metal mesh or cages.

Hazelnuts should be gathered when they begin to fall and before birds get them. Store them at 50° F or shell and freeze them. For toasted hazelnuts, spread them in a thin layer on a baking sheet and toast them at 350° F for about 15 minutes, or until brown.

Q. We have 2 English walnut trees. For the past 3 years, 1 tree has had nuts, but the other tree has not. They were planted at the same time. Do you have any idea why 1 tree has not had any nuts on it? Also, what should I spray for worms? Last fall we lost more than ½ of the nuts because of worms. Also, can the leaves from English walnut trees be put in a garden?

A. Several factors could keep the tree from producing. Nut trees are wind-pollinated, and cross-pollinators should be planted within 50 feet of each other. If one tree is decidedly upwind of the other, it may not be pollinated. Trees require 2–8 years to reach maturity, and the one tree may still be immature. Perhaps the barren tree is a cultivar that flowers earlier and is damaged by late frosts. A hard freeze after growth has started in the spring will destroy new growth and the potential nut crop.

Walnuts may be infested with walnut husk flies, codling moth larvae, weevils, and curculios. Certain insecticides may be used to control these insects, but timing is dependent upon proper identification of the pest.

The black walnut contains a chemical called juglone, which causes some plants, especially tomatoes, to wilt or die. All other walnuts produce the same toxin to a lesser degree. It is best to avoid putting any walnut leaves on the garden.

Q. I'm planning on mulching my shrub beds this fall. What material would look good?

A. Mulch can be marvelous stuff. It conserves moisture, keeps the ground cool, reduces weeds, and can provide an attractive accent. The different kinds of decorative mulches have both positive and negative aspects.

Shredded hardwood bark mulch accomplishes the goals listed above at a reasonable cost. As it decomposes, it adds valuable organic matter to the soil, and the shredded form helps it hold on slopes. A thick layer of shredded bark mulch reduces but does not eliminate weeds.

Cypress mulch looks similar to hardwood mulch, but it costs about twice as much, is more orange, retains its color longer, and breaks down more slowly. Choose it if you love the color and don't mind the cost. Cypress mulch may become difficult to find, since some southern states are protecting the cypress tree by no longer permitting its harvest.

Stone mulches are a low-maintenance choice, but they require a fabric or plastic barrier beneath them to reduce weeds. What's more, it is difficult to plant annuals or perennials in a bed mulched with stone. Over time, the stones may end up in the lawn, where they can become dangerous flying objects coming out of your lawn mower. Stone is tough to remove if you ever want to switch to another kind of mulch, so be certain it is what you want before putting it down.

When you order mulch in bulk, it may be sold by the cubic yard. A cubic yard of mulch covers 108 square feet 3 inches deep.

2. How do I pick out strong, healthy spring bulbs? Some of the specials I see advertised in magazines and catalogs seem too good to be true.

A. To an extent, you get what you pay for! The best bulbs come from reputable sources. Ask friends and neighbors if they can recommend local or mail-order companies. Purchase bulbs as soon as they become available, and choose firm, plump bulbs. Pass up the ones that are soft, bruised, or blemished. Avoid dehydrated bulbs by choosing the heavier ones. Some "too good to be true" offers send you smaller bulbs that may not flower or even have the energy to live past the first year.

2. I have to replant tulips every few years. They look great the first year and then produce fewer and fewer blooms each year. Am I doing something wrong?

A. Most hybrid tulips decrease their production each year. It is common for older tulips to produce fewer blooms each year until they quit flowering completely. Underground, they are forming bulblets that produce foliage. These bulblets need to grow for several years before they have enough strength to flower. You can speed the process by lifting the bulbs after blossoming, removing the small bulblets from the bulbs and replanting the bulbs and bulblets.

Some tulips will naturalize, or spread. Darwin hybrids in red, rose, orange, and yellow, and species tulips (nonhybrids) will provide repeat performances. Plant them 8 inches deep in a well-drained site.

Q. We want to plant shade trees on our property this year, but our yard doesn't drain very well. It's compacted, clay soil. My neighbors recommend digging deep and putting gravel in the bottom of the hole. Will this help?

A. A deep basin of gravel or amended backfill creates a "bathtub" effect. The clay forms a bowl that holds water around the tree's root ball, and the amended soil allows water to percolate into the "bathtub." Researchers have found that trees in unamended soil send roots out several feet in a year or two, while the roots of those in amended soil stay within the original planting hole.

Either plant trees on a raised mound, or berm, or choose plants suited to your site. Shade trees that tolerate wet soil include sweet gum (*Liquidambar styraciflua*), red maple (*Acer rubrum*), river birch (*Betula nigra*), and white ash (*Fraxinus americana*). This list may not include your favorite tree, but these are all fine trees that would grace any lawn.

Q. I'm planning a landscape bed under some walnut trees. I know you have to be particular about what you plant under walnuts. Do you have any recommendations?

A. You're wise to plan ahead in order to avoid problems with juglone, the chemical given off by walnuts. You'll save time, money, and heartache by choosing plants that will coexist with walnut trees.

The woody plants in your new beds might include Japanese maples (*Acer palmatum*), arborvitaes, Exbury hybrids of rhododendron, and most viburnums. Tolerant perennials include daylilies, ferns, iris, shasta daisies, coral bells, phlox, sedums, astilbes, and violets. Fibrous begonias, pot marigolds (*Calendula officinalis*), morning glories, and pansies can provide annual color to a walnut bed. Certain spring-flowering bulbs, such as crocus, winter aconite (*Eranthis hyemalis*), and Siberian squill (*Scilla siberica*) grow under walnut trees.

Q. My vegetable garden is overcome with foxtail weeds. What can I do to get rid of them and other weeds?

A. Hindsight has probably proven to you that preventing weed establishment is the most effective means of control. Black plastic mulch or a heavy layer of organic material will keep weed seeds from germinating.

Preemergent herbicides are effective on foxtail if applied before seeds germinate. There are some labeled for use on many vegetable crops, but none are safe for all vegetables. Follow the directions carefully. You cannot directly seed your garden plants into soil treated with a preemergent herbicide, so use these herbicides around vegetable transplants or after germination of seeded crops. Unfortunately, by the time the vegetable seeds germinate, the foxtail may germinate, too.

After weeds have germinated, regain control by pulling, tilling, or hoeing. A scuffle, or action, hoe works well where mulch is thin. This tool has a flat blade on the bottom of a handle-shaped loop of metal. It provides a relatively easy way of slicing the tops off plants, which eventually starves the roots.

Outside the vegetable garden, you can spray actively growing weeds with a nonselective postemergent herbicide. These kill all green plant tissue, so use care and follow label instructions.

OCTOBER

October's bright colors—clear blue sky, fiery foliage, and bright red apples—gladden the heart. The decorations of pumpkins, Indian corn, and multicolored gourds symbolize the fall season as a time for preparing and storing our harvests, and many of this month's activities involve the proper storage of produce. The frosty October nights, which bring on the annual leaf drop, are a call to action as you prepare plants for their dormant season.

The fallen leaves crackling underfoot are just begging to be composted into a garden investment. Today's fallen leaves become tomorrow's "brown gold." Planting bulbs, too, is an investment where a bit of hard work this month pays off big next spring.

Garden Calendar

HOME

Water indoor plants less frequently and discontinue fertilizing as plants slow down or stop growing for the winter.

Poinsettias saved from last year can be encouraged to reflower for this year's holiday season by providing complete darkness for 15 hours daily beginning about October 1 until about December 10 (see pages 241–42).

Pot spring-flowering bulbs to force into bloom indoors (see pages 245–46).

YARD

Continue mowing lawn as needed.

Keep plants, especially newly planted ones, well watered until the ground freezes.

Rake large leaves, such as maple and oak, to prevent them from matting down and smothering lawn grass. Raking smaller leaves, such as honey locust, is not necessary.

Have soil ready for mounding over roses for winter protection. Do not mound or cover the roses until temperature is consistently below freezing.

Apply winter mulch to strawberries when plants are dormant but before temperatures drop below 20° F.

GARDEN

Harvest root crops and store in a cold (32° F), humid location. Storing produce in perforated plastic bags in the refrigerator is a convenient and easy way to increase humidity.

Harvest brussels sprouts as they develop in the axils of the leaves from the bottom of the stem. Sprouts will continue to develop up the stem.

Harvest pumpkins and winter squash when rind is hard and fully colored but before frost. Store in a cool location until ready to use.

Harvest gourds when stems begin to brown and dry. Cure at 70–80° F for 2–4 weeks.

Asparagus top growth should not be removed until foliage yellows. Let foliage stand over the winter to collect snow and leaves for insulation and moisture unless insects or disease were a problem.

Dig and store tender flowering bulbs and tubers for winter storage (see pages 239–41).

Remove plant debris from the garden to protect next year's planting from possible overwintering insects and disease. Compost plant refuse (see pages 243–44).

Have garden soil tested for fertilizer needs every 3–5 years.

Prepare garden soil this fall for earlier planting next spring (see pages 259–60).

Carve a Halloween jack-o'-lantern.

Complete planting of spring-flowering bulbs.

STORING APPLES FOR THE WINTER

Apples tend to bear bumper crops most years, and many home growers will be searching for new recipe ideas to use up the heavy yields. Why not store some of your crop for fresh eating through the winter?

As a general rule, the later-maturing cultivars—such as 'Red Delicious,' 'Northern Spy,' 'Stayman,' 'Winesap,' 'Rome Beauty,' 'Turley,' and 'Idared'—will store much longer than earlier cultivars, up to 5 months under ideal conditions.

Only good-quality fruit that is free of bruises, cuts, or other damage should be selected for storage. One bad apple really can spoil the whole lot by introducing rot organisms and releasing increased levels of ethylene gas, which hastens the ripening and aging process. Store only those apples that have reached maturity but have not fully ripened. The fruit's skin should have a greenish yellow undercolor, and the flesh should be sweet, hard, and crisp. Use up fruits that have developed a more yellow undercolor, softened flesh, and a mellow flavor.

Apples are best stored at 30–32° F with 90% relative humidity and some air circulation. Warmer temperatures will cause the apples to age faster, and low humidity can cause excessive shriveling. These conditions may be difficult to find in the home but can be achieved with a little effort. The most practical solution for home storage is the refrigerator. However, the air inside refrigerators is very dry, particularly in frost-free types. Pack the apples in perforated plastic bags to keep the humidity high yet still allow some air circulation.

A cool cellar or an unheated room or outbuilding can be used as long as the temperature can be kept at 30–40° F with high humidity. Apples will freeze at 27.8–29.4° F, depending on the cultivar, and frozen fruit will deteriorate rapidly. Such storage methods as straw-lined pits and buried tiles are at the mercy of the weather and may give satisfactory results some years but may be a loss in others.

If reliable fresh storage is not feasible for you, other methods of preservation are available. Many apple cultivars are well adapted to freezing either as sauce or slices. Apples are delicious in pies, crisps, salads, or baked. If all else fails, try sharing your bounty with a fruitless neighbor!

HARVESTING AND PRESERVING GOURDS

While gourds are often a part of today's Halloween and Thanksgiving decorations, they date back to 2200 B.C., making them among the oldest cultivated plants in history. Since the times of the ancient Egyptians, gourd shells have been used as dippers or containers for grain storage.

The term "gourd" is most correctly applied to the hard-shelled members of the vining plants known as cucurbits and includes several species. Gourds can still be used for functional items such as birdhouses, dippers, lanterns, and storage bins. But nowadays most gourds are used to add a harvest look to autumn decorations.

Although each gourd may have its own characteristics, in general, gourds are ready to harvest when the rinds are firm and the stem of the plant begins to turn brown and dry. Gourds should be harvested when they are fully mature, but before frost.

Gourds should be cured or air dried prior to use. First wash them with warm soapy water and then place them on layers of newspaper to dry for about a week. During that time, the outer skin hardens, and surface color sets. Replace the newspaper with fresh sheets and allow the gourds to dry for an additional 3–4 weeks to finish drying. To encourage drying and good color retention, dry gourds in a warm, dry, dark area, such as a closet or under a bed.

Decorative gourds can be displayed in their natural state for 3–4 months. Applying wax, shellac, or varnish can prolong their shelf life for several more months and will lend a shiny coat to the exterior.

LUFFA: THE NATURAL SPONGE

The luffa gourd, also known as the vegetable sponge, dishrag gourd, and loofah, has gained much popularity in recent years. A member of the same family as cucumbers and squash, luffa has a very similar habit to the other vine crops, only much bigger.

The luffa plant itself is a rambling vine that can reach up to 15 feet long. A support to train this huge plant is a must. Like other members of the family, the plant bears the male and female structures on separate bright yellow flowers. Bees carry the pollen from the male flowers to the female flowers. After pollination occurs, the female flowers produce a large cylindrical fruit up to 2 feet long.

Young fruits of a few inches can actually be harvested for eating and are popular in Oriental cooking. However, once the fruits enlarge, tough fibers are produced throughout the pulp. These fibers form the sponge.

Luffas require a long growing season, and the fruits usually need to be left on the vines until a killing frost takes the plants. The longer they mature on the vine, the sturdier the sponge. Prepare the sponge by peeling the outer layers of tissue away to reveal the inner fibrous mass. Use one of the following pretreatments to soften the outer rind, making the sponge easier to peel.

1. Soak the gourd in a tub of water until the outer covering softens.

2. Boil the gourd in water for about 15 minutes, allow to cool, then peel. Finding a kettle large enough to accommodate the entire gourd is not practical, but it can be cut in halves or quarters.

3. Freeze the gourd for 2 hours, then thaw and peel.

4. Microwave the gourd for 5–10 minutes on high power. Cutting the gourd in half will speed processing and make it easier to fit it in the oven.

The plant's seeds are within the fibers of the sponge and must be removed by shaking and pulling them out with your fingers. Then wash the sponge in mild soapy water and rinse several times to remove the soap residue. Allow the sponge to dry to a dull beige color. If a whiter sponge is desired, soak it in a solution of household bleach and water.

The finished sponge can be used as a bath sponge, back scratcher, dishrag, or scouring pad. A luffa sponge can last for years, depending on how it's used. Don't be afraid to put it to hard work; you can always grow more next year!

COOL POTATOES TO PREVENT SPROUTING

If you've marveled at how productive your potato patch is only to find that many of the tubers turned soft or sprouted during storage, you're probably not alone.

The most important concern for home storage of vegetables is maintaining low temperatures to slow down the maturing process. Getting temperatures low enough, down to 40° F, is a problem shared by many gardeners, since most storage areas are in the basement of a home or an unheated room. Outdoor temperatures just aren't cool enough until long after harvest for most vegetables. Later on, outdoor temperatures are much too cold.

Potatoes pose a special problem because they will not only turn soft or shrivel but also sprout at warm temperatures. Home growers often ask if they can chemically treat their potatoes to prevent sprouting. The answer is both yes and no.

Commercial growers usually treat their potatoes by spraying the plants about 4–6 weeks before harvest. By the time the tubers are harvested, it is too late to apply the chemical. The major problem for home growers is that the chemical used is expensive and just not available in small packages suitable for home growers' needs. The smallest package commonly sold is one gallon, but only 4 tablespoons are needed to treat 1,000 square feet of plants!

There is another chemical used by some commercial growers that can be applied to potatoes after harvest, but again it is not readily available in packages sized for the homeowner. Moreover, the amount of the chemical applied must be very accurate because applying too low a dosage can actually promote sprouting.

For home growers, the best solution to prevent potatoes from sprouting is to keep the temperature close to, but not below, 40° F. You may just have to accept a few bad potatoes along with the good.

Although there is a vast number of plants that will grow much better in southern climates, there are a few plants that actually prefer our cooler weather. Horseradish is such a plant. The cool temperatures of fall and winter prompt the plant to store its starches in its roots. More than two thirds of our nation's horseradish supply is produced in southwestern Illinois, around the East St. Louis area.

Horseradish is a perennial plant that is grown for its sharply flavored roots. It is said to have been one of the bitter herbs eaten by the Jews during Passover and is still widely used today as part of the modern observance of the holiday.

Horseradish has nothing to do with horses and is not a radish, although it is a member of the same mustard family. The word may have come from the German name *Meerrettich*, which sounds like "mareradish."

Horseradish puts on most of its root growth in the late summer and early fall. The best roots have been exposed to several frosts before harvest. Generally, all roots are harvested in October or early November, and the smaller branch roots are saved for replanting the following spring. Store the roots at 30–32° F and 90–95% relative humidity for up to 10 months. Packing the roots in perforated plastic bags and storing them in the refrigerator is convenient and effective. Roots can be left in the ground all winter and harvested as long as the ground can be dug, but they should be lifted before they resprout in spring. The roots will become quite woody if left in the ground for several growing seasons.

The hot, penetrating flavor and aroma of horseradish are brought out by grating or slicing the root. The root contains highly volatile sulfured oils that are released only when the root cells are broken. Horseradish loses its pungency rapidly after grinding, particularly if it is exposed to air or stored improperly, so roots are best kept whole for long-term storage. Prepared horseradish will keep up to 6 weeks if tightly covered and refrigerated or frozen.

POSSUM
IN THE
PAWPAW
TREE

PAWPAW: THE MIDWESTERN BANANA?

Although the pawpaw is native to the eastern and central United States, it is a surprisingly well-kept secret. But those who do know the fruit are not likely to forget its delightful aroma and flavor.

The pawpaw has been called the Hoosier banana, but probably only by Hoosiers themselves. The same plant is also known as the Michigan banana in other circles. Botanically, the tree is known as *Asimina triloba* and can be found growing in low woods in much of the Midwest, with the heart of its territory in the Ohio Valley. In earlier times, strands of the inner bark of pawpaws were used by Native Americans as a fiber for fishnets and clothes. Later, a medicinal extract that induces vomiting was harvested from the seed. Recent studies have examined pesticidal properties of an alkaloid contained in highest quantity in the bark. Pawpaw extract also shows promise as a cancer-fighting drug.

You may have guessed by now that the pawpaw tastes somewhat like a banana, although others have described the flavor as similar to a mango's. The fruit is a greenish yellow berry that turns brownish black when fully ripe. Each fruit is about 2–5 inches long and can weigh up to 8 ounces. They are borne in clusters of as many as 7 fruits. Each fruit contains several very large brown seeds.

Some backyard growers complain of poor fruit set on their pawpaws. There is still some controversy over which insects are the primary pollinators. We do know that a pawpaw flower cannot pollinate itself, so other flowers must be nearby to provide a pollen source. (See page 200.)

Harvest pawpaws when the fruit yields slightly when gently squeezed, usually in late September or October. The fruits have excellent flavor when eaten fresh, but unfortunately they bruise easily and do not keep well even when refrigerated. Pawpaws can be dried or frozen for later use or processed into ice cream, cakes, cookies, breads, and pastries.

The pawpaw tree usually grows up to about 20 feet, although it can grow taller in

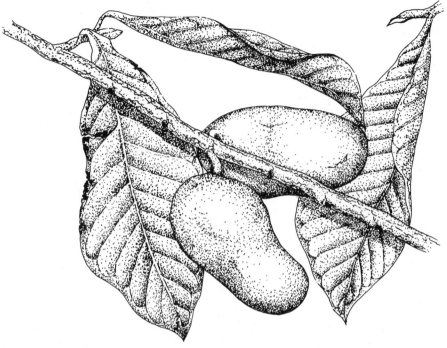

Pawpaw, a native Midwestern treat.

a favorable location. A sunny location with moist, fertile, slightly acid soil is best. The leaves can turn a brilliant yellow in the fall on some specimens.

TENDER PERENNIALS NEED INDOOR PROTECTION

Most flowering plants either die after one year in the garden or come up year after year indefinitely. But because of their susceptibility to cold temperatures, some plants must be dug up, and their roots or other underground structures stored indoors overwinter. The most common garden plants in this category include gladiolus, caladium, tuberous

239

begonia, canna, and dahlia. Although these plants are all considered tender, each is best handled a bit differently for winter storage.

Gladiolus grows from a corm, which should be dug when the foliage just begins to fade, usually after a frost. Use a spading fork to carefully lift the plants and save any of the miniature corms (called cormels). These cormels will grow larger if planted next year and eventually reach a size that supports flowers as well as foliage.

The corms should be cured before storing to help prevent disease from developing. Cure the corms for 2–4 weeks in a warm (about 75–80° F) room where air can circulate around the corms. Once cured, the corms should be stored dry in a cool location, about 35–40° F. Old nylon stockings or onion bags hung from the wall allow good air circulation throughout storage.

Caladiums, often called elephant ears, are much more sensitive to cold temperatures. Their tubers, which look like small potatoes, should be dug up just before frost. Surface moisture should be dried off by placing the tubers in a warm location for 7–10 days. To prevent excessive drying in storage, pack the tubers between layers of dry vermiculite, peat moss, sawdust, or a similar material in a sturdy box. The optimum storage temperature for caladiums is 60° F.

Tuberous begonias should also be dug up just before frost. Cut the tops back to 2 inches and air dry the tubers for 2–3 weeks in a warm location. Then store them in boxes as you would caladiums but decrease the temperature to about 45–50° F.

Dahlias should be cut back to about 3–4 inches after the first light frost. Then carefully lift the plants, leaving as much soil attached as possible to prevent breaking the fleshy roots. Because they are so susceptible to drying, dahlia roots should be air dried for only a few hours or so. Then pack them in boxes as you would caladiums and store them at 35–40° F.

Cannas need not be dug up until after a hard frost. Cut the tops back to 4 inches, lift the roots with a spading fork, and air dry them in a warm spot for 1–2 weeks. Canna roots do not require covering—they can simply be placed in shallow boxes. The roots hold best at 45–50° F.

These procedures may seem like a lot of bother, but with care, your tender perennials will put on another magnificent show next summer—and spare your wallet!

FERTILIZE WOODY PLANTS THIS FALL

Although most people think of spring as the time to fertilize, fall feeding can give trees and shrubs a boost. Not all landscape plants need fertilizer, but young plants and those that are recovering from stress can benefit from it.

Timing the fall fertilizer application is important because a too early feeding can promote late-fall growth. Young tissue will not have a chance to harden off properly before winter and is thus likely to be killed. Fertilizer applied too late in the fall will not be taken up by the plants and will be wasted.

Roots continue to grow and take in fertilizer as long as soil temperatures are above 40° F. The trees and shrubs themselves are a good indicator of when to fertilize: make your application immediately following leaf fall.

For most plants, 1–2 pounds of actual nitrogen per 1,000 square feet should be adequate for a late-fall fertilization. Cut the application in half for evergreens, since their root systems are more shallow. The surrounding lawn will also benefit from fall fertilization. (See pages 65–66.)

POINSETTIAS CAN REBLOOM FOR THE HOLIDAYS

If you're still saving last year's poinsettia, you can make it bloom in time for this year's holidays if you give your plant some special attention. Poinsettias are sensitive to photoperiod, the length of daylight. Actually, it is the number of hours of darkness each day that is important to poinsettia flowering.

Poinsettias initiate flowers when days are short and long periods of uninterrupted darkness occur. In the home environment, even a dimly lit lamp at night is enough to prevent flower initiation in poinsettias.

To get your poinsettia to bloom again, place the plant in complete darkness for 15 hours each day—say, between 5:00 P.M. and 8:00 A.M. Any interruption of the dark period, including simply opening the door of the closet you store the plant in, can result in delayed flowering. The plant should be given a sunny location during the light treatment.

To have your poinsettia bloom in time for the holidays, you'll need to begin the treatment by early October. The treatment can be discontinued once the bracts begin to show good color, usually by early December.

FALL COLOR SIGNALS END OF SEASON

According to a Native American legend, trees change color because of the slaying of the Great Bear in the heavens. The bear's blood turns some leaves red, and the spattering fat from the pot in which the heavenly hunters cook the meat provides the yellow colors.

The scientific explanation is that there is a chemical change in the leaves. The orange and yellow that we see in the fall are actually present in the leaf all summer. However, those colors are masked by the presence of chlorophyll during the growing season, the pigment responsible for the green color in plants. The plant uses light and chlorophyll to manufacture carbohydrates from carbon dioxide and water in the plant environment. Trees continually replenish chlorophyll as it is used up in making food during the growing season.

Contrary to popular belief, frost is not needed for the fall color change, but as the days grow shorter and temperatures cool, the tree uses up chlorophyll faster than it can replace it. The green color fades as the level of chlorophyll decreases, allowing the other pigments to show through.

The yellow, brown, and orange colors common to such trees as birches, hickories, aspens, and some maples, come from pigments called carotenoids, the same pigments that are responsible for the color of carrots, corn, and bananas.

The red and purple colors common to oaks, sweet gums, dogwoods, and some maples are produced by another type of pigment, anthocyanin, which is also contained in cherries, grapes, apples, and blueberries. Unlike chlorophyll and carotenoids, anthocyanins are not always present in the leaf but are produced in late summer when prompted by environmental signals. Anthocyanins also combine with carotenoids to produce the fiery red, orange, and bronze colors found in sumacs, oaks, and dogwoods.

The intensity of fall color varies from year to year, depending on the weather. Red colors tend to be most intense when days are warm and sunny but nights are cool— below 45° F. The color intensifies because more sugars are produced during warm sunny days, and cool night temperatures cause the sugars to remain in the leaves. Pigments are formed from these sugars, so the more sugar in the leaf, the more pigment and thus more intense colors. Warm, rainy fall weather decreases the amount of sugar and pigment production. Warm nights cause what sugars are made to move out of the leaves, so that leaf colors are muted.

Leaf color can also vary from tree to tree and even from one side of a tree to another. Leaves that are more exposed to the sun tend to show more red coloration, while those in the shade turn yellow. Stress such as drought, poor fertility, disease, or insects may cause fall color to come on earlier but usually results in less intense coloration.

BACKYARD COMPOSTING

Composting is a great way to recycle the plant debris in your garden, including both crops and weeds. Composting can also help cities lower the costs of collecting trash and operating landfills.

The main gardening benefit of composting is in the improved soil structure that results from working compost into the garden. Compost also returns some nutrients back to the soil.

A properly constructed compost pile should be done in layers, beginning with about a 2-inch layer of soil, which contains the microorganisms that are responsible for breaking down organic matter. Then add 6–8 inches of plant debris, such as leaves,

lawn clippings, and garden plants. Since the microorganisms need nitrogen to break down the plant material, if your pile does not have a good balance of fresh green material—such as grass clippings—sprinkle about a cup of commercial nitrogen fertilizer as your next layer. Manure is also an excellent source of nitrogen, and 1–2 inches can be substituted for the commercial fertilizer. Water the pile thoroughly and repeat each layer until the pile is of a workable height.

As the materials decompose, the temperature in the center of a good-size pile can reach as high as 160° F, which will kill off some insect pests, disease organisms, and weed seeds. The minimum size for heat generation is about 3 feet by 3 feet by 3 feet. If your compost pile is small or you are otherwise in doubt about the level of heat generated, it may be best to avoid heavily infested plants. You'll want to turn the pile every 2–4 weeks to be sure that all the materials will be heated to that temperature. Moist compost will heat more uniformly, so be sure to water the compost occasionally if needed.

Having a compost bin or wall structure to contain the pile can help keep the pile neat, but heaping the contents on the ground can work just as well. However, some urban areas have mandated that compost piles must be contained; check with your local health department. If a structure is used to contain the compost, removable horizontal slats will help make the structure adapt to the size of the pile as it grows or shrinks and will allow for easier turning.

Compost is ready to use when it's dark and crumbly and looks like good soil. No signs of the original material should be recognizable. Depending on what outdoor temperatures are like and how well you tend the pile, your compost may be ready to add back to the garden by next spring.

PLANT SPRING-FLOWERING BULBS THIS FALL

If thinking about the coming winter season is getting you down, start planning your spring-flowering bulb show. Autumn is the time to plant crocus, daffodils, tulips, and many other spring bloomers.

Spring-flowering bulbs are planted in the fall to allow them to establish roots before top growth begins in the spring. Planting too early may cause the bulbs to sprout this fall, only to be killed back by winter weather. Planting too late may not give the bulbs adequate time to root before winter. Ideally, bulbs should be planted in late September through October, but it is better to plant late rather than try to store the bulbs over the winter.

Start your bulb garden on the right path by planting only quality bulbs from local garden centers or reputable mail-order sources. It's best to shop early to obtain the best selection of variety and quality. Select large, firm bulbs and avoid those that are sprouting or molding.

While many bulbs can adapt to a wide range of soil types, none can tolerate poorly drained soil. Prepare the planting bed by adding organic matter, such as peat moss, well-rotted manure, or compost. Adequate fertility can be achieved by adding a low-analysis, balanced fertilizer, such as 5-10-5 or 6-10-4, at the rate of 2–3 pounds per 100 square feet of bed. Mix all amendments thoroughly with the soil in the bed before you plant the bulbs.

The size of the bulb and the species will dictate the proper planting depth and spacing. The bulbs should come with planting instructions specific to that particular flower.

Spring will be here before you know it, and your bulbs will make it beautiful!

FORCING BULBS FOR INDOOR COLOR

Forcing spring-flowering bulbs for indoor color will brighten up the short, dark days of winter and make waiting for your outdoor spring-flowering bulb show more bearable. All it takes is a little planning ahead.

Hardy bulbs, such as tulips, daffodils, hyacinths, and crocuses, require a cold period of about 10–13 weeks to trigger the bulbs to grow roots and initiate flowers. Thus, if you want to have blooms in time for the holidays, you have to start the cooling process in October.

Pot up your bulbs in good-quality potting soil so that the narrow end is pointing up. Planting depth will depend on the type of bulb. Tulips and hyacinths should be planted so that just the tip of the bulb is showing above the soil. Because tulips have large leaves, place the flat side of the bulb facing the wall of the pot so the leaf will face outward. Plant daffodils so that ½ of the bulb is showing. Crocus, snowdrops, and grape hyacinths should be planted 1 inch deep. For a more showy display, plant 3–7 bulbs of the same kind in one large pot.

Water thoroughly and store in a cold area where the temperature can be maintained between 40 and 50° F. The potted bulbs can be placed in a cold frame, mulch-lined soil trench, unheated garage, basement, or refrigerator.

After 10–13 weeks of cold storage, water the soil and place the pots in a cool area (60–65° F) and gradually increase the amount of light. For a sequence of blooming, remove pots from storage every two weeks.

If you're a "late bloomer" like many of us, you can purchase precooled hardy bulbs, which need only be exposed to a few weeks of 60° F temperatures to bring springtime indoors.

Once your bulbs have begun to bloom, keep the plants in a cool location, away from heat vents and direct sunshine, to prolong their beauty. It's usually best to discard hardy bulbs after forcing, since their food reserves are used up. If you do plant them outdoors after the blooms fade, choose a location where the foliage will receive maximum sunshine to help rebuild the bulb's food reserves. It may take a year or two for the bulbs to put on a good show again.

Gardening Questions

2. We moved last year and brought with us 2 good stocks of small seedless grapes that have produced each year. This year, the stocks produced again, but the grapes were large and had seeds. What happened?

A. Several problems may have caused you to lose the tops of your grafted grape plants. Suckers may have overtaken the planting. These will often be more vigor-ous and produce less desirable fruit than that of the scion, or grafted top. Or you may have cut off the scions if you pruned them severely in order to move them. It is also possible that the tops are not hardy in your new area.

If last year's crop was not satisfactory, you will need to order new plants, mak-ing certain they are hardy in your new location. Keep a careful eye on all grafted plants and remove suckers promptly.

Q. We planted shade trees on our property this fall. We were told to wrap them with tree wrap, but we don't know why. How long do we leave the wrap on and what is the purpose?

A. Tree wrap protects young trees from sunscald, borers, and rodent damage. Thin-barked trees, especially maples, are vulnerable to damage. Paper tree wrap, avail-able at most garden centers, or burlap strips should be wound around the trunk from the ground to the first tier of branches. Apply the wrap in late fall and remove it in March to keep the trunk dry and healthy. Wrap the tree for 2–3 winters, at which time you will probably notice the tree has developed a tougher coat of bark.

Some recent research conducted in the South has found little benefit to wrapping, but it has not yet been researched in our area. For now, winter tree wrap-ping is still recommended here for young, thin-barked trees.

Q. I'd like to plant some maple trees along my driveway. How far apart should I put them? My driveway is approximately 100 feet long.

A. There are many kinds of maples, and they grow to different mature heights. I don't recommend the silver maple: it grows very quickly, but it's weak-wooded, so the limbs break easily in ice, wind, and snow.

The sugar maple grows more slowly and is renowned for its brilliant fall col-ors. A 1½-inch caliper sugar maple may attain a height of 20 feet with an equal rounded spread in 4 or 5 years. They eventually reach 60–100 feet.

Red maples grow more quickly than sugar maples, more slowly than silver maples, and turn shades of red in autumn. Many cultivars exist, but in general, if

you plant a 1½-inch caliper red maple, it will reach 20 feet in 5–7 years and eventually become 50–70 feet tall.

Spacing is a matter of personal choice. I would space red maples 20 feet apart and sugar maples 25 feet apart to have the tree row fill out in about 15 years without wasting money or sacrificing the form of the trees.

Q. This fall my burning bush shrubs showed a small amount of color. Last year, there was no hint of fall color at all. What is the problem?

A. Sunlight is necessary for the brilliant red coloring of burning bush, *Euonymus alatus*, to appear, so trimming back any overhanging branches from nearby shrubs might help. If the plants are not too large, you could transplant them to a site where they will receive full sun.

If your plants already receive some sunlight, then a soil test may be the next step. Burning bush prefers a slightly acidic soil and will not color well in an alkaline soil.

Burning bush normally shows its fall color even when deficient in nutrients, so nutrient deficiency is not a likely problem. Regular fertilization is always a good idea, and it is possible that your shrubs, if severely deficient, will respond to fertilization.

Finally, some similar shrubs turn a pale yellow in the fall. Perhaps your shrubs are showing their true colors after all!

Q. My community offers free chipped wood that I could use as mulch. Are there any problems that this mulch might cause? Will it attract termites to my house?

A. Fresh wood chips are not likely to attract termites, although the moist environment may attract sow bugs, slugs, and millipedes. These insects may enter your home, but they do not damage the structure.

A large pile of wood chips can be quite hot. Spread the pile out and let it air for a week. Avoid using this mulch on tender transplants until the pile has cooled for several weeks. Apply a balanced fertilizer when you mulch, since decomposing mulch ties up the available nitrogen.

NOVEMBER

As the last brilliant leaves fall from the trees and the days grow shorter, gardeners prepare for the upcoming winter. On some days, inclement weather keeps you indoors to plan the garden activities you'll pursue when a warm spell comes. Other November days may bring a burst of Indian summer, allowing you outdoors to protect roses and strawberries and remove garden debris to add to the compost pile. This is the time to make sure your plants are all well protected against the midwestern winter ahead.

At the end of the month, we observe the first American immigrants' commemoration of the harvest. The Thanksgiving table may be laden with harvests from your garden, including fresh broccoli or a pumpkin pie made from your very own pumpkins.

Garden Calendar

HOME

Move plants closer to windows or to sunnier exposures, such as west- and south-facing windows, if plants are dropping many leaves. Artificial lights may be needed to supplement natural light.

Pot up spring-flowering bulbs to force into bloom indoors.

YARD

Late-fall fertilizing can help keep lawn green into winter and boost early spring recovery. Apply 1 pound actual nitrogen per 1,000 square feet of lawn.

Clean up and discard fallen leaves and fruits around fruit plants to reduce disease carryover.

Remove dead, diseased, or damaged branches.

Prevent rabbit and rodent feeding damage by erecting physical barriers, such as metal mesh (¼-inch) hardware cloth. Pull mulch away from the trunk a few inches because the mulch provides a warm winter home for rodents. Chemical repellents are also available, but their effectiveness is temporary and not foolproof.

Protect trees from frost cracking (or sunscald) by wrapping trunks with commercial tree wrap or painting the south and southwest sides of the trunk with white latex outdoor paint.

Protect the graft union on rose bushes by mounding soil up around the plants and adding mulch on top.

If you are planning to order a "live" Christmas tree, prepare its planting hole before the soil freezes (see pages 273–74).

GARDEN

If frost hasn't taken your garden away yet, continue harvesting.

Remove plant debris, both crop residue and weeds, from the garden and discard or compost. This will help reduce the carryover of diseases, insects, and weeds to next year's garden.

Apply winter mulch to strawberries when plants are dormant but before temperatures drop below 20° F.

ANTI-FREEZE FOR ROSES

Most gardeners don't think about burying their roses, but that is essentially what they should do to protect grafted roses through the winter.

The first step to winterizing roses is to keep them healthy throughout the growing season. Protecting roses from insect and disease damage and maintaining adequate fertility and moisture will go a long way in getting them through the winter unscathed.

After several freezes in the late fall, plants become dormant, and this is the time to put on the winter protection. If applied too early, the materials meant to protect may actually smother the plants, or at least encourage disease.

Pick up and remove debris, such as leaves and dead stems, on and around the plants to prevent diseases from overwintering. If the soil is dry, give it a thorough soaking. Plants underneath overhangs of buildings are often very dry, even during wet seasons.

The most foolproof method of protection is to mound the soil up around the plant to protect the graft union. A 12-inch mound, or approximately 5 gallons, of soil provides excellent protection. A soil mound will also prevent rabbits from feeding on the stems.

Prepare the plant by tying the canes up with twine, not only to prevent excessive wind whipping but also to make mounding easier. Begin by tying twine to the base of a lower branch and wind the twine up the plant in a spiral. Save pruning chores until late winter or early spring, as branches cut in the fall tend to die back from the cut later during the winter.

Dig the soil for the mound from an area away from the roses, so as not to damage their roots. For further protection, pile additional mulch, such as straw or chopped leaves, on top of the soil mound.

Commercially available rose cones have been used with varying success. Even with cones, some soil mounding is still advisable—about 6–8 inches to protect the graft union and to anchor the cone. Plants must be pruned to fit under the cone. Cut slits in the tops of the cones to provide air ventilation because excessive moisture buildup encourages fungus growth. A heavy rock or brick placed on top of the cone will help secure it in place.

In early spring, both soil mounds and cones must be removed as soon as plants begin new growth. Don't forget to remove the twine, and be careful not to injure old canes or new growth.

Soil from the mounds should be placed in another area rather than on top of the plant's root area. Adding more soil thickness may prevent proper aeration, which is needed for root growth.

PREPARING LANDSCAPE PLANTS FOR WINTER

Winterizing your landscape plants is just as important as winterizing your car. Those bright, sunny days of winter may be a welcome sight to us humans, but they can spell trouble for some landscape plants. Direct sunshine on young, thin-barked trees warms the bark considerably. As the temperature drops rapidly at sundown, the outer bark cools down and contracts faster than the inner bark. Thus the outer bark must split to accommodate what's below.

Other common types of winter injury include breakage from heavy snow and ice, severe drying, and animal feeding damage. However, you can help protect your plants by properly preparing them for the winter season.

Shading young, thin-barked trees, such as maples and fruit trees, on the south and southwest sides will help prevent bark splits from temperature extremes. Wrapping the trunks with commercial tree wrap in late fall provides some protection (see page 247).

You can't do very much about excessively low temperatures. But you can be sure that the plants chosen for the landscape are hardy for your area and are otherwise adapted to the individual site conditions.

All plants, but especially evergreens, are susceptible to drying out over the winter. The above-ground parts, such as twigs and evergreen leaves, are very much alive and are continuously losing water through transpiration. Once the ground is frozen, the plant's roots are not able to take up water to replace that which is lost through the tops. The result is drying leaves, buds, and twigs. Sunny, windy conditions cause water to be lost from the tops more rapidly, further aggravating the situation. Broad-leaved evergreens are particularly susceptible, since they have a greater leaf surface to lose water from.

Making sure the plants have a sufficient supply of soil moisture before the ground freezes will help create healthier specimens to fight the winter battle. Water thoroughly every 7–10 days if fall rains are not sufficient. Shading susceptible plants from winter sun and wind can also be helpful. Burlap can be fastened to stakes, but even just a section of snow fencing should be adequate. Plant highly susceptible plants, such as rhododendrons, on the north side of the house or a hedge to avoid strong winter sun.

Multistemmed shrubs seem to be particularly prone to damage from heavy snow and ice loads. The intense weight of snow and ice bends branches to the ground, breaking the bark and cutting off circulation to the roots of the food manufactured by the leaves. Starving roots eventually die, which leaves the tops without a supply of water, and eventually the whole plant will die. The process could take several years.

To prevent damage from heavy loads, support multistemmed plants by bundling the stems together with burlap, canvas, or chicken wire. Simply binding the stems together with cord will do in a pinch. Be sure to remove heavy snow as soon as possible, but don't try to remove ice. More damage to the branch will probably occur than if the ice is allowed to melt on its own.

STRAWBERRIES NEED WINTER PROTECTION

Strawberries have already set their buds for next spring's flowers, and the crop can be lost unless you protect them from harsh winter conditions. Flower buds can be damaged at temperatures below 15° F, and with each 5°-drop in temperature, the damage is even worse. Strawberries are also susceptible to heaving in the erratic midwestern winter.

Mulching strawberry plants will help protect the flower buds from extreme low temperatures and prevent heaving. Be sure to wait until plants are dormant before you pile on the mulch. Applying mulch too early, before growth stops, can cause the crowns of the plants to rot. Plants should be mulched before the temperature drops below 20° F.

Several materials can be used for winter mulch, including clean straw, chopped cornstalks, hay, corncobs, or bark chips. Don't try to use grass clippings or tree leaves (unless shredded), since they tend to mat down and smother the plants. About a 2–3-inch layer, after settling, should provide adequate protection.

Make sure you uncover the plants in the spring as new growth begins. Rake off most of the mulch as soon as the first new leaves develop. The new growth will probably look a little yellow but should turn green as it is exposed to light. Rake the mulch between the rows to provide weed control and emergency cover in case frost threatens. Mulching around the plants will also help keep the berries clean.

MULCH FOR WINTER PROTECTION

Winter mulch isn't necessary for all garden plants, but it can mean survival for some less hardy plants. Winter mulch has a different purpose than summer mulch. The main benefits of winter cover are to protect against heaving from wide temperature fluctuations in the soil and to prevent extreme cold temperatures from harming plants.

Heaving is most harmful to relatively shallow-rooted plants, such as strawberries and newly planted specimens of any kind that have not yet had a chance to develop solid footing. The insulation that winter mulch provides keeps the soil temperatures from fluctuating, thus preventing heaving of plants. Winter mulch also prevents extreme cold damage to above-ground plant parts.

In most cases, 2–4 inches of mulch, such as straw, pine needles, hay, or bark chips, give adequate protection. For some more tender plants, such as grafted roses, more elaborate protection is needed.

Timing is critical when applying winter mulch. It's best to wait until after temperatures are consistently below freezing to apply the mulch. After all, you aren't trying to keep the soil from freezing; rather, you want to keep it from alternately freezing and thawing. Applying the winter mulch too early can smother the plant and encourage disease development.

PLEASE DON'T BURN AUTUMN LEAVES

Ah, the aroma of burning leaves in autumn! A sure sign that winter can't be far away. But did you realize that you could be breaking the law when you set your yard waste on fire? Open burning of any material is prohibited in some areas.

Burning leaves leads to pollution of our air as well as fire hazards. The smoke from burning leaves contains a number of toxic and/or irritating particles and gases.

The tiny particles contained in smoke from burning leaves can accumulate in our lungs and stay there for years, increasing the risk of respiratory infection and reducing the amount of air reaching the lungs. For those who already suffer from asthma and other breathing disorders, leaf burning can be extremely hazardous.

Moist leaves, which tend to burn slowly, give off more smoke than dry leaves and are thus more likely to give off chemicals called hydrocarbons, which cause irritation of the eyes, nose, throat, and lungs. Some of these hydrocarbons are known to be carcinogenic.

Carbon monoxide is an invisible gas that results from incomplete burning, such as smoldering leaf piles. Carbon monoxide is absorbed into the blood after one inhales the gas, where it reduces the amount of oxygen that the red blood cells can carry. Children, seniors, smokers, and persons suffering from chronic lung and heart disease are more susceptible to carbon monoxide effects than healthy adults.

What are the alternatives to burning leaves? Many states have passed legislation banning the disposal of yard waste in landfills. Some communities will offer leaf pick-up service for large-scale composting. The finished compost can then be used in home gardens and landscapes.

You could also compost those leaves yourself. Dry leaves alone will break down slowly over time, but you can speed that process by mixing the leaves with nitrogen-containing green plant materials, such as grass clippings, garden refuse, and produce scraps. (See pages 243–44.)

Shredded leaves can also be used as a mulch around garden and landscape plants. Mulch provides many benefits, including weed suppression, moisture conservation, and moderation of soil temperature. Leaves can be applied to dormant plants in the winter to prevent young plants from heaving out of the ground. Leaf mulch can help keep soil cooler and prevent it from drying out in summer. No more than a 2–3-inch layer of leaves should be used around actively growing plants. Chop or shred the leaves first to prevent them from matting down and preventing air from reaching roots.

Directly applying the leaves to a garden or unused area of soil is another option. Spread the leaves over as large an area as possible and then till or plow them under. Chopping or shredding the leaves will help them to break down more quickly.

So when it's time to dispose of leaves, take a lesson from Mother Nature. She'd much sooner recycle than pollute!

WOOD PRESERVATIVES FOR GARDENING STRUCTURES

Wood is an attractive material for raised beds, flower boxes, trellises, and other gardening structures. However, recent controversy regarding chemical wood preservation treatments has left many gardeners wondering about the safety of such products.

If chemically preserved wood must be used, choose wood that has been pressure-treated. The most common chemical used in pressure-treated lumber is chromated copper arsenate (CCA). Although this chemical sounds pretty formidable, it is applied to the wood under pressure and is bound so tightly to the wood that only a minute amount may leak out into the immediate soil. However, in small areas such as a greenhouse flat, plant damage is possible.

Although many tests indicate that this type of treated wood is safe to use in outdoor gardens, some have questioned the data, leading to much discussion in popular gardening magazines. Most gardeners have used this type of lumber in garden structures for years without apparent problems of toxicity to people or plants. However, it is a good idea to wear a dust mask when sawing on pressure-treated lumber to avoid breathing in the sawdust. It is also best not to burn such lumber to avoid potentially harmful fumes. If you are concerned about the safety of treated lumber, there are plenty of other materials available for use as containers and raised beds, including chimney tiles, barrels, cinder blocks, bricks, and naturally rot-resistant wood, such as redwood and cedar.

Pressure-treated wood, which appears greenish in color, is treated at several different levels, depending on the intended use of the wood. The most common ratings available are above-ground use, ground-contact use, and structural support. Be sure to ask for ground-contact wood if you're building a cold frame, raised bed, or other soil-holding structure.

Creosote is familiar to many as the brownish-black tar used to preserve railroad ties and telephone poles. Although the EPA restricts the sale of creosote, access to railroad ties or other lumber treated with the substance is still possible. Creosote can give off plant-damaging fumes for many years after treatment. Thus freshly treated wood can damage or even kill plants that are sensitive to it and may result in allergic reactions in some people as well. Old, weathered railroad ties are not likely to give off damaging fumes.

Pentachlorophenol, or penta, is used much like creosote in durable lumber materials such as railroad ties, utility poles, and structural supports. It, too, has volatile fumes that may damage nearby plants and has been restricted by the EPA. Unlike creosote, penta only causes a slight darkening of the wood, so penta-treated wood can be very difficult to recognize if untreated wood is not available for comparison.

Some types of wood are naturally resistant to decay, including cedar and redwood, but these woods are becoming more scarce, and the prices are escalating accordingly. So for now, it looks like the best bet for garden construction is to use pressure-treated wood.

PREPARE YOUR SPRING GARDEN THIS FALL

Just as you thought you finished your garden work this year, it's time to start work on your spring garden. Fall is a great time to get your soil ready for next year's planting.

The first order of business is to remove this year's plant debris, which is a good general sanitation practice. Plant refuse makes a great place for insects and disease to overwinter. Why not turn that refuse into valuable compost? Once the compost has decomposed (hopefully by spring), it can be worked into the soil to add organic matter and some nutrients.

Other types of organic matter can be incorporated into the soil in the fall to help improve soil drainage and water-holding capacity and loosen up heavy soils. Plowing and incorporating organic matter in the fall avoids the rush of garden activities and often waterlogged soil in spring. Materials such as leaves, grass clippings, manure, or

summer mulch should be well decomposed by spring if plowed under in the fall. Work these materials into the top 5–7 inches of soil with a tiller or shovel. However, garden sites that are prone to erosion by wind or water over the winter should not be worked until the spring.

This is a good time for soil testing, which helps you keep current on your garden's nutritional status. Testing in the fall every 3–5 years allows plenty of time to receive your results and act on test recommendations for fertilizer and other amendments if needed. Private laboratories and some state universities offer soil testing services, but the test recommendations will only be as good as the sample of soil that you send in. Make sure your sample is representative of your garden. Small cores of soil 6–8 inches deep should be taken from several spots throughout the garden and then mixed together. A total of 1–2 cups of this mixed soil should then be submitted for testing.

POPCORN WITHOUT THE POP

Gardeners are often faced with a big disappointment when trying to pop their home-grown popcorn. Properly conditioned popcorn should begin to pop in 80–90 seconds in a preheated popper. Poor popping quality can usually be blamed on improper moisture content. This could be either too much or too little moisture.

Probably the most common mistake is not allowing the corn to dry long enough before storing. Test pop the corn to see if it has dried sufficiently. Popcorn that pops slowly with a lot of loud noise and lots of steam is too moist. Popcorn should be allowed to dry thoroughly on the stalk and then cured in a warm, well-ventilated area for about 2–3 weeks. After curing, remove the kernels from the cob by rubbing one ear against another, starting at the tip of one ear and working down to the base.

On the other hand, popcorn that is too dry will not pop well, either. Excessively dry popcorn tends to scorch rather than pop. Overly dry popcorn can be rescued by adding about 1 tablespoon of water per quart of popcorn. Shake well twice a day for a couple of days. You may need to add more water if test popping still doesn't measure up.

To maintain proper moisture content, keep the kernels in an airtight container and store it in a cool location. A sealable glass jar in the refrigerator works well.

GROWING TREES FROM SEED

Many trees can be grown from seed collected in your own backyard, but you should be prepared for what lies ahead. Plants may not grow true from seed, so don't be too disappointed if the new plants are not what you expected. Moreover, seeds of many woody plants require special treatment before they can germinate.

Many of our modern ornamental and fruit trees must be propagated by means other than seeds to ensure that specific characteristics will endure. These plants are most often propagated by cuttings, grafting, or other vegetative methods that provide clones, or exact duplicates, of the mother plants. Reproduction by seed can be variable, and while the offspring may be similar to one or both parents, some desirable characteristics may be lost.

Sprouting seeds from fruits purchased at the grocery can be particularly disappointing, since many of these fruits have come from growing areas that are very different than the Midwest. These plants may not be able to withstand our growing conditions.

Most woody plants grown in the Midwest bear seeds that are dormant and must go through some physiological maturation before they can germinate. These changes are often referred to as after ripening. The most common type of dormancy is overcome by moist chilling, or stratification. In nature, seeds are stratified by lying in moist soil over the winter but may never actually germinate. The seeds may be buried too deep or damaged by insects, animals, or excessively dry conditions.

Gardeners can stratify seeds in a more controlled manner by placing the seeds in a moist medium, such as peat moss, vermiculite, or sand. The refrigerator provides just about the right temperature to provide the chilling. Although the length of the chilling period varies with the plant species, most seeds are adequately stratified for 3–4 months at 35–40° F.

After the chilling period, seeds can be sown in pots, flats, or other suitable containers with a loose, well-drained medium, such as a mixture of peat moss and vermiculite. Maintaining high moisture and relative humidity is crucial to germinating the seeds. You can raise relative humidity by enclosing the seed tray in a plastic tent. Poking some holes through the plastic will allow air circulation. Keep the trays in a warm, dimly lit location.

Germination can be as quick as a few days or as slow as several months, depending on the species and environmental conditions. Once the seeds germinate, move the seedlings to a brighter area. You may need to nurse the seedlings indoors for several months before planting outdoors. Try to give the young plants as much light as possible and feed with a fertilizer for houseplants according to label directions.

Your home-grown seedlings may not be prize winners, but they can provide a fun project for the adventurous gardener. Other special handling techniques may be needed for some plants. If you're truly interested in experimenting with home-grown trees, take a trip to your library and become more familiar with the individual plant. Ask the reference librarian for books on plant propagation and seeds of woody plants.

Gardening Questions

Q. The prices of dried flower wreaths are beyond my budget, but they are so beautiful. I dried some flowers from my garden this summer, and I'd like to try to make my own wreath. How do I go about it?

A. Many garden flowers can be air dried, including baby's breath, strawflower, statice, yarrow, and hydrangea. With a bit more effort, you can dry roses, marigolds, stock, and many others. Don't forget the seed plumes of grasses and attractive foliage. (See pages 92–93, 99, 199–200 on how to dry flowers.)

My favorite way to make a wreath is to begin with a straw wreath base, which is available at most craft stores. I cover this with dried foliage by lashing it on with clear fishing line. The silvery gray of artemesia or lavender foliage is a good choice as a background to the flowers.

You'll soon discover why the wreaths are so expensive: it requires lots of flowers and the time and patience to place each one. With a glue gun, apply a dab of glue on the back of each flower and press it into place on the wreath. Vary the size and texture of the flowers as you work around the wreath to give the finished piece an overall balance. Remember to leave room for a bow of ribbon or lace. A clear craft spray sealer or hairspray will help preserve the wreath.

Q. Our daughter is getting married next year and will carry fresh flowers from our garden. They will have sentimental value to us, and I'd like to keep them in some way. Someone once sent me a card made of pressed flowers. Can I press the flowers in her bouquet?

A. Pressing flowers is simple if you choose the right blossoms. Obviously, a fully double, ruffled rose will be difficult to flatten. Select flowers that are thin and flat, such as pansies, bleeding hearts, coral bells, and daisies. Press some foliage too, including fern, ivy, and clover. Put the flowers facedown on white paper. Spread the petals into an attractive position with as little overlap as possible. Place another sheet of paper on top of the plant material and press it with books, phone directories or a plant press. Check them in a few weeks.

You can make an arrangement of pressed flowers on paper and frame it for a nice wall hanging. You can also make bookmarks, place mats, stationery, picture frames, and candles. A good craft book will help you get started.

Q. Last spring we planted rhododendrons, boxwood, and azaleas. How do you treat these in the winter? I was thinking of putting straw around them in a wire cage. Winter winds are quite harsh where we live.

A. Broad-leaved evergreens, such as the shrubs you mentioned, benefit from some winter protection because winter winds continue to draw moisture out of the

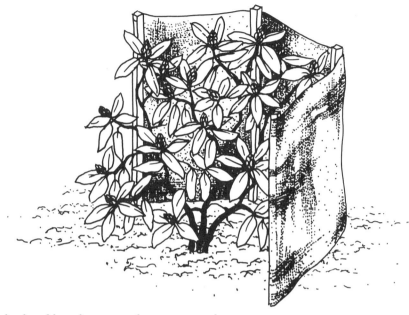

Shelter broad-leaved evergreens from winter winds.

foliage after the roots are dormant and unable to draw moisture out of the frozen soil. Straw, canvas, or burlap over a wire cage provides adequate shelter. A screen made of burlap or plastic on the windward side would also offer adequate protection. Keep plants well watered until the ground freezes.

Antidessication sprays on the market have been used with variable reports of success. They help prevent dessication, but additional protection is usually necessary.

 We had mums this fall. We mulched them but didn't cut them off. We were told

not to cut them off in the fall because the cold would get down in the stems and make them weak. Do you cut them off in the spring? How far do you cut them back?

A. The advice you received earlier is a garden myth. Cut your chrysanthemums back in the fall, as the debris provides overwintering sites for insects and diseases. Garden sanitation is one of the best organic methods of disease control, so make fall garden cleanup a priority.

Garden mums are generally referred to as hardy, but they have a high mortality rate compared to many other perennials. Florists' mums are meant to be enjoyed indoors and are not hardy. Cut garden mums back to 1 inch from the ground and apply a mulch in late fall or early winter after plants are fully dormant for protection and to prevent heaving.

Q. We have a lot of hog manure. Can we use it on our garden, or is it too hot? It has a lot of straw mixed in it.

A. It is best not to apply fresh manure of any kind to growing plants. Compost the manure for one year or apply it to the garden in the fall to avoid nitrogen burning.

Q. I have voles in the compost, garden, and flower bed. How do I get rid of them?

A. Voles prefer some vegetative cover, so you can limit their activity by clearing ground vegetation from a 3-foot radius around the base of trees and shrubs. Tree guards are helpful, since voles feed on green-barked trees and shrubs. Guards should be constructed from hardware cloth with a mesh no larger than ¼ inch. They should enclose the tree trunk and extend to at least 18 inches above the soil surface. Tree guards will reduce the damage caused by meadow and prairie voles but will not stop pine voles from attacking tree and shrub roots.

A compost pile, especially one containing brush, is an ideal habitat for voles. Try containing the compost pile to exclude the voles. Again, clear the vegetation from around the compost. Baiting and trapping may be an alternative solution.

Q. I'd like to know of some good ways to mark where plants are set out. I don't want to injure any dormant plants when I'm adding new flowers.

A. Everyone you ask will have a different answer to this question. I make homemade labels for my perennials out of the excess slats from vinyl miniblinds. Some plastics I've tried become brittle and break in one growing season, but vinyl miniblinds last several years. I cut them into 6-inch lengths and write the plant names on them with a black permanent marker.

Attach labels to woody plants by tying them onto a branch so they can't be dislodged or lost. Make sure to tie them on loosely, otherwise the tie might injure the plant. Some mail-order garden supply catalogs sell metal tags. These are sturdy and long lasting but more expensive than a homemade variety.

My spring-flowering bulbs take up large, irregularly shaped portions of my garden beds, so they're hard to label. Instead, I photograph the bulbs in the spring and check the photos before planting in those areas.

Ask you gardening friends for their favorite plant-labeling methods. There isn't a perfect solution, but you should be able to come up with a satisfactory option.

DECEMBER

December brings our garden season to a close, and it is sweet parting. We're sorry to see the season end, but we know it will come again. Shakespeare wrote:

> At Christmas, I no more desire a rose
> Than wish a snow in May's new-fangled mirth;
> But like of each thing that in season grows.

Likewise, we are glad to put away our garden tools, and we welcome the horticultural delights of December. From earliest times, evergreens, including holly and mistletoe, had a special part in traditions, as they symbolized the continuity of life in a way that deciduous plants could not. This is the season of gift giving, including poinsettias, holiday greenery, and dried flower crafts. You didn't dry flowers this fall? Well, that's the most wonderful thing about gardening. There's always next year.

Garden Calendar

HOME

When shopping for a Christmas tree, check for green, flexible, firmly held needles and a sticky trunk base—both indicators of freshness. Make a fresh cut and keep the cut end under water at all times.

Evergreens, except pines and spruce, can be trimmed now for a fresh supply of holiday greenery.

Extend the lives of holiday plants, such as poinsettias and Christmas cactus, by placing them in a cool, brightly lit area free from warm or cold drafts.

Move plants closer to windows but avoid placing foliage against cold windowpanes. Artificial lighting may be helpful.

Check houseplant leaves for brown, dry edges, which indicate too little relative humidity in the house. Increase humidity by running a humidifier, grouping plants together, or using pebble trays.

To force bulbs for the holidays, bring them into warmer temperatures after they have been sufficiently precooled.

Check stored produce and tender flower bulbs and roots for rot, shriveling, or excess moisture. Discard damaged material.

YARD

Protect shrubs from extensive snow loads by tying their stems together with twine. Carefully remove heavy snow loads with a broom to prevent limb breakage.

Protect broad-leaved evergreens or other tender landscape plants from excessive drying by winter sun and wind.

Provide winter protection for roses by mounding soil approximately 12 inches high to insulate the graft union.

GARDEN

Clean up dead plant materials, synthetic mulch, and other debris in the vegetable garden as well as in flower beds, rose beds, and orchards.

To protect newly planted or tender perennials and bulbs, mulch with straw, chopped leaves, or other organic material after plants become dormant.

Store leftover garden chemicals where they will stay dry, unfrozen, and out of the reach of children and pets.

Order seed catalogs and make notes for next year's garden.

HOLIDAY GREENERY

Give your home the festive mood of the holidays by bringing a bit of your landscape evergreens indoors. Wreaths, swags, garlands, and centerpieces can all be made from plants that are commonly found in the home landscape.

Some of the best materials to cut include balsam and Douglas firs, yew, holly, boxwood, and juniper. Pines are very attractive in arrangements, but this is not a good time to prune them. If pine branches cannot be cut from your tree inconspicuously, look for boughs at nurseries, garden centers, florists, or Christmas tree sales. Needles of hemlock and spruce drop quickly and should not be used for indoor decorations.

Privet, barberry, English ivy, and rhododendron provide an attractive contrast to the needled foliage. Dried grasses, herbs, berries, cones, and seedpods can help add color to a holiday display.

Careful pruning is the key, since plants can be damaged by a careless pruning job. In the warm, dry environment of the home, cut greens will dry out very quickly, so keep the cut ends of the branches in water whenever possible. Sprays are available to help cut down on moisture loss and somewhat extend the life of cut greens. Plastic or lacquer hobby sprays or plant resin antitranspirants can be used. However, these sprays leave a very sticky residue and should only be used if decorations will be placed outdoors or out of reach indoors.

Evergreen decorations can be a fire hazard when they age and dry. Avoid placing them near fireplaces, heat ducts, televisions, candles, or other sources of heat or flame. A home-made flame retardant of 4 tablespoons of boric acid, 9 tablespoons of borax, and 2 quarts of water can be sprayed on the foliage. Another recipe calls for 5 tablespoons of borax and 4 tablespoons of Epsom salts in 2 quarts of water. These flame retardants are not foolproof, so the best precaution is to discard the decorations when they become dry and brittle.

BE CHOOSY WHEN SELECTING CHRISTMAS TREES

It's time to begin the search for that perfect holiday tree. Careful selection for quality and proper maintenance of trees can help keep the holidays cheerful and safe.

When choosing a specific tree, keep in mind that different trees vary in their characteristics. One important feature is needle retention. Spruces tend to drop their needles most quickly, while firs are a little slower. Pines have the longest-lasting needles, with Scotch and red pine holding their needles longer than white pine.

Regardless of the tree you choose, be sure it is freshly cut. Fresh trees should have green, pliable needles that are firmly attached. One way to check for freshness is to tap the bottom of the tree trunk lightly against the ground. If many dry, brittle needles fall

out, the tree is not very fresh. The cut end of a fresh tree should be sticky with sap. Needles of fresh trees should be quite fragrant, but firs and white pines tend to have greater natural fragrance than other evergreens.

Prices will vary among tree species as well as with the size of the tree. Generally, Scotch pine is the least expensive, followed by Douglas and balsam firs, white pine, and Colorado blue spruce.

Once a tree is selected, proper care in the home will extend its life. Just prior to placing it in a stand, make a fresh cut across the bottom of the trunk to aid in water uptake. Keep the cut end of the trunk under water at all times. A tree goes through a lot of water in a warm, dry room, so be sure to check the water level at least once a day. Commercial tree preservatives are available and may help keep the foliage fresh and pliable. Avoid placing the tree near hot or cold drafts because these conditions promote needle drop.

Allowing the needles to dry out can cause the tree to become a fire hazard. Be sure to keep the tree away from heat sources, such as warm-air vents, fireplaces, and television sets. Flame-retardant sprays are available for Christmas trees and other holiday greenery. Although these sprays do not make the trees fireproof, they can help reduce flammability.

Maintaining a fresh tree with proper care is probably the best fire prevention. But no matter how well you care for a tree, it is not likely to remain fresh much longer than 3 weeks. So it pays to be a little patient and not buy your tree too early in the holiday season.

Think twice before you throw your Christmas tree in the trash. That tree can be recycled; winter birds will appreciate the cover of the tree in your backyard, especially when you decorate it with bird-food ornaments. Suet, molded seeds, or disposable hangers should be readily available. Don't just throw the tree into the yard—you'll need to secure the trunk to the ground to prevent it from rolling away in winter winds.

If feeding the birds isn't your cup of tea, try chopping the tree and using the broken limbs as a mulch for perennial flower beds. Be sure to remove the branches in the spring as the plants begin to grow again. Many areas have special collection times for discarded trees so that they can be chipped up for use as mulch in city parks.

CUT YOUR OWN CHRISTMAS TREE

The harvest season isn't over yet. Why not harvest a Christmas tree this year?

Cutting your own tree can give you some insight into what it takes to produce this important part of the agricultural industry. Christmas trees are planted and cared for much like any other crop. The major difference is the amount of time invested: 6–7 years to harvest size.

Buying a tree straight from the grower may keep your costs lower, but the major advantage in cutting your own tree is in the assurance of a very fresh product. So even if prices aren't any lower, you're still getting better value for your money. You may also have a better selection of tree sizes and species to choose from.

Choosing and cutting your own tree can also be a fun family outing. Many Christmas tree growers provide refreshments, ornament sales, and a wagon or sleigh ride.

Because your tree will be freshly cut, you won't have to worry as much about it lasting the 3–4 weeks of the holiday season. But just like any other real tree, you'll have to provide a fresh supply of water to the tree at all times. Make a fresh cut across the base of the trunk when you get the tree home. Then put the tree in a stand that will hold an ample supply of water, preferably a gallon. Check your tree regularly to make sure the water supply doesn't dry out. Keep the tree away from sources of heat, which cause the needles to dry rapidly.

Check your local newspaper for advertisements of local Christmas tree growers.

LIVING CHRISTMAS TREES

A unique gift for the holidays might be a living Christmas tree that can be planted outdoors and enjoyed for years to come. Sounds great, but such a gift does require advanced preparation.

A living Christmas tree is a live plant, which still has its own root system intact. The idea is to enjoy the tree indoors during the holidays and then plant it outdoors. The catch is that weather conditions usually do not allow for planting trees outdoors once the holidays are past. So unless you've prepared the planting hole earlier in the fall when the weather was warmer, you may not be able to get the tree into the ground.

Even if you are able to plant, soil temperatures will probably be colder than that required for new roots to develop. Winter sun and wind can cause excessive drying, even in plants that have well-established root systems. Just imagine the damage that could follow if plants had no opportunity to establish roots.

Conditions indoors may be acceptable for short-term storage but not for the long haul. Ideally, a living tree should not be kept indoors for more than a few days, but certainly no longer than a week or two. You want the plant's buds to stay dormant and not produce new growth, which would subsequently be killed by winter conditions. Keep your living Christmas tree in a cool room away from hot or cold drafts and water it as needed to prevent the roots from drying.

When you're ready to plant the tree outdoors, let it spend a few days in a cool garage before planting it to help it adjust to the extreme change in temperature. After planting, water thoroughly and stake or guy the tree in place if needed. Shading the plant to the south and west sides will help protect it from excessive drying from the sun.

POINSETTIA CARE

The poinsettia, the most popular holiday plant, is most often perceived as having bright red flowers on a green background. But what most people think of as the flowers are actually colored bracts, or leaves that surround a small, yellowish green structure, which is the true flower.

Today's poinsettia is much improved from the poinsettia of even 10 years ago thanks to plant breeders. Although red is certainly the most popular color, pink, white, and even speckled bracts are also available now.

New cultivars tend to have a greater number of larger bracts on more compact plants. Poinsettia trees are also popular, as are hanging baskets. Modern poinsettias last longer in the home, but the improved longevity of today's poinsettias can only be enjoyed if they receive proper care.

The best way to extend the life of your poinsettia is to match as closely as possible the conditions under which it was produced. Poinsettias are grown in greenhouses, where cool temperatures can be maintained between 60–75° F, with high relative humidity and high light intensity.

These conditions will be difficult if not impossible to match in the home. Natural light intensity tends to be quite low and of shorter duration in the winter. And as we heat the air indoors, the air becomes drier, so that relative humidity often drops too low to maintain good plant health.

You can remedy the situation by placing your plant near a sunny window, but do not allow the foliage to contact the cold windowpane. Running a humidifier or grouping plants together on a pebble tray will help raise humidity. Both hot and cold drafts can cause leaf drop, so avoid placing plants near doors or heating vents.

Both under- and overwatering reduce your plant's vigor. Plants that are allowed to wilt will begin to brown along the edges of the leaves or may drop leaves entirely. Watering too often will prevent proper aeration of the soil, and roots will begin to decay. Poinsettias should be watered when the top inch of soil feels dry to the touch. If your pot was wrapped in foil, be sure to poke a few holes through the bottom to allow the water to drain away.

Poinsettias can be saved and brought back into bloom for next year if given the proper attention. The typical home environment does not provide the ideal conditions for maintaining the health of a poinsettia plant beyond the holidays. But for the dedicated indoor gardener, the poinsettia can provide an interesting challenge throughout the year.

Leaves and floral bracts usually fall once the flowers fade. Cut back on watering as the leaves begin to fall until the soil becomes completely dry. The plant should then be in a dormant condition and should be stored in a cool, dark location at about 50° F.

Water only enough to keep the stem of the plant from shriveling, but not enough to promote growth.

Repot the plant when new growth begins in about midspring and then place it near a sunny, south-facing window. Plants that receive inadequate light will be tall and spindly. Keep the air temperature at about 70–75° F and water the plant only when the soil begins to dry. Apply balanced fertilizer either for a foliage plant, such as 10-10-10, or for a blooming plant, such as 5-10-5, following the label recommendations for rate and frequency.

Poinsettias can be moved outdoors to a semishady area after the danger of frost is past. If a shorter, stockier plant is desired, pinch out the growing tips when there are two fully expanded leaves on each shoot. Do not pinch after mid-August. Be sure to bring plants back indoors before outdoor temperatures dip below 55° F (usually by the end of August). Check plants for signs of insect pests and control as needed before you bring the plants indoors.

To bring poinsettias back in to bloom for the holidays, you'll need to keep the plant in complete darkness for at least 15 hours each night for 10 weeks (see pages 241–42).

HOLIDAY GIFT PLANTS

'Tis the season for giving, so why not give a gift that lasts all year? A plant is a special gift that brings beauty to the home and to the heart as you help a living thing grow.

Poinsettias are undoubtedly the most popular gift plant, but many others are just as appropriate for the holiday season. Christmas cactus, begonias, cyclamens, kalanchoe, and azaleas offer attractive blossoms on compact plants and can brighten any room in the house. Jerusalem cherries and ornamental peppers feature festive fruits to help celebrate the season.

Try to match the gift to the recipient in terms of the kind of care the plant needs. Christmas cacti need bright sunlight to continue blooming and growing after the holidays, as will Jerusalem cherries and ornamental peppers. Most flowering plants, including azaleas, begonias, kalanchoe, and cyclamens, will tolerate indirect bright light but demand cool temperatures, especially at night. Jerusalem cherries are poisonous and so are best suited for families that do not have young children. Many garden suppliers carry flowering bulb packages for cheerful spring color indoors. Amaryllis, tulips, hyacinths, and paper-white narcissus are among the favorites.

Some gift plants will continue to bloom throughout the new year if given proper care. Others may need a period of rest before they can be brought back to life. Ask the sales clerk for a plant care sheet when you make your purchase, or include a book on plant care as part of your present.

Plants make great gifts, but be sure that your gift is delivered with the same care you took to select it. During cold weather, even the healthiest plant can be damaged during delivery. Exposure to cold and wind for as short a period as it takes to walk to your car can damage some plants. Have the sales clerk wrap your purchase in paper to protect it and get the plant from the store to your car as quickly as possible. If the temperature is below freezing, preheat the car beforehand to prevent further chilling injury.

Plants left in an unheated car can be injured or killed quickly, so drop the plants off at home before running other errands. If the plant must be in cold air for any length of time, insulate it by placing it in a box with several layers of newspaper bundled around the tops as well as around the plant's container. Packing plants in boxes with newspaper also will help protect them from tipping over. Besides breaking stems and leaves, tipping often causes soil to spill from the pot, breaking roots along the way.

Once the plant is indoors, keep it away from warm and cold drafts. Most plants, particularly those in flower, prefer moderately cool temperatures, such as 60–70° F during the day and a little cooler at night.

Bright light is also important. Light will be brightest near a window, but remember that leaves can be injured by contact with cold glass.

If a plant isn't a practical gift, there are many other ideas for your gardening friends and family. Good gardening tools often head the gardener's wish list. A sturdy new rake,

hoe, or spade can save a tired back and time for the busy gardener. Small hand tools, such as pruners, trowels, and cultivators, are handy both inside and out. For bulb gardeners, a long-handled bulb planter or a bulb drill bit can help make the job easier.

Indoor gardeners would surely appreciate a lighting system to help their houseplants thrive during the dreary winter months. Lighting systems can be as small as a fluorescent tube or as large as a multiple-shelved unit.

Gardening books are available on a wide variety of subjects and can help your special gardener improve his or her gardening skills. A subscription to a garden magazine is also a welcome gift.

If you're still undecided on what to get for your gardener, try a gift certificate from a favorite seed company or local garden shop. Or give a membership to a nearby botanic garden, conservatory, or arboretum (see Appendix B).

POMANDERS MAKE FRAGRANT GIFTS

Many of us are familiar with pomanders, though we may not recognize the name. Pomanders are perforated containers or fabric sacks filled with fragrant herbs and spices and make unusual holiday gifts.

The word pomander comes from the French *pomme d'ambre*, meaning "apple of ambergris." Originally, pomanders were small pieces of the strongly scented ambergris from the sperm whale. These little apple-shaped pieces were placed in beautiful cases of gold, silver, ivory, or wood and worn around the neck or waist to protect against infection and unpleasant odors.

Today, pomanders take on a variety of forms. Most common are glass and ceramic pomanders, which are available in gift shops and from mail-order houses. These usually round containers with small perforations at the top are filled with a potpourri of flowers, herbs, and spices.

You can make an old-fashioned pomander using either lemons or oranges, whole cloves, and powdered orris root (check specialty coffee stores or spice shops for bulk quantities). Punch holes close together into the fruit using a meat skewer or ice pick. Push the whole cloves into the holes until the fruit is completely studded with the cloves. Place the powdered orris root in a bowl and roll the fruit in the powder until it is completely covered and shake off the excess powder. A spicier scent can be made by rolling the pomander in a mixture of orris root, cinnamon, nutmeg, and allspice.

Air dry the pomander in a warm, dry location for about a week or so. After the pomander is dry, tie a ribbon around the fruit, place a bow at the top, and hang it in a closet or place it in a drawer to freshen linens.

Gardening Questions

Q. I like to make holiday decorations for the house. Can I cut the evergreens in my yard for wreath material?

A. This is a good time of year to snip off any stray spurts of growth from many evergreens. Junipers, arborvitaes, and yews won't miss a few selectively pruned shoots. Arranging can be as simple as laying the cuttings on a mantel with a holiday bow or several ornaments. Not much effort is required to fill the house or office with the scents of the holidays.

Your outdoor plantings can provide accent color, too. Look for berries on holly, winterberry, viburnum, hawthorn, and pyracantha. It's easy to wire a few pine cones to tuck into an arrangement. Try colored twigs from kerria, willow, and red- and yellow-twigged dogwood.

Of course, you want to keep the plant's appearance in mind when taking cuttings. I don't want to be responsible for gaping holes in your plants. As with eggnog and cookies, moderation is the key, so snip wisely and avoid cutting spruce and pine trees.

Q. We found an old aquarium while cleaning out the attic. We'd like to make a large terrarium for ourselves and maybe some smaller ones to give to friends during the holidays. Do you have any advice?

A. A terrarium makes a nice gift and provides a sheltered, humid home for a plant collection. Technically, any glass container can be used as a terrarium. The container should have clear glass to provide the best light for the plants and some kind of lid to control the moisture and humidity. Bottles, goblets, fish bowls, and tanks are attractive choices, but be sure the opening is large enough to get the plants into the container.

Choose plants that like high humidity (no cacti!), similar habitats, and are suitable for the size of the container. The mature size of many houseplants is far too big to fit the small, enclosed area of a terrarium. Mosses, orchids, and small ferns all prefer a woodland habitat. Tropical plants for terrariums include ivies, peperomias, and African violets.

Begin the planting process by covering the bottom of the container with 1–3 inches of small gravel. Top this with a thin layer of sheet moss, which grows on stones or fallen logs in the woods and is available at most florists and craft stores. Top it all off with a layer of soil. The sheet moss keeps the soil from falling through to the gravel.

Plant the terrarium, then moisten the plants with a fine mist and put the cover in place. Use the cover to regulate the moisture. If there is too much water in the bottom of the terrarium, or if water condenses on the inside of the glass, remove the cover for several hours each day. If the soil is dry, mist the plantings again. Keep your terrarium in a bright place without direct sunlight. Fertilize only if the plants become pale green or show other signs of nutritional deficiency. Fertilization is not an automatic activity with a terrarium, since dissolved minerals can't escape and lead to salt build-up. Because of the difficulty in adding nutrients, most terrariums need to be replaced or refreshed in about a year, so you could give terrariums to friends annually!

2. What is missing from my holly bushes? Each year my 8-year-old bushes bloom, but there are no berries. I fertilized, used leaf mulch around the roots, and put peat moss on top to hold moisture in our sandy soil, but nothing makes them produce berries.

A. Holly, winterberry, and bittersweet are dioecious plants, meaning the sexes are separated into male (staminate) and female (pistillate) plants, and you need both in close proximity to form berries. You probably need to plant a male holly. Put it in the background, where it can pollinate the pistillate plants but won't obstruct them from view when they produce berries.

2. My house is engulfed by junipers. They are probably 20 years old and now cover the windows and reach the eaves. Can I cut them back to stubs and have them grow out next year?

A. If you cut them back to stubs, you'll have stubs next year! Yews are the only ever-greens with latent buds on older wood that will produce foliage when pruned. With all other evergreens, including your junipers, you should not cut back beyond the living foliage portion of the branches.

Years ago, someone chose the wrong plant for your site. The easiest way to avoid maintenance is to choose the right plant for the right place. If you want plants at your window sills, which are 3 feet from the ground, you can choose a plant that will reach 3 feet at maturity, or choose a taller plant and trim it year after year. Obviously, it pays to do your homework before purchasing plants.

I would remove the shrubs and replace them. If you have access to a truck or tractor, you can hook a chain around the base of the plant and pull it out. With monsters like yours, it may be easier to cut them back to the ground rather than try to remove the root system. If you leave the root system in place, plant the replacements off to the side of the original juniper.

Junipers are available in a wide range of mature heights, from 1 to 16 feet. Check the plant labels carefully. Other low-growing evergreen options include

nest spruce (*Picea abies* 'Nidiformis') and dwarf gold-thread cypress (*Chamaecyparis pisifera* 'Aurea').

Q. I would like to cut starts from my crown of thorns plant (*Euphorbia milii*), but it has a milky substance that flows when I cut it. Can I start it from cuttings, and how?

A. Use a sharp knife to take 3–4-inch tip cuttings in the spring or early summer. Immediately spray the cut surfaces with water to stop the milky latex flow. Allow the cuttings to dry overnight before sticking them in pots of vermiculite or peat and sand. Keep the medium moist but not wet. Set the cuttings in bright, indirect light. You can use a perforated plastic bag around the plant to boost humidity during the rooting procedure. Your cutting should root around 5–8 weeks later, at which time you should transplant it into regular potting mix.

Q. My houseplants seem to be healthy, but they have a white crust over the soil. I fertilize and water regularly. What is it, and what should I do about it?

A. The crust is an accumulation of salts that come from fertilizer or minerals in your water. Eventually, the salts build up to a dangerous level. Remove the white, crusty layer of soil and add fresh, new soil if needed to maintain the original soil depth on the roots.

Flushing the soil with water will leach the salts out. Set the plants in a sink and water them thoroughly until water comes out the bottom. Let the plant drain and repeat this procedure several times until the water draining out of the soil looks clear.

To prevent salt accumulation, put houseplants in pots with drainage holes. At least once a month, water until some water drains through the soil and out the bottom of the pot. Discard the excess water. Some water softeners add high levels of sodium to the water. If your water is softened, bypass the treated water or use distilled water, rain water, or water from a dehumidifier.

Q. After reading garden magazines and books, I usually have a list of plants I would like to try. Sometimes I can find them at a local nursery, but sometimes the seeds or plants are so unusual that my nursery can't help me. I get a few mail-order garden catalogs, but they aren't always helpful. How do I find the garden oddities?

A. You're off to a good start by first checking with local nurseries and greenhouses. Even if they don't carry a particular item, they may be able to order it for you. If the items are not available locally, your county extension service or librarian can help you locate references about gardening by mail and source guides for plant material or an actual source for the plant you want. Additionally, many botanic gardens offer telephone help lines. Plant societies or clubs at the local or national level could also offer assistance.

Appendix A

Midwest Plant Hardiness Zone Map

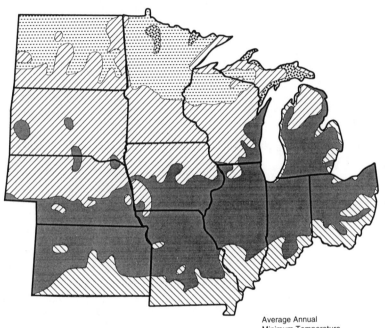

Adapted from the USDA Plant Hardiness Zone Map;
courtesy Sharon Katz and the Purdue University
Agricultural Communication Service.

Average Annual
Minimum Temperature

Zone		Temperature (°F)
2		-50° to -40°
3		-40° to -30°
4		-30° to -20°
5		-20° to -10°
6		-10° to 0°

Appendix B

Public Gardens and Arboreta of the Midwest

Public gardens and arboreta can be abundant sources of information about plants that can be grown in the Midwest. The following list of selected gardens includes some of the larger public collections as well as more intimate green spaces. Descriptions of these as well as many other points of horticultural interest can be found in the following books:

Thomas M. Barrett, ed, *North American Horticulture: A Reference Guide* (New York: MacMillan, 1992).

Sharon Lappin Lumsden, *Green Byways: Garden Discoveries in the Great Lakes States* (Champaign, Ill.: Lime Tree Publications, 1993).

Diane MacKenzie and Gordon Thomas, *Gardens of North America: A Complete Directory & Traveler's Guide* (Jacksonville, Fla.: Advanced Energy Systems, 1993).

ILLINOIS

Rivendell Botanic Garden
P.O. Box 17
Beardstown, IL 62618

Garfield Park Conservatory
300 N. Central Park Blvd.
Chicago, IL
(312) 533-1281
Send correspondence to:
425 E. McFetridge Dr.
Chicago, IL 60605

Lincoln Park Conservatory
2400 N. Stockton Dr.
Chicago, IL 60614
(312) 294-4770

Merrick Rose Garden
Oak at Lake Streets
Evanston, IL
(708) 866-2911
Send correspondence to:
Evanston Parks Dept.
2100 Ridge Rd.
Evanston, IL 60201

Shakespeare Garden
220 Sheridan Road
Evanston, IL
Send correspondence to:
Garden Club of Evanston
2703 Euclid Park Place
Evanston, IL 60201

Chicago Botanic Garden
Lake-Cook Rd.
P.O. Box 400
Glencoe, IL 60022
(708) 835-5440

Morton Arboretum
Rt. 53
Lisle, IL 60532
(708) 968-0074

Moline Garden Center
3300 Fifth Ave.
Riverside Park
Moline, IL 61265

Oak Park Conservatory
617 Garfield St.
Oak Park, IL 60304
(708) 386-4700

George Luthy Memorial Botanical
Garden
Peoria Park District
2218 N. Prospect
Peoria, IL 61603
(309) 686-3362

Starhill Forest
RR 1, Box 272
Petersburg, IL 62675

Washington Park Botanical Garden
Fayette & Chatham Rds.
P.O. Box 5052
Springfield, IL 62705
(217) 787-2540

Abraham Lincoln Memorial Garden
2301 East Lake Dr.
Springfield, IL 62707
(217) 529-1111

INDIANA

Foellinger-Freimann Conservatory
1100 South Calhoun St.
Fort Wayne, IN 46802
(219) 427-1267

Huntington College Arboretum
2303 College Ave.
Huntington, IN 46750
(219) 356-6000, extension 2001

Eli Lilly Botanical Gardens
Indianapolis Museum of Art
1200 West 38th St.
Indianapolis, IN 46208-4196
(317) 923-1331

Garfield Park Conservatory
2450 S. Shelby St.
Indianapolis, IN 46203
(317) 784-3044

Holcomb Botanical Garden
Butler University
4600 Sunset Ave.
Indianapolis, IN 46208
(317) 283-9413

Jerry E. Clegg Foundation Botanical
Gardens
1782 North 400 East
Lafayette, IN 47905
(317) 423-1325

Christy Woods
Ball State University
200 W. University Ave.
Muncie, IN 47306
(317) 285-8838

Hayes Regional Arboretum
801 Elks Rd.
Richmond, IN 47374
(317) 962-3745

Purdue University Horticulture Gardens
1165 Horticulture Bldg.
West Lafayette, IN 47907-1165
(317) 494-1298

E. G. Hill Memorial Rose Garden
828 Promenade
Richmond, IN 47374

IOWA

Iowa State University Horticulture
Garden
Elwood Dr. and Haber Rd.
Ames, IA 50001
(515) 294-2751

Bickelhaupt Arboretum
340 South 14th St.
Clinton, IA 52732
(319) 242-4771

Des Moines Botanical Center
909 East River Dr.
Des Moines, IA 50316
(515) 283-4148

Dubuque Arboretum & Botanical
Gardens
3125 West 32nd St.
Dubuque, IA 52001
(319) 556-2100

Iowa Arboretum
Box 44A, Rt. 1
Madrid, IA 50156
(515) 795-3216

Pearson Memorial Garden Center
Maquoketa, IA 52060

Marshalltown Garden Center
709 Center St.
Marshalltown, IA 50158

KANSAS

Bartlett Arboretum
301 N. Line
Belle Plaine, KS 67013
(316) 488-3451

Dyck Arboretum of the Plains
Hesston College
P.O. Box 3000
Hesston, KS 67062
(316) 327-8127

Independence Garden Center
Riverside Park
Independence, KS 67301

Merritt Horticultural Center
411 North 61st St.
Kansas City, KS 66102
(913) 299-9254

Kansas State University Gardens
U.S. 24
Manhattan, KS 66506
(913) 532-6250

Manhattan Horticulture Center
1600 Laramie St.
Manhattan, KS 66502

E. F. A. Reinisch Rose & Test Gardens
Gage Park
4320 West 10th St.
Topeka, KS 66604
(913) 272-6150

Meade Park Botanic Gardens
124 North Fillmore
Topeka, KS 66606

Kansas Landscape Arboretum
Milford Lake
Wakefield, KS 67487

Botanica, The Wichita Gardens
701 Amidon
Wichita, KS 67203
(316) 264-0448

MICHIGAN

Matthaei Botanical Gardens
University of Michigan
1800 North Dixboro Rd.
Ann Arbor, MI 48105
(313) 998-7061

Detroit Garden Center
1460 E. Jefferson
Detroit, MI 48207
(313) 259-6363

Anna Scripps Whitcomb Conservatory
Belle Isle
Detroit, MI 48207
(313) 267-7133

Michigan State University
Horticulture Gardens
East Lansing, MI 48823
(517) 355-0348

Chadwick Garden Center
Public Museum East Bldg.
233 Washington, S.E.
Grand Rapids, MI 49503

Grosse Pointe Garden Center
32 Lake Shore Dr.
Grosse Pointe Farms, MI 48236
(313) 881-4594

Cooley Gardens
South Capitol Ave. and Main St.
P.O. Box 14164
Lansing, MI 48901
(517) 351-5707

Dow Gardens
1018 West Main St.
Midland, MI 48640
(517) 631-2677

Fernwood Garden and Nature Center
13988 Range Line Rd.
Niles, MI 49120
(616) 695-6491

Hidden Lake Gardens
M-50
Tipton, MI 49287
(517) 431-2060

MINNESOTA

Minnesota Landscape Arboretum
3675 Arboretum Dr.
P.O. Box 39
Chanhassen, MN 55317
(612) 443-2460

Sibley Gardens
Parklane and Given Sts.
Mankato, MN 56001
(507) 625-3161

Eloise Butler Wildflower Garden and
Bird Sanctuary
3800 Bryant Ave., South
Minneapolis, MN 55409
(612) 348-5702

Como Park Conservatory
Midway Pkwy. and Kaufman Dr.
St. Paul, MN 55103
(612) 489-5378

MISSOURI

Cape Girardeau Rose Test Garden
Perry and Rose Sts.
Cape Girardeau, MO 63701
(314) 335-0706

Woodland and Floral Gardens
Interstate 70
Columbia, MO
Send correspondence to:
I-43 Agriculture Building
University of Missouri
Columbia, MO 65211
(314) 882-7511

Shaw Arboretum
State Hwy 100
P.O. Box 38
Gray Summit, MO 63039
(314) 742-3512

Flower and Garden Demonstration
Gardens
4521 Pennsylvania Ave.
Kansas City, MO 64111
(816) 531-5730

Kansas City Garden Center
5300 Pennsylvania Ave.
Kansas City, MO 64112

Powell Gardens
Rt. 1, Box 90
Kingsville, MO 64061
(816) 566-2213

Jewel Box Conservatory
1501 Oakland Ave.
St. Louis, MO 63122
(314) 535-1503

Missouri Botanical Garden
4344 Shaw Blvd.
P.O. Box 299
St. Louis, MO 63166
(314) 577-5100

POSSUM
IN THE
PAWPAW
TREE

NEBRASKA

Sallows Conservatory and Arboretum
11th and Nebraska Sts.
P.O. Drawer D
City of Alliance
Alliance, NE 69301
(308) 762-7422

Alice Abel Arboretum
Nebraska Wesleyan University
5000 St. Paul Ave.
Lincoln, NE 68504-2796
(402) 466-2371

Chet Ager Nature Center
2470 A. St.
Lincoln, NE 68502
(402) 471-7895

Earl Maxwell Arboretum
40th and Holdrege Sts.
University of Nebraska
East Campus
Lincoln, NE 68583
(402) 472-2679

Nebraska Statewide Arboretum
112 Forestry Sciences Laboratory
University of Nebraska
Lincoln, NE 68583-0823
(402) 472-2971

University of Nebraska West Central
Research & Extension Center
Rt. 4, Box 46A
North Platte, NE 69101
(308) 532-3611

NORTH DAKOTA

Berthold Public School Arboretum
P.O. Box 185
Berthold, ND 58718
(701) 453-3484

International Peace Garden, Inc.
P.O. Box 116, Rt. 1
Dunseith, ND 58329
(701) 263-4390

OHIO

Wartinger Park
1368 Research Park Dr.
Beavercreek, OH 45385
(513) 426-5100

Canton Garden Center
1615 Stadium Park, N.W.
Canton, OH 44718

Civic Garden Center of Greater
Cincinnati
2715 Reading Rd.
Cincinnati, OH 45206
(513) 221-0981

Ault Park
Cincinnati Park Board
950 Eden Park Dr.
Cincinnati, OH 45202
(513) 352-4080

Krohn Conservatory
950 Eden Park Dr.
Cincinnati, OH 45202
(513) 352-4080

Mt. Airy Arboretum
5083 Colerain Ave.
Cincinnati, OH 45223
(513) 541-8176

Garden Center of Greater Cleveland
11030 East Boulevard
Cleveland, OH 44106
(216) 721-1600

Cleveland Cultural Gardens
East and Liberty Blvds.
Rockefeller Park
Cleveland, OH   •
Send correspondence to:
Westgate Legal Bldg.
20088 Center Ridge Rd.
Rocky River, OH 44116
(216) 664-3103

Chadwick Arboretum
The Ohio State University
2120 Fyffe Rd.
Columbus, OH 43210
(614) 292-0473

Franklin Park Conservatory
1777 East Broad St.
Columbus, OH 43203
(614) 222-7447

Whetstone Park of Roses
4015 Olentangy Blvd.
Columbus, OH 43214
(614) 645-6648

Cox Arboretum
6733 Springboro Pike
Dayton, OH 45449
(513) 434-9005

Dayton Council Garden Center
1820 Brown St.
Dayton, OH 45409

Wegerzyn Horticultural Center
1301 East Siebenthaler Ave.
Dayton, OH 45414
(513) 277-6545

Kingwood Center
900 Park Ave. West
Mansfield, OH 44906
(419) 522-0211

Falconskeape Gardens
7359 Branch Rd.
Medina, OH 44256
(216) 723-4966

Holden Arboretum
9500 Sperry Rd.
Mentor, OH 44060
(216) 256-1110

Dawes Arboretum
7770 Jacksontown Rd. S.E.
Newark, OH 43055
(614) 323-2355

Gardenview Horticultural Park
16711 Pearl Rd.
Strongsville, OH 44136
(216) 238-6653

Stranahan Arboretum
University of Toledo
33 Birckhead Pl.
Toledo, OH 43608
(419) 882-6806

Toledo Botanical Garden
P.O. Box 7304
5403 Elmer Dr.
Toledo, OH 43615
(419) 536-8365

Inniswood Botanical Garden and Nature
Preserve
940 Hempstead Rd.
Westerville, OH 43081
(614) 895-6216

Secrest Arboretum
Ohio Agricultural Research and
Development Center
1680 Madison Ave.
Wooster, OH 44691-4096
(216) 264-3761

SOUTH DAKOTA

McCrory Gardens
South Dakota State University
Brookings, SD 57007
(605) 688-5136

McKennon Park
Dept. of Parks and Recreation
600 E. 7th St.
Sioux Falls, SD 57102
(605) 339-7060

WISCONSIN

Boerner Botanical Gardens
5879 South 92nd St.
Hales Corner, WI 53130
(414) 425-1130

Mitchell Park Conservatory
524 South Layton Blvd.
Milwaukee, WI 53215
(414) 649-9830

Olbrich Botanical Gardens
3330 Atwood Ave.
Madison, WI 53704
(608) 246-4551

University of Wisconsin Arboretum
1207 Seminole Highway
Madison, WI 53711
(608) 262-2746

Botanical Garden of the University of
Wisconsin
Dept. of Botany
144 Birge Hall
430 Lincoln Dr.
Madison, WI 53706
(608) 262-2235

Jones Arboretum and Botanical Gardens
US 14
Readstown, WI 54652
(608) 629-5553

Appendix C

State Cooperative Extension Service Offices

Every state has a Cooperative Extension Service, which serves as an educational outreach for the Land Grant Universities. The extension offices can provide gardening publications that are targeted for local growing conditions. Also available is information about the Master Gardener Program, a volunteer-development program that enlists local gardeners to share their knowledge with their communities.

Consumer Horticulture Extension
University of Illinois
104 Ornamental Horticulture Bldg.
Urbana, IL 61801

Consumer Horticulture Extension
Purdue University
1165 Horticulture Bldg.
West Lafayette, IN 47907-1165

Consumer Horticulture Extension
Iowa State University
Department of Horticulture
Ames, IA 50011

Consumer Horticulture Extension
227 Waters Hall
Kansas State University
Manhattan, KS 66506

Consumer Horticulture Extension
Michigan State University
Department of Horticulture
East Lansing, MI 48824

Consumer Horticulture Extension
University of Minnesota
1970 Folwell Ave.
St. Paul, MN 55108

Consumer Horticulture Extension
University of Missouri
Department of Horticulture
Columbia, MO 65211

Consumer Horticulture Extension
University of Nebraska
Plant Science Bldg.
Lincoln, NE 68503

POSSUM
IN THE
PAWPAW
TREE

Consumer Horticulture Extension
North Dakota State University
Department of Horticulture
Fargo, ND 58105

Consumer Horticulture Extension
The Ohio State University
Howlett Hall
Columbus, OH 43210

Consumer Horticulture Extension
South Dakota State University
Department of Horticulture
Brookings, SD 57007

Consumer Horticulture Extension
University of Wisconsin
Department of Horticulture
Madison, WI 53706

Glossary

actual nitrogen: The amount of nitrogen in the form of nitrate (NO_3) contained in a fertilizer.

annual plant: A plant that completes its life cycle in one growing season.

anther: The part of a flower that produces pollen.

bark: The outer layers of a woody stem or root.

biennial plant: A plant that completes its life cycle in 2 growing seasons, generally producing foliage only the first year and flowers and seeds the second year.

bolting: The unwanted production of flowers.

bone meal: A fertilizer derived from powdered animal bones used as a source of phosphorous.

bract: A leaf-like structure in some plant species that occurs just below the flower(s). May be mistaken for flower petals, as in poinsettia and dogwood.

broadcast: An even distribution of dried material over an area, including fertilizers or pesticides.

broad-leaved evergreen: A non-needled plant that retains some or all of its leaves throughout the year.

bulb: A type of underground storage structure made up of modified stem and leaves.

bulblet: A baby bulb produced alongside the mother bulb.

callus: A proliferation of cells produced in response to a wound.

chlorophyll: The plant pigment responsible for green color that captures light energy from the sun used in photosynthesis.

chlorosis: The absence of chlorophyll.

clay: Soil particles that are so small that they pack tightly (<.002 mm.). Clay soils may be the cause of poor water drainage and aeration.

cold frame: An outdoor structure used to protect tender plants from cold temperatures, usually constructed of framed window glass, allowing for solar heating.

compost: A dark, loose, organic material made from decomposed plants.

conifer: A cone-bearing plant with needle-like leaves.

corm: A short, swollen underground stem, often mistaken for a bulb.

cover crop: A crop planted to stabilize soil and provide organic matter. Sometimes called green manure.

cross-pollination: The transfer of pollen from a flower to another flower on a different plant.

crown: The part of the plant where the stem meets the roots, or a modified, shortened stem, as in strawberry.

cultivar: A cultivated variety; a name given to a group of plants within a species that is distinguished by certain characteristics.

cutting: A section of stem or root used for plant propagation.

damping off: A fungal disease that attacks young seedlings as they germinate.

deciduous: A woody plant that is leafless sometime during the year (usually in the winter in the Midwest).

division: A method of propagation where a plant is separated into 2 or more sections.

dieback: Death of shoot tips of plants, generally indicating stress caused by insects, diseases, or environmental conditions.

division: A method of propagation where a plant is separated into 2 or more sections.

dormancy: A period of rest when plants are alive but not growing.

dormant oil: A type of horticultural oil applied during the dormant season to control some overwintering insect pests.

evergreen: A plant that retains some or all of its foliage throughout the year.

fertilizer: A material containing nutrients essential to plant growth. The numbers on a fertilizer package indicate the percentages of nitrogen, phosphorus, and potassium contained, in that order.

fibrous roots: A finely branched root system.

flower: The part of a plant bearing reproductive organs, often, but not necessarily, colorful and showy.

fruit: A mature ovary containing seeds.

fungicide: A pesticide used to prevent fungal infections.

genus: A group of closely related species.

germination: Sprouting of seeds.

girdle: An injury or growth that interferes with sap flow.

grafting: Splicing together of different plants so that the combination grows as a single plant.

ground cover: A low-growing, spreading plant generally under 2 feet tall.

harden off: To gradually expose young plants to outdoor growing conditions.

hardwood cutting: A section of mature woody stem taken late in the season for propagation.

hardy: Capable of surviving local seasonal extremes.

heaving: The uprooting of plants caused by alternate freezing and thawing of soil.

herb: Any plant used wholly or in part for flavoring, fragrance, or medicine.

herbaceous: A plant that dies back to the ground each year; a non-woody plant.

herbicide: A pesticide used to prevent or control unwanted plants.

horticulture: The art and science of growing plants for food and ornament.

hot bed: A cold frame with an additional source of heat.

hybrid: The offspring of 2 genetically different parents.

insecticide: A pesticide used to control unwanted insects.

internode: The portion of a stem between the nodes.

larva: An immature stage in the life cycle of an insect.

layering: A method of propagation where rooting is induced on the stem prior to separating it from the mother plant.

leaching: The movement of minerals through the soil beyond the plants' reach.

loam: An ideal soil mixture made up of sand, silt, clay, and organic matter.

miticide: A pesticide used to control mites.

monoecious: A species in which male and female flowers are produced separately on the same plant.

mulch: A soil covering used to prevent weeds, retain soil moisture, reduce erosion, modify soil temperature, and/or improve the appearance of a planting.

mycorrhiza: A mutually beneficial association between specific combinations of fungi and plant roots.

node: The portion of a stem where leaves are attached and buds are produced.

nut: A type of fruit with a hard shell.

organic matter: Decomposed plant or animal material.

ovary: The part of a female portion of a flower that becomes a fruit when it matures.

overwinter: To survive the winter.

parasite: An organism that, during some or all of its life cycle, obtains food or shelter at the expense of another plant or animal.

peat moss: Partially decomposed plant material derived primarily from bog plants.

perennial: A plant that lives and can produce seed year after year.

perlite: A white, granular material made from expanded volcanic lava, often used to improve aeration and water-holding capacity in soils.

pesticide: A product that claims to control or repel pests, including insecticides, fungicides, herbicides, and rodenticides.

petiole: The stalk that attaches a leaf blade to a stem.

pH: A measure of acidity or alkalinity.

photosynthesis: The process by which plants capture energy from the sun to make carbohydrates, which are later used as fuel for growth.

pollen: Tiny grains that contain male sperm cells.

pollination: The transfer of pollen from the male to the female flower structures.

potbound: A potted plant whose roots have grown to fill the entire available space.

propagate: To increase the number of plants.

respiration: A physiological process in which plants break down carbohydrates as a fuel source.

rhizome: A horizontal underground stem often enlarged for storage of food reserves.

root: The part of the plant that anchors the plant and is responsible for uptake of water and nutrients.

runner: A horizontal stem that grows along the soil surface.

run-off: Water that flows over the soil surface rather than being absorbed into the soil.

sand: Soil particles that are relatively coarse (.05–2.0mm), increasing aeration and drainage.

seed: A structure consisting of a plant embryo and food reserves.

seedling: A recently germinated plant.

shrub: A woody, perennial, multistemmed plant smaller than a tree.

side-dress: To apply a material (usually fertilizer) to the soil next to a plant.

silt: Medium-sized soil particles (between .05 and .002 mm.).

softwood: Young, green stem tissue of a woody plant.

species: A group of closely related plants that are generally able to interbreed.

sphagnum moss: A type of moss from decayed sphagnum plants.

stamen: The male part of the flower that bears the anther.

stem: The above-ground portion of the plant that bears leaves, flowers, and fruits and conducts water and carbohydrates between the roots and leaves.

succulent: A plant with enlarged stems or leaves for water storage.

sucker: Unwanted shoots originating from the roots.

superior oil: A high-quality pest-controlling oil applied when plants are dormant.

symbiotic: A mutually beneficial relationship between 2 or more living organisms.

taproot: A large, main root usually growing downward.

tender: Easily injured.

tendril: A modified, thread-like leaf used by the plant to cling to a support.

thin: To remove excess seedlings, giving the remaining plants optimum room for growth.

topsoil: The upper layer of soil.

transpiration: The natural loss of water as vapor from the leaves.

tuber: A swollen underground stem that stores food reserves.

variety: A naturally recurring variation of a species.

vegetative propagation: A method of increasing the number of plants using pieces of leaves, stems, or roots, resulting in new plants genetically identical to the parent.

vermiculite: A tan, granular material made from expanded mica, often used to improve aeration and water-holding capacity in soils.

virus: An infectious disease, generally incurable, often spread by insects.

water in: To water a newly installed plant to settle the soil around the roots.

weed: Any plant growing where it is not wanted.

woody plant: A perennial plant whose above-ground portions persist and continue to grow each year.

Index

Bold page numbers indicate that there is an illustration on the page.

African violet, spots on, 43–44
Algae in water garden, 178
All-America Selections, 97
Allelopathy, 196
Almond, 223–24
Alternaria leaf spot, and geranium, 173–74
Amaryllis, 9–**10**
Annuals, flowering, 88–89; overwintering of, 208
Anthocyanins, 243
Anthracnose, and raspberry, 150–51
Aphids, and grapes, 130
Apple: and fireblight, 129; and insect control, 45–46;
   pollination of, 111–12; seed propagation of, 8;
   storage of, 232–33
Apricot, pollination of, 112
Arbor Day, 77, 82
Arboreta, 287–94
Asparagus: harvesting of, 106; planting of, 83–85,
   84; spring care of, 54; summer care of, 136,
   148–49; top removal of, 95–96, 149, 232;
   weed control of, 96
Asparagus fern, 22
Aubrieta, 126–27
Avocado, indoor propagation of, 7
Azalea: and lack of flowers, 71; winter protection of,
   263–64
Azalea, florist, 36

Baby's breath, drying of, 199–200
Bacillus thuringiensis (Bt), 150, 173
Bacterial leaf spot, and geranium, 173–74
Bacterial wilt, 140–41
Balled-and-burlapped plants, 82
Band planting, 81
Bare-root plants, 82
Bark split, 34, 253

Bean, and rust, 172
Begonia, fibrous, 227
Begonia, tuberous, overwintering of, 240
Belamcanda, 99
Bermuda grass, 201–2
Birch, and sap loss, 73
Bittersweet, and lack of berries, 281
Blackberry lily, 99
Black rot, and grape, 95
Blossom-drop, and tomato, 161
Blossom-end rot, and tomato, 161
Bluegrass, 157, 202
Blue wild rye grass, 203
Bolting, 136; of lettuce, 79; of rhubarb, 175–76
Bonemeal, 71
Botanical names, 16–18
Boxwood, winter protection of, 263–64
Branches, forcing to bloom, 5, 6–7
Broad-leaved evergreen, winter protection of, 263–64
Brussels sprouts, 185–86
Bulbs: division of, 127; fertilization of, 56, 71; and
   foliage removal, 55, 99, 136, 137; forcing of,
   15, 245–46; late planting of, 14–15; planting
   of, 208–9, 244–45; precocious blooming of,
   32–33; selection of, 225; sequence of bloom of,
   55; in shade, 97; spring-flowering, 54; trans-
   planting of, 56
Burning bush: and lack of coloration, 248; and spider
   mites, 151
Butterflies, plants to attract, 122–23

Cacti, 21–22
Cactus, Christmas (Thanksgiving), 207
Caladium, overwintering of, 240
Calceolaria, 36
Canna, overwintering of, 240

Capsaicin, 219–20

Capsicum, 219

Carex, 203

Carotenoids, 242

Carrot, indoor propagation of, 7

Catfacing, and tomato, 162

Cats, and houseplants, 25

Cauliflower, 78–79

Ceropegia, 36–37

Cherry: pollination of, 112; seed propagation of, 8, 176–77

Chinese silver grass, 202

Chlorophyll, 67–68, 242

Chlorosis, 141–43

Christmas trees: cut-your-own, 273; indoor care of, 272; live, 251, 273–74; recycling of, 272–73; selection of, 269, 271–73

Chrysanthemum: pinching of, 149; top removal of, 264–65

Cilantro, 59–60

Cineraria, 36

Clay, 39–40

Clematis: propagation of, 153; rejuvenation pruning of, 72

Codling moth, 224

Cold injury, 33–34

Colorado potato beetle, 149

Composting, 243–44

Container gardening, 117–18

Containerized plants, 82

Containers; 13–14, 117

Coriander, 59–60

Corn, sweet, 116–17; harvesting of, 158; and racoons, 197

Cortaderia selloana, 202

Cover crop, 186–87

Crab apple: and fireblight, 129; forcing branches of, 6–7

Crabgrass, prevention of, 54, 77

Creeping charlie, 70

Creosote, 259

Cross-pollination: of corn, 116–17; of fruit trees, 109, 111–12; of nuts, 176, 203; of vine crops, 169–70

Crown of thorns, propagation of, 282

Cucumber: and bacterial wilt, 106, 140–41; bitterness of, 163–64; burpless, 163; female flower

of, 163; gynoecious, 163; male flower of, 163; pollination of, 162–63, 169–70; and squash vine borer, 173

Cucumber beetle, 106, 141

Cultivar: definition of, 17–18; selection of, 56–57, 97

Curculios, 224

Cut-flower care, 37–38, 158

Cuttings: of flowers, 181; of herbs, 191–92; of trees and shrubs, 147–48

Cyclamen, 35–36

Dahlia, overwintering of, 240

Daylily, division of, 189

Dead-heading, 137

Dehumidifier, water from, 203

Dessication, 33–34

Dioecious, 281

Dish gardens, 21–22

Division: of bulbs, 127; of iris, 123–24, 189; of oriental poppy, 127; of perennials, 188–89

Dogwood, forcing branches of, 6–7

Dried flowers, in wreaths, 262–63

Drought, 159–61

Drying: of flowers, 92–93, 99, 199–200; of herbs, 90

Easter lily, 93–94

Edible landscaping, 108–9

Elymus, 203

Erianthus ravennae, 202

Euonymus alatus, 248

Euphorbia milii, propagation of, 282

Eustoma, 126

Evergreens: as foundation plants, 281–82; and needle drop, 222–23; pruning of, 61–63

Evergreens, broad-leaved, winter protection of, 263–64

Extension service state offices, 295–96

Fall color, 242–43

False rock-cress, 126–27

Ferns, 227; indoor, 12–13

Fertilization: of bulbs, 56, 71; of houseplants, 77; of landscape plants, 53, 65–66, 241; of lawn, 105, 181, 207, 251; of strawberry, 85–86, 168

Fescue, 203

Festuca, 203

Finocchio, 43
Fireblight, 129
Firethorn, and fireblight, 129
Flame retardants, 271
Floating row covers, 122
Floral preservatives, 37
Florence fennel, 43
Flower bed design, 41–43
Flowers: cool-season planting of, 54; deadheading of,
    136, 137; dried, in wreaths, 262–63; drying of,
    92–93, 99, 199–200; edible, 171; pinching of,
    106, 137; pressing of, 263
Flowers, lack of, 128–29; and azaleas and rhododen-
    drons, 71; and bulbs, 127; and clematis, 72;
    and houseplants, 23; and hydrangea, 176; and
    iris, 123; and kaffir lily, 23; and lilac, 128–29;
    and lipstick plant, 23; and peony, 123; and
    phlox, 174; and wisteria, 151–52
Forsythia, forcing branches of, 6–7
Foundation plants, evergreen, 200–201, 281–82
Fountain grass, 202
Foxtail, 227
Frost-cracking, 34, 253
Frost date, 122
Frost protection, 69, 122, 215–16
Fruit cracking, and tomato, 162
Fruit trees: and fruit drop, 139; and lack of fruit,
    164–65; pollination of, 111–12, 165; pruning
    of, 46; and thinning fruit, 135, 139–40

Garbage, new plants from, 7
Garlic, 96; fall planting of, 218; harvesting of, 182
Geranium: and alternaria leaf spot, 173–74; and bac-
    terial leaf spot, 173–74; mosquito-repelling,
    144–45; and rust, 173–74
Gladiolus, 170–71; overwintering of, 240
Glycerin, 200
Gopher purge, 15
Gourd: cross-pollination of, 169–70; harvesting and
    preservation of, 234; luffa sponge, 234–35
Grape, 246–47; and black rot, 95; distorted leaves
    on, 130; harvesting and storage of, 210–11;
    pruning of, 46, 54, 77
Grass clippings, recycling of, 91–92
Grasses, ornamental, 202–3
Green manure, 186–87
Ground covers, 109–11, 152–53; in shade, 70

Groundhogs, 44
Ground ivy, 70

Hardiness zones, 26, **285**
Hawthorn: and fireblight, 129; seed propagation of,
    176–77
Hazelnut, 223–24
Heaving, 256
Hedge, pruning of, **72**
Herbicide drift, 130
Herbs, 89–91; propagation of, 191–93
Holiday gifts, 276–78
Holiday greenery, 270, 279
Holly, and lack of berries, 281
Honeysuckle, forcing branches of, 6–7
Horseradish, 237
Hosta: division of, 189; and slugs, 152
Houseplants: fall care of, 220–21, 251; fertilization
    of, 77; as gifts, 35–36, 276–77; and humidity,
    5, 11–12; poisonous, 25; propagation of, 181;
    spring care of, 53, 105; summer care of, 121,
    135; and white crust on soil, 44, 282; winter
    care of, 5, 11–12, 31, 269
Hybrid, 183
Hydrangea, 176

Impatiens, poor germination of, 98
Insecticidal soaps, 130, 204
Intensive gardening, 80–82
Intercropping, 81
Interplanting, 81
Iris: division of, 123–24, 189; and lack of flowers,
    123
Iron deficiency, 141–43

Jade plant, 23, 49
Japanese beetle, 174–75
Juglone, 56, 196–97, 224, 226–27
Juniper, overgrown, 281
Juvenility, of wisteria, 151–52

Kaffir lily, 23

Labels, plant, 266
Landscape plants: and chlorosis, 141–43; fertilization
    of, 53, 65–66, 241; planting of, 53, 77,
    217–18; propagation of, 135, 147–48; pruning

of, 31, 60–63, **61**; removal of, 221–22; rodent protection of, 251; and topping, 63–64; winter injury of, 33–34; winter protection of, 53, 251, 253–55

Latin names, 16–18

Lawn: fertilization of, 105, 181, 207, 251; planting of, 190–91; summer dormancy of, 157, 159; and thatch, 208; watering of, 135; weed control of, 105, 208

Lawn-mower blight, 157

Layering, **192**

Leaching, 282

Leaves: burning of, 256–58; recycling of, 257

Lettuce, 79–80

Light, 67–68

Lilac: and lack of flowers, 128–29; pruning of, 73

Lilium longiflorum, 93–94

Limonium, 98

Lipstick plant, 23

Lisianthus, 126

Loam, 39

Lupine, 199

Magnolia, forcing branches of, 6–7

Mail-order, 15–16

Manure, 265

Maple: red, 226; and sap loss, 73; selection of, 247–48; and slime flux, 73

Mealybugs, 24

Melon, and squash vine borer, 173

Microwave drying: of flowers, 92–93; of herbs, 90

Miscanthus sinensis, 202

Miscanthus sinensis 'Gracillimus,' 202

Moles, 74, 177

Mosquito-repelling plant, 15–16, 144–45

Mulch, 119–20, 136; black plastic, 113, 120; freshly chipped wood, 248; and fungal growth, 99; and termites, 248; types of, 224–25; as winter protection, 256

Multipurpose Fruit Spray (MPFS), 45–46

Muskmelon: and bacterial wilt, 140–41; and cucumber beetle, 141

Nectarines, pollination of, 112

Nut sedge, 131–32

Oak twig girdler, 175

Onion: harvesting of, 182; seed, 47–48; sets, 47–48; sweet Spanish, 198

Orange, seed propagation of, 8

Orchard, and pest control, 105

Organic matter, 40

Oriental poppy, 127, 198–99

Ornamental grasses, 202–3

Overwintering indoors: of annuals, 126, 208; of tender perennials, 240

Oxygenators, 178

Pampas grass, 202

Pampas grass, hardy, 202

Pansy, 227

Parsley, Chinese, 59–60

Pawpaw: 238–39; planting of, 69; pollination of, 200; and possums, xiii; seed propagation of, 70

Peach: pollination of, 112; seed propagation of, 176–77

Peanuts, 214–15

Pear: and fireblight, 129; harvesting and storage of, 211–12; pollination of, 112

Peas, and root maggots, 94

Peat moss, in growing media, 40

Pecan, 176

Pennisetum alopecuroides, 202–3

Penta, 259

Peony, 125; and ants, 123; and botrytis blight, 125; division of, 188–89; and lack of flowers, 123

Pepper, and lack of fruit, 172

Peppers, hot, 219–20

Perennials, 88–89; for butterflies, 122–23; division of, **188–89**; long-blooming, 48; for shade, 97–98; tender, overwintering of, 209, 239–41; for vertical accent, 199

Pesticide injury, 165–66

Petunia, leggy, 127

pH: and chlorosis, 142–43; and wood ash, 19–20

Phlox: and lack of flowers, 174; and powdery mildew, 174

Photosynthesis, 67

Pinching: of chrysanthemum, 149; of flowers, 106, 137

Pineapple, indoor propagation of, 7, **8**

Plant labels, 266

Plant sources, 283

Plum, pollination of, 112

Plumosa asparagus fern, 22
Poinsettia, 5, 274–76; reblooming, 231, 241–42
Poison ivy, 143–44
Poisonous plants, 25
Pomanders, 278–79
Pond, and algae, 178
Popcorn, and failure to pop, 260
Poplars, fast growing, 15–16
Potato: discoloration of, 223; fruits of, 168–69; green, 213; harvesting of, 182, 212–13; planting of, 58–59; storage of, 236
Potato beetles, 149
Pot marigold, 227
Potpourri, 193–94
Pressing flowers, 263
Pressure-treated lumber, 258
Propagation: of clematis, 153; of crown of thorns, 282; by cuttings, 147–48, 181, 191–92; by division, **124**, 188–89; of herbs, 191; of houseplants, 181; from kitchen scraps, 7–9; of landscape plants, 135, 147–48; by layering, **192**; of raspberries, 190; from seed, 54, 136; of trees from seed, 177, 261–62
Pruning: of broken limbs, 27; of evergreens, 61–63; of fruit trees, 46; of grapes, 46, 54, 77; of hedges, **72**; of hydrangeas, 176; of landscape plants, 31, 60–63, **61**; of low branches, 73; of raspberries, 158, 189–90; of roses, 64–65; and sap loss, 73; of tomato, 198; and topping, 63–64; of wisteria, 152
Public gardens, 287–94
Pumpkin: cross-pollination of, 169–70; planting of, 146–47; storage of, 213
Pussy willow, forcing branches of, 6–7
Pyracantha, and fireblight, 129

Raccoons, 197
Raised beds, 118–19; treated lumber for, 258–59
Raspberry: and anthracnose, 150–51; propagation of, 189–90; pruning of, 54, 158, 189–90; and sucker removal, 106; and virus, 151
Redbud, forcing branches of, 6–7
Rhododendrons: and lack of flowers, 71; winter protection of, 263–64
Rhubarb: bolting of, 175–76; harvesting of, 106; spring care of, 54; summer care of, 136, 148
River birch, 226

Rodent injury, prevention of, 5, 251
Root maggots, 94
Roots, surface, 27
Rose: American Rose Society, 210; and black spot, 65, 105; and Japanese beetle, 174–75; planting of, 86–88; pruning of, 64–65; types of, 86–87; winter protection of, 251, 252–53
Rose hips, 209–10
Rust: and bean, 172; and geranium, 173–74

Saffron, 20–21
Salt accumulation, and houseplants, 44, 282
Salts, de-icing, 5, 18–19
Sand, 39–40
Season extenders, 69, 80
Seed: collecting of, 183–84; germination of, 31, 98; growing transplants from, 47; selection of, 47; starting indoors, 54, 136; storage of, 145–46, 207
Shade, plants for, 70, 97–98, 203
Silt, 39–40
Slime flux, 73
Slugs, and hosta, 152
Soil: amendment of, 39–40, 226; preparation of, 259–60; sterilant, 201; testing of, 260
Solanine, 169, 213
Spider mites, and burning bush, 151
Squash: cross-pollination of, 169–70; harvesting of, 182–83; spaghetti, 213–14
Squash vine borer, 173
Staking trees, 83
Statice, 98–99
Stone wall, perennials for, 127
Stratification, 261–62
Strawberry: and blossom removal, 106; fertilization of, 168; planting of, 85–86; renovation of, 158, 166–68, **167**; winter protection of, 54, 252, 255
String of hearts, 36–37
Succession planting, 80, 106
Suckers: on landscape plants, 157; on raspberry, 106; on tomato, 136
Sunflower, 194–96, **195**
Sunroom, 46
Sunscald, and tomato, 162
Superior oil, 53
Sweet gum, 226

Terrarium, 12, 280

Thinning, of fruits, 135, 139–40

Tomato: and blossom drop, 161; and blossom-end rot, 161; caged vs. staked, 130–31; and cat-facing, 162; culture of, 113–15; determinate, 114, 198; and fruit cracking, 162; green, 208, 216; indeterminate, 114, 198; and lack of fruit, 197–98; leggy, 115–16; and suckers, 136; and sunscald, 162

Tomato, tree, 15–16

Tomato hornworm, 150

Topping, 63–64

Toxicodendron radicans, 143–44

Transplants: growing of, 40–41; hardening off of, 54

Trapping: of groundhogs, 45; of racoons, 197

Tree guards, 265

Trees: fall planting of, 217–18; planting of, 82–83, 226; seed propagation of, 261–62; and wet soil, 226

Tree wrap, 34, 247, 253

Trickle irrigation, 138–39

Tulips: and lack of flowers, 225–26; naturalizing of, 226

Twig girdler, oak, 175

Valentine gifts, 35–37

Vanilla, 38–**39**

Variety, plant, 17–18

Vegetable garden: fall, 182, 184–85; and pest control, 57; planning of, 56; planting of, 57

Vegetables: cool-season, 54, 58, 77, 78; warm-season, 105, 112–13

Venus flytrap, **100**–101

Vermiculite, 40, 58

Voles, 265

Walnut, 203, 224; and companion plants, 226–27; toxicity of, 56, 196–97

Watering: guidelines for, 138, 159–61; and household gray water, 160–61; and trickle irrigation, 138–39

Watermelon: cross-pollination of, 169–70; harvesting of, 182

Watersprouts, 157

Weed control, 227; in asparagus, 96

Weeping fig, 48–49

Weevils, 224

Wildflowers, 106–8

Wildlife, plants to attract, 26

Winterberry, and lack of berries, 281

Winter injury, of landscape plants, 33–34

Winter protection: of broad-leaved evergreens, 263–**64**; of landscape plants, 53, 251, 253–55; of roses, 251, 252–53; of strawberry, 54, 252, 255

Wisteria: and lack of flowers, 151–52; pruning of, 152

Wood ash, 19–20

Woodchucks, 44–45

Wood preservatives, 258–59

Wound dressing, 34

Wounds, treatment of, 27

Wreath, dried flower, 262–63

Yew, and failure to survive, 200–201

Zoysia, 201–2